KEY MATHS

8²

First published in 1996
Second edition published in 2001 by:
Nelson Thornes (Publishers) Ltd

Reprinted in 2001 by:
Nelson Thornes Ltd
Delta Place
27 Bath Road
CHELTENHAM
GL53 7TH
United Kingdom

08 09 / 10

A catalogue record for this book is available from the British Library

ISBN 978 0 7487 5985 9

Original design concept by Studio Dorel
Cover design by John Christopher, Design Works
Cover photographs: Roger Howard / Ace Photo
Agency (front); Chris Fairclough, Colour Library
(spine); Baron Wolman / Tony Stone Images (back)
Cartoons by Clinton Banbury
Page make-up by Tech Set Ltd

Printed and Bound in China by Midas Printing International Ltd.

Acknowledgements

The publishers thank the following for permission to reproduce copyright material: Aerofilms, p. 149; ED142018 The Thinker, Bronze by Rodin (front view) Musee Rodin, Paris/Bridgeman Art Library, London, p. 207; British Broadcasting Corporation, p. 52; British Mensa Ltd, p. 341; Central Statistical Office, p. 289; Channel Four Television, p. 52; Collections, pp. 257 (Michael Allen), p. 300 (bottom right – Brian Shuel); The Hulton Deutsch Collection, p. 51; Independent Television, p. 52; Kraft Jacobs Suchard, pp. 314, 318; Milepost 9½, p. 144; National Savings, p. 164; The National Blood Service, p. 299; Reproduced from the Ordance Survey mapping with permission of The Controller of Her Majesty's Stationery Office © Crown copyright (07000U), pp. 232, 247, 249, 267; Sky Television, p. 52; Sporting Pictures (UK) Ltd, pp. 169, 255; Tony Stone Images, pp. 94 (John Lawrence), 244 (Dale Durfee), 272 (Tim Davis), 300 (bottom left – Kevin Kelley), p. 310 (David Sutherland); York City Archives, p. 256. All other photographs by Martyn F. Chillmaid.

The publishers have made every effort to contact copyright holders but apologise if any have been overlooked.

▶ **David Baker**
The Anthony Gell School, Wirksworth

▶ **Paul Hogan**
Fulwood High School, Preston

▶ **Barbara Job**
Christleton County High School, Chester

▶ **Renie Verity**
Pensby High School for Girls, Heswall

T

Contents

v

1 Graphs

QUESTIONS

EXTENSION

SUMMARY

TEST YOURSELF

The map shows the time in different parts of the world when it is 12 noon in UK winter time.

Do you have any relations in New Zealand?
Be careful if you telephone them.
It is nearly 12 midnight in New Zealand when it is 12 noon in the UK!

Look in a world atlas to find out:
- how continents such as Africa arrange time zones to fit countries' borders
- what happens when a traveller crosses the International Date Line.

1 Conversion graphs

Class 8J are in Paris on an exchange visit. They are buying presents for their friends.
They want to convert the prices from francs to pounds.
They have a conversion graph.

Exercise 1:1

This is the graph that 8J are using:

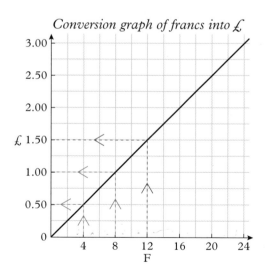

Conversion graph of francs into £

1 Anne is buying a model of the Eiffel Tower. It costs 12F.
Find 12F on the bottom scale of the graph.
Follow the red line to the graph.
Read off the price in £ from the side scale.

2 Ned is buying a picture of Paris. It costs 8F.
Follow the green line to see how much this is in £.

3 Danielle is buying two pens. They cost 4F each.
   a Follow the blue line to find out how much one pen costs in £.
   b How much do the two pens cost in £?

4 Terry wants to buy three boxes of chocolates. A box costs 16F.
   a How much does one box cost in £?
   b How much do three boxes cost in £?
   c Terry has 50F.
      Has he enough money to buy the chocolates *and* a pen?

| **Conversion graph** | We use a **conversion graph** to change from one unit to another. Conversion graphs are always straight lines. | |

Exercise 1:2

1 Here is a conversion graph for US dollars ($) into £.

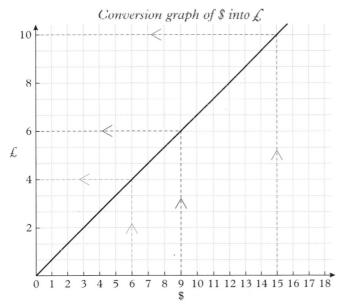

   a Convert $9 into £ (red line).
   b Convert $15 into £ (blue line).
   c Convert $6 into £ (green line).

2 This graph converts miles into kilometres.
It can also convert kilometres into miles.

Conversion graph of miles into km

a Convert 5 miles to km (red line).
b Convert 15 miles to km.
c Convert 16 **km to miles** (blue line).
d Convert 28 km to miles.

3 This graph converts kilograms into pounds (lbs).

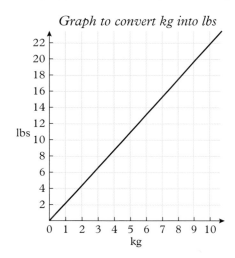

Graph to convert kg into lbs

a Convert 7 kg into pounds.
b Convert 10 kg into pounds.
c A bag of sugar weighs 1 kg.
About how many pounds is this?
d A large bag of potatoes weighs 5 lbs.
About how many kilograms is this?

2   Graphs and rules

Exercise 1:3

1   David is taking part in the school sponsored walk.
He is being sponsored £2 per mile by his family. The further he walks
the more money he will collect.
He works out the amount in a table.

Number of miles	1	2	3	4	5
Amount £	2	4			

a   Copy the table.
b   Fill in the last three columns of the table.

Here is a graph of David's table:

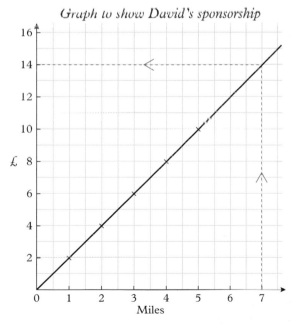

Graph to show David's sponsorship

c   Follow the red line.
How much will David get if he walks 7 miles?

2 Nicky is also doing the sponsored walk.
He is being sponsored £3 per mile.

    a Copy the table for Nicky.
    Fill it in.

Number of miles	1	2	3	4	5
Amount £					

    b Draw a graph for Nicky.
    Use the same scales as David's graph but make the vertical axis go
    up to 22.
    c How much will Nicky get if he walks 7 miles?
    d How much will he get if he walks $4\frac{1}{2}$ miles?
    e About how far would Nicky have to walk to get £20?
    f How much will he get if he walks 15 miles?
    (This is not shown on the graph but you can work it out. How?)

3 Yasmin is being sponsored £1.50 per mile.

    a Make a table to show the amount Yasmin will get.
    b Draw a graph using the same scales as before.
    c Use your graph to work out how much Yasmin will get if she
    walks $3\frac{1}{2}$ miles.
    d How far would Yasmin need to walk to get £10.50?
    e Compare Nicky's graph with Yasmin's.
    Describe the main difference between the two graphs.
    Explain why this difference has happened.
    f Describe what the graph of someone being sponsored £5 per mile
    would look like.

· ·

◄◄REPLAY►

Formula	A rule written out in algebra is known as a **formula**.
Example	Nicky is being sponsored £3 per mile. The *t*otal he collects equals £3 × number of *m*iles. In short form this is: $t = 3 \times m$
	Remember that we do not write × signs in algebra. This means that the rule should be written $t = 3m$

Exercise 1:4

Write down the short form of these rules.
Use the red letters and numbers.

1 The *t*otal amount raised in a sponsored walk at £2 for each *m*ile.

2 The *t*otal amount raised in a sponsored swim at £6 for each *l*ength.

3 The *w*ages earned by someone earning £4 per *h*our.

4 The *h*eight of a plant which grows at 3 cm per *m*onth.

5 The *d*istance covered by a car travelling at 30 miles per *h*our.

6 The *a*mount of money Joanna saves if she saves £6 per *m*onth.

7 The amount Andy earns is calculated using the formula $w = 4h$.
w is his wages and h is the number of hours he works.

Work out Andy's wages if he works for:
a 5 hours
b 7 hours
c $3\frac{1}{2}$ hours
d $6\frac{1}{4}$ hours

Sometimes it is useful to draw a graph of a rule.

Example

Tim has a part-time job as a waiter.
He earns £3 per hour that he works.
He works out a table to show how much he can earn.

Number of hours	1	2	3	4	5
Wages £	3	6	9	12	15

His rule is: *w*ages equals £3 × number of *h*ours worked.
In algebra this is: $w = 3 \times h$ or $w = 3h$

Tim draws a graph of his table (see next page).

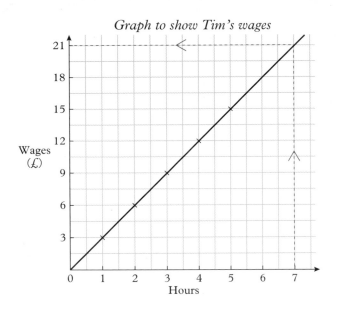

Graph to show Tim's wages

He can now see how much he would earn for 7 hours' work.
Follow the red line.

Exercise 1:5

1 Anisha works in the same cafe as Tim.
She is older and earns £4 per hour.

Her rule is: *w*ages equals £4 × number of *h*ours worked
a Write Anisha's rule in algebra.
b Copy the table and fill it in.

Number of hours	1	2	3	4	5
Wages £					

c Plot a graph to show Anisha's wages.
Use this scale.

d Use your graph to work out how much
Anisha will earn if she works:
(1) 4 hours
(2) $3\frac{1}{2}$ hours
(3) 8 hours
(4) $4\frac{1}{2}$ hours

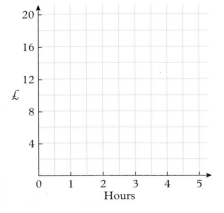

2 Nathan's new video recorder has a counter on it.
He plays a video and works out a rule for the counter.

Nathan's rule is
counter equals **50** × number of *m*inutes.
a Write Nathan's rule in algebra.
b Here is Nathan's table.
Copy it and fill it in for Nathan's rule.

Number of minutes	10	20	30	40	50
Counter					

c Draw a graph for this table.
Put the time along the bottom and the counter up the side.
d Use your graph to find out what the counter will show after:
  (1) 30 minutes
  (2) 50 minutes
  (3) 35 minutes
  (4) 45 minutes
  (5) 75 minutes

3 Joel and Lianne are jogging together. Lianne soon gets ahead of Joel.
Lianne jogs at 4 metres per second (m/s).
Joel jogs at 3 metres per second.
They each work out a rule for the distance they jog.

a Write Lianne's rule in algebra using the letters *d* and *s*.
b Copy this table for Lianne's rule.
Use your formula to fill it in.

Number of seconds	10	20	30	40	50
Distance					

c Draw a graph for this table.
d Write Joel's rule in algebra.
e Make a table for Joel's distances.
Draw the graph on the same diagram as Lianne's.
f Describe the differences between the two graphs.
Explain why the graphs are different.

3 Time

The time is 7.55 am.
Stan's bus journey to school takes 47 minutes.
He wants to know if he will be at school by 8.45 am.

At 7.55 am it is 5 minutes to the next hour.
$47 - 5 = 42$
The bus arrives at 8.42 am.

Exercise 1:6

1 Work out the times when these buses arrive.
   a Bus leaves at 7.50 am and takes 45 minutes.
   b Bus leaves at 3.35 pm and takes 50 minutes.
   c Bus leaves at 7.25 am and takes 36 minutes.
   d Bus leaves at 10.17 am and takes 52 minutes.
   e Bus leaves at 3.46 pm and takes 28 minutes.
   f Bus leaves at 11.27 am and takes 25 minutes.

am	**am** stands for ante meridian.	This means before noon.
pm	**pm** stands for post meridian.	This means after noon.

7.55 am is in the morning.   3.04 pm is in the afternoon.

Timetables for buses and trains use the 24-hour clock.

Examples

We always have four figures.
7.55 am is the same as **07 55**
3.04 pm is the same as **15 04**
Midnight is 00 00
Midday is 12 00

2   Convert these to 24-hour clock times.
   a 4.20 pm   **c** 10 am   **e** 9 pm   **g** 12.15 am
   b 5.30 pm   **d** 6.38 pm   **f** 1.25 pm   **h** 12.06 pm

3   Convert these to am or pm times.
   a 03 05   **c** 17 16   **e** 08 55   **g** 12 45
   b 19 00   **d** 21 35   **f** 23 00   **h** 00 30

4   Work out the times when these buses arrive.
    Use the 24-hour clock.
   a Bus leaves at 15 52 and takes 14 minutes.
   b Bus leaves at 08 05 and takes 39 minutes.
   c Bus leaves at 14 19 and takes 55 minutes.
   d Bus leaves at 21 43 and takes 26 minutes.

Example

A train leaves at 08 36.
The journey takes 2 hours 45 minutes.
When does the train arrive?

Work out the minutes first.
At 08 36 it is 24 minutes to the next hour.
$45 - 24 = 21$
A train taking just 45 minutes would arrive at 09 21.
A train taking 2 hours 45 minutes would arrive at 11 21.

5 Work out the times when these trains arrive.
Use the 24-hour clock.
   a Train leaves at 12 44 and takes 1 hour 37 minutes.
   b Train leaves at 08 52 and takes 3 hours 18 minutes.
   c Train leaves at 18 25 and takes 2 hours 19 minutes.
   d Train leaves at 15 38 and takes 4 hours 26 minutes.

6 Ms Davies has an important meeting.
She needs to be in Manchester at 9.45 am.
Her train leaves at 7.52 and takes 1 hour 34 minutes.
Will Ms Davies be early or late and by how many minutes?

7 Sarah catches a train and then a bus to school.
The train takes 27 minutes and leaves at 07 52.
The bus leaves at 08 22.
How long does Sarah have to get from the train to the bus?

8 A film lasts 112 minutes.
   a How long does it last in hours and minutes?
   b If the film starts at 8.15 pm, when will it finish?

· ·

Example   How long is it from 8.35 am to
            9.12 am?

            From 8.35 to 9.00 is 25 minutes.
            From 9.00 to 9.12 is 12 minutes.
            25 + 12 = 37
            Answer: 37 min

Exercise 1:7

1 How long is it between these times?
- **a** 7.25 am to 8.17 am
- **b** 09 34 to 10 28
- **c** 6.48 pm to 7.15 pm
- **d** 16 25 to 17 33

Example   How long is it from 8.35 pm to 11.42 pm?

8.35 to 9.00 is 25 min   11.00 to 11.42 is 42 min

9.00 → 11.00
= 2 h

25 minutes

12 minutes

$$25 + 42 = 67 \text{ min}$$
$$= 1 \text{ h } 7 \text{ min}$$
$$2 \text{ h} + 1 \text{ h } 7 \text{ min} = 3 \text{ h } 7 \text{ min}$$

---

2 How long is it between these times?
- **a** 5.15 pm to 7.37 pm
- **b** 19 29 to 21 08
- **c** 09 20 to 13 46
- **d** 9.05 am to 3.54 pm
- **e** 17 28 to 21 43
- **f** 16 42 to 23 15

3 Sian's school day starts at 8.50 am and finishes at 3.35 pm.
- **a** How long is Sian at school?
- **b** Morning break is 15 minutes and lunch is 1 hour.
  How long is Sian with her class?

4 On Saturday Matthew works in a supermarket.
He starts at 8.45 am and finishes at 4.15 pm.
He has two 15-minute tea breaks and 45 minutes for lunch.
How long does Matthew work?

You can use a calculator with a **DMS** key to do calculations with time.

The symbols stand for degrees, minutes, seconds. They are meant for calculating angles.

You can use them for time.

If your calculator has a **° ' "** key ask your teacher for help.

Example 1   Enter 9 h 30 min on the calculator.

Key in: **9** **DMS** **3** **0** gives a display $9°30$

Key in: **2nd F** **DMS** gives a display 9.5

This shows that 9 h 30 minutes = 9.5 h

Example 2   Enter the time 15 25 on the calculator.

Key in: **1** **5** **DMS** **2** **5** gives a display $15°25$

Key in: **2nd F** **DMS** gives a display 15.41666667

This shows that 15.25 = 15.41666667 h

Exercise 1:8

1   Copy this table and fill it in.

Time	h min display	Decimal display, h
6 h 30 min		
8 h 15 min		
15 45		
18 20		
23 35		
12 midday		

Example   How long is it from 9.40 am to 1.08 pm?

1.08 pm is 13 08 in the 24-hour clock.
The calculation is   13 08 − 09 40
Key in:

1 **3** **DMS** **8** **−** **9** **DMS** **4** **0** **=**

The display shows $3°28'00.00$

Answer: 3 h 28 min

---

2 Use a calculator to find how long it is between these times.
   a 9.25 am to 11.37 am   **d** 6.23 pm to 8.49 pm
   b 10 05 to 15 38   **e** 10.04 am to 3.52 pm
   c 9.36 pm to midnight   **f** 8.45 pm to 11.19 pm

· ·

Exercise 1:9

Liverpool Lime Street	0600	—	0710	0745	—	0845	0945
Runcorn	0617	—	0727	0802	—	0902	1002
Hartford	—	0648	—	—	0856	—	1013
Crewe	0639	0702	0753	—	0914	0925	1025
Stafford	0700	—	—	0837	0935	0944	1047
Tamworth	0720	—	—	—	—	—	—
Nuneaton	0735	—	—	—	—	1008	—
Rugby	—	0802	—	—	—	1023	1125
Milton Keynes Central	—	—	—	0933	1031	1049	—
Watford Junction	—	—	0930	—	—	—	1214
London Euston	0853	0912	0953	1020	1117	1136	1237

The timetable shows some trains from Liverpool to London.

1 a What time is the earliest train from Runcorn that stops at
   Watford Junction?
   b How long does the train take to get from Runcorn to
   Watford Junction?

2 Donna has an important appointment in Milton Keynes at 10 45.
   Which train should she get from Liverpool?

3 a What time does the 10 13 from Hartford get to Rugby?
   b How long does this train take to get from Hartford to Rugby?

4 I have just missed the 06 39 from Crewe to London Euston.
   a How long will I have to wait for the next train?
   b What time will I arrive in London?
   c How much later will I arrive than if I had caught the 06 39?

5 There are five trains on this timetable that go from Liverpool to
   London Euston.
   a Work out the time each train takes to get from Liverpool to
   London Euston.
   b What time does the fastest train leave Liverpool?
   c What time does the slowest train leave Liverpool?

4 Travel graphs

Carl and Sian enjoy train spotting.
They know that express trains
travel very fast.
Other trains go more slowly.

Exercise 1:10

Copy the axes on to squared paper.
Use them for all the questions in this exercise.

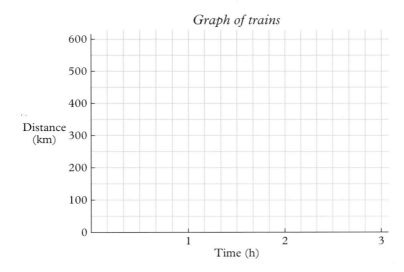

Graph of trains

1 a Copy the table for an express train travelling at an
average speed of 200 km/h.
Fill it in.

Time from start (h)	0	1	2	3
Distance travelled (km)	0	200		

b Plot the points from the table.
Join them to get a straight line.
Label your line 'express train'.

2 **a** Copy the table for a goods train travelling at an average speed of 100 km/h.
Fill it in.

Time from start (h)	0	1	2	3
Distance travelled (km)	0	100		

b Plot the points from the table.
Join them to get a straight line.
Label your line 'goods train'.

3 A cross-country train travels at an average speed of 150 km/h.
a Describe where the line for this train will go on your graph.
b Copy this table for the cross-country train.
Fill it in.

Time from start (h)	0	1	2	3
Distance travelled (km)	0	150		

c Plot the points from the table.
Join them to get a straight line.
Label your line 'cross-country train'.
d Was your answer to part **a** correct?

4 **a** Describe how the speed of a train affects its graph.
b Describe the graph of a train that is not moving.

5 The axes you have used for this exercise use six divisions for one hour.
How many minutes does one division represent?

6 How many minutes does one division represent on these scales?

7 What are the times shown on these scales?

Exercise 1:11

1

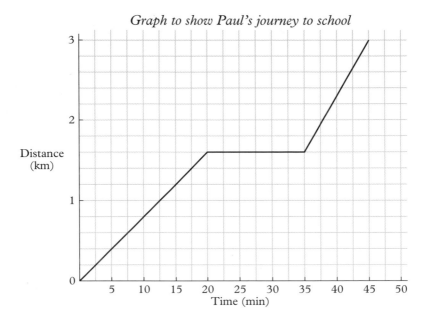

Graph to show Paul's journey to school

The graph shows Paul's journey from home to school.

a Paul started by walking.
How long did he walk?

b Paul stopped at a shop to buy a pen.
(1) How does this show on the graph?
(2) How long did Paul stop?

c Paul was late and started to run.
(1) How long did he run?
(2) How far did Paul run?

d How long did Paul's journey take altogether?

e If he left home at 8.05 am, what time did Paul arrive at school?

f How far does Paul travel to school?

2 Copy the axes from question **1**.
Draw a graph of Anne's journey from home to school.

a Anne walks 1 km in 15 minutes from home to the bus stop.
Draw a line to show this on your graph.

b Ann waits 10 minutes for a bus.
Draw a horizontal line to show this on your graph.

c The bus travels 2 km in 15 minutes to get to Anne's school.
(1) How far has Ann travelled altogether?
(2) How many minutes does Ann take to get from home to school?
(3) Use your answers to (1) and (2) to help you complete your graph.

3   Copy the axes on to squared paper.

Graph to show the Patels' journey

The Patel family are travelling on the motorway in their car.
a   They travel at 60 miles/h.
   How far do they travel in one hour?
   Plot this point on your graph.
b   They continue at 60 miles/h for another 30 minutes.
   (1) How far do they travel in 30 minutes?
   (2) How far have they travelled altogether?
   (3) Plot this point on your graph.
   (4) Draw the line for the first part of the journey.
c   The Patels stop for coffee for 30 minutes.
   Draw this on your graph.
d   They continue for one more hour.
   They are now 120 miles from home.
   (1) Plot the point they have reached on your graph.
   (2) Draw a line for this part of the journey.
e   At what speed did they travel after coffee?

4   Copy the axes on to squared paper.

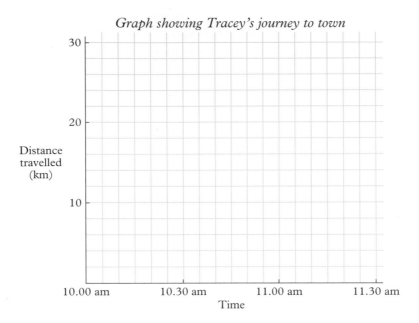

Graph showing Tracey's journey to town

Tracey goes out on her bicycle on Saturday morning.
She leaves home at 10 o'clock.

a   Tracey starts cycling at 32 km/h.
  (1) How far does she cycle in 30 minutes?
  (2) Plot this point on your graph.
  (3) Draw the line for the first part of Tracey's journey.
b   Tracey spends 20 minutes in the library.
  Draw this on your graph.
c   Tracey leaves the library with a friend.
  She walks 2 km pushing her bike. This takes 20 minutes.
  Draw Tracey's walk on your graph.
d   Tracey rides 8 km into town in 20 minutes.
  Draw this on your graph.
e   How far does Tracey travel altogether?
f   At what time does Tracey arrive in town?

1   This graph converts inches into centimetres.

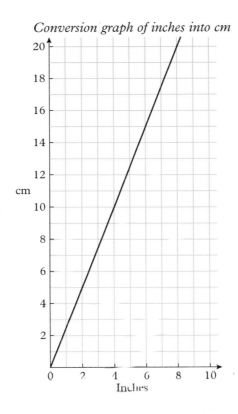

Conversion graph of inches into cm

cm

Inches

a A ruler is 6 inches long.
     About how many centimetres is this?
b A book measures 4 inches by 8 inches.
     What is the size of the book in centimetres?
c A television has a 67 cm screen.
     What is this in inches?

2   Keeping a cat costs about £4 per week.
    a This table shows the costs.
         Copy it and fill it in.

Number of weeks	1	2	3	4	5
Cost £	4	8			

b Plot a graph of the cost.
c Continue the line.
     How much does it cost to keep a cat for 6 weeks?

3 This timetable gives the times of trains from London to Norwich. The times are given using the 24-hour clock.

Mondays to Fridays	✕	✕	✕						
London Liverpool Street	1330	1430	1530	1555	1630	1700	1725	1730	1800
Colchester	1418	1518	1618	1645	1718	—	1824	—	—
Harwich International Port	—	—	—	—	—	—	1855	—	—
Ipswich	1436	1536	1636	1711	1736	1801	—	1841	1905
Stowmarket	1447	1547	1647	—	1747	—	—	1852	1916
Diss	1459	1559	1659	—	1800	—	—	1905	1929
Norwich	1523	1623	1723	—	1824	1836	—	1929	1953

Restaurant ✕

a Three trains have restaurants.
  (1) Write down the times that these three trains leave London.
  (2) Convert these times to am or pm times.

b Only one train stops at Harwich International Port.
  (1) What time does the train arrive at Harwich?
  (2) Convert this time to am or pm time.

c (1) What time does the 17 30 from London arrive at Norwich?
  (2) Convert this time to am or pm time.

d Mary arrives at London Liverpool Street at 4.15 pm.
  (1) What time does the next train leave for Norwich?
  (2) How long does the train take to get to Norwich?

4 Maureen wants to record *Mission of the Shark*.

  a Maureen programmes her video using the 24-hour clock. Write down the start time and the finish time of the film in this way.

  b Maureen has a blank 240-minute tape. How much time will be left on her tape? Give your answer in hours and minutes.

7.20	**Pets Win Prizes (T) (S)** Including racing millipedes and llamas. *686320*
8.00	**The National Lottery Live (S)** *118097*
8.15	**Casualty** Facts of Life **(T) (S) (R)** Ash (Patrick Robinson) is in the limelight this week, suspended in mid-shift after an article in the local paper. *134287*
9.05	**News; Sport; (T)** weather *364320*
9.25	**Bob Monkhouse On The Spot (S)** *225897*
9.55	**Film** **Mission Of The Shark** (Robert Iscove, 1991, TVM) **(T)** Stacy Keach leads this fact-based survival drama as the commander of a US warship torpedoed in shark-infested waters in 1945. *935436*
11.30	**Film** **The File Of The Golden Goose** (Sam Wanamaker, 1969) Yul Brynner is an American agent sent to London to infiltrate a counterfeiting gang in this strictly formulaic crime drama. **(T)** *577981*
1.15	**Weather;** close *950036*

5 Jaswinder is revising for GCSE. He wants to do three hours' revision each night.
Jaswinder starts at 4.25 pm. He breaks for tea which takes 45 minutes.
At 7.40 pm he stops to watch television.

  a How long has Jaswinder worked?

  b The television programme ends at 8.35 pm. Jaswinder starts his revision again.
  When will he finish his three hours?

1 This table shows the exchange rate for Spanish pesetas and £.

£	1	2	3	4
Spanish pesetas	200	400	600	800

a Draw a conversion graph.
Use these scales.

b Continue your graph to the edge of the scale.

c Use your graph to work out the cost of these items in £:
  (1) A toy donkey costing 1000 pesetas
  (2) A picture of Madrid costing 700 pesetas

d How many pesetas would you get for £50?

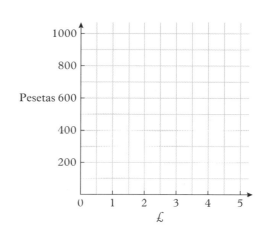

2 Copy the axes on to squared paper.
Draw a graph of Mr Brown's car journey.

Mr Brown drove for 30 minutes at 70 miles/h. He stopped for lunch for 30 minutes. After lunch Mr Brown drove for 45 minutes at 60 miles/h. During the last hour of his journey he slowed to 40 miles/h.

Use your graph to find out how far Mr Brown travelled altogether.

Graph of Mr Brown's car journey

3 Luke goes into town after school. He leaves at 4 pm.
Copy the axes.
Draw a travel graph of Luke's trip.

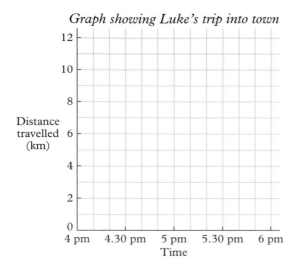

Graph showing Luke's trip into town

	Distance	Time taken
walk to library	4 km	40 min
choose books	–	30 min
bus to town	5 km	20 min
walk through town	2 km	30 min

a (1) When was Luke travelling the fastest?
(2) How can you tell this from the graph?
b How far did he travel altogether?
c The average speed for the whole trip $= \dfrac{\text{total distance travelled}}{\text{total time taken}}$

What was Luke's average speed for the whole trip?

4 How long is it between these times?
Give your answers in hours and minutes.
a 11.24 am to 2.15 pm   **d** 8.51 pm to 10.44 pm
b 08 45 to 11 37   **e** 00 43 to 05 28
c 4.26 pm to 7.55 pm   **f** 6.21 am to 2.42 pm

5 The school play is due to start at 7.30 pm. It starts seven minutes late.
The interval is 15 minutes. The play finishes at 9.44 pm.
How long is the play?

- ### Conversion graph

  We use a **conversion graph** to change from one unit to another.
  Conversion graphs are always straight lines.

- ### Graphs and formulas

  Nicky is being sponsored £3 per mile
  The *total* he collects equals £3 × number of *miles*.
  In algebra this is $t = 3 \times m$
  We write $t = 3m$

  To draw a graph of a formula first fill in a table:

Number of miles	1	2	3	4	5
Amount £	3	6	9	12	15

  Then draw the graph.

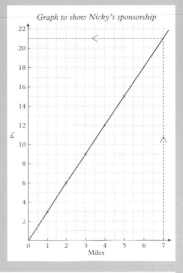

- ### Time

  am stands for ante meridian. This means before noon.
  pm stands for post meridian. This means after noon.

  24-hour clock times always have four figures.
  6.35 am is the same as 06 35
  5.25 pm is the same as 17 25

  You can enter times in your calculator using the **DMS** or ``ᵒ ,, ,,`` keys.

- ### Travel graphs

  Time is always shown along the horizontal axis.
  Distance is always shown on the vertical axis.

1 This is a conversion graph for German marks (DM) into £.
  a Convert DM10 into £ (red line).
  b Convert DM12 into £ (blue line).
  c Convert DM6 into £.

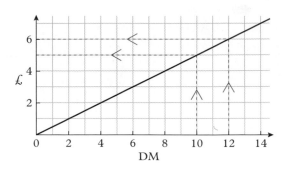

2 Alison earns £5 per hour as a waitress.
  a This table shows her wages. Copy the table and fill it in.

Number of hours	1	2	3	4	5
Wages £	5	10			

  b Draw a graph of Alison's wages. Use these scales.

3 **a** Convert these to 24-hour clock times.
    (1) 6.45 am   (2) 8.20 pm   (3) 12 noon
  b Convert these to am or pm times.
    (1) 18 25   (2) 07 45   (3) 22 10

4 The graph shows Mohammed's journey to work.
  a On the way he stopped at the paper shop. How long did he stop for?
  b How far was Mohammed's journey to work altogether?
  c Mohammed travelled at different speeds before and after stopping.
    (1) Which part of the journey was faster?
    (2) Explain how the graph shows this.

Graph of Mohammed's journey to work

2 Estimating your mental power

The number 10^{100} is called a googol.

This is a 1 and one hundred zeros.

$10^{100} =$ 10 000 000 000 000 000 000 000 000 000 000 000 000 000 000 000 000 000 000 000 000 000 000 000 000 000 000 000 000 000 000 000 000 000 000 000

It takes Kerry $\frac{1}{4}$ second to write a zero and $\frac{1}{5}$ second to write the 1.
How long does it take her to write a googol?

1 Powers and roots

· ·

This number pattern is special.

The dots always form a square.

◄◄**REPLAY**►

. . .

. . . .

. . . .

·   · ·   · · ·

$1 \times 1 = 1$ $2 \times 2 = 4$ $3 \times 3 = 9$

For 1×1 we write 1^2 (one squared).
For 2×2 we write 2^2 (two squared).
For 3×3 we write 3^2 (three squared).

| **Square numbers** | The **square numbers** are 1, 4, 9, ...
We get them from 1^2, 2^2, 3^2, ... |

Exercise 2:1

1 Copy this table of square numbers.
    Fill it in.

1^2	2^2	3^2	4^2	5^2	
1	4	9			36

We can use the x^2 key on a calculator to work out square numbers.

Example　　　Work out 6^2

Key in: **6** x^2 **=**

Answer: 36

2 Use x^2 to work out:
　　a 3^2　　**b** 5^2　　**c** 7^2　　**d** 9^2　　**e** 10^2　　**f** 13^2

3 Use x^2 to work out:
　　a 21^2　　**b** 26^2　　**c** 31^2　　**d** 43^2　　**e** 29^2　　**f** 45^2

4 Use x^2 to work out:
　　a 20^2　　　　　　**b** 30^2　　　　　　**c** 40^2
　　Without using your calculator, write down the answers to:
　　d 50^2　　　　　　**e** 60^2　　　　　　**f** 70^2

5 Use x^2 to work out:
　　a 4.3^2　　**b** 7.5^2　　**c** 2.6^2　　**d** 31.2^2　　**e** 100^2　　**f** 130^2

Example　　　Find the area of this square.

Area = length × width
　　　= 4 × 4
　　　= 16 cm^2

4 × 4 is 4^2. You can use x^2

Key in: **4** x^2 **=**

Answer: 16 cm^2

4 cm

4 cm

6 Use x^2 to find the areas of these squares:

a

7 cm

7 cm

b

12 cm

12 cm

c

2.3 cm

2.3 cm

7 This bowling green is a square.
The length of a side is 25 m.
Find the area of the bowling green.

8 Mrs Brown has a square carpet.
The length of a side is 3.6 m.
Find the area of the carpet.

9 Find the area of this square
chessboard.
The length of a side is 48 cm.

Example   The area of this square is 25 cm².
What is the length of a side?

We know that
    5 × 5 = 25
So the length of a side is 5 cm.

area = 25 cm²

Exercise 2:2

1 Find the length of a side of these squares.

a

area = 4 cm²

c

area = 9 cm²

b

area = 16 cm²

d

area = 1 cm²

| **Square root** | On a calculator there is a $\sqrt{}$ key. |

This is called a **square root** key.

This key will find the length of a side of a square for you.

Example

The area of this square is $16\,\text{cm}^2$.

The length of a side is $\sqrt{16}$

Key in: $\sqrt{}$ ▢1 ▢6 ▢=

Answer: 4 cm

area = $16\,\text{cm}^2$

---

2 Use $\sqrt{}$ to find the length of a side of a square with area:

   a $36\,\text{cm}^2$ **b** $49\,\text{cm}^2$ **c** $121\,\text{cm}^2$ **d** $81\,\text{cm}^2$

3 Work out:

   a $\sqrt{25}$ **d** $\sqrt{169}$ **g** $\sqrt{361}$ **j** $\sqrt{676}$

   b $\sqrt{64}$ **e** $\sqrt{196}$ **h** $\sqrt{225}$ **k** $\sqrt{900}$

   c $\sqrt{144}$ **f** $\sqrt{324}$ **i** $\sqrt{256}$ **l** $\sqrt{3136}$

The area of this square is $7\,\text{cm}^2$.

The length of a side is $\sqrt{7}$

$\sqrt{}$ ▢7 ▢= on the calculator gives

$2.6457513\,11$

area = $7\,\text{cm}^2$

2.6   2.7

2.64 is nearer to 2.6 than to 2.7

The length of the side is 2.6 cm correct to one decimal place (1 dp).

Exercise 2:3

1 Copy this table.
Fill it in.

Area of square	√ from calculator	Length of side (to 1 dp)
11	3.3166248	
20		4.5
34		
19		
43		

2 Find the length of a side of these squares.
Add two more rows to your table from question **1**.
Write your answers in the new rows.

a
area = 14 cm²

b
area = 15.4 cm²

3 Work these out.
Give your answers correct to 1 decimal place.

a $\sqrt{29}$ **c** $\sqrt{42}$ **e** $\sqrt{200}$ **g** $\sqrt{378}$

b $\sqrt{60}$ **d** $\sqrt{189}$ **f** $\sqrt{569}$ **h** $\sqrt{206}$

4 This record sleeve is a square.
The area is 920 cm².
Find the length of a side.

◄◄REPLAY►

You sometimes have to multiply a number by itself lots of times.
$$2 \times 2 \times 2 \times 2 \times 2$$
A quick way of writing this is 2^5
The small number 5 is called a **power**.
$$2^5 = 2 \times 2 \times 2 \times 2 \times 2$$

Power	4^3 is 4 to the **power** of 3. The **power** '3' tells you how many fours are multiplied together.
Cube	Another name for a power of 3 is **cube**. So you can read 4^3 as '4 cubed'. $4^3 = 4 \times 4 \times 4 = 64$

Exercise 2:4

1 Write these numbers using a power.

  a 3×3 **c** $6 \times 6 \times 6 \times 6 \times 6$ **e** $9 \times 9 \times 9 \times 9 \times 9 \times 9$

  b $5 \times 5 \times 5$ **d** $8 \times 8 \times 8 \times 8$ **f** $4 \times 4 \times 4 \times 4 \times 4 \times 4 \times 4$

2 Work out the values of:

  a 4^2 **c** 2^4 **e** 2^5 **g** 4 cubed

  b 3^4 **d** 3^2 **f** 5 squared   **h** 6 cubed

Example	You can use the key on your calculator to work out powers. To find the value of 5^3 Key in: Answer: 125

3 Use to work out:

  a 5^4 **d** 6^4 **g** 8^3 **j** 15^3

  b 3^6 **e** 4^7 **h** 6^5 ● **k** 4.1^3

  c 7^3 **f** 2^8 **i** 21^2 ● **l** 3.7^5

● **4** Copy this number pattern.
Fill it in.
The numbers in the last column have a special name.
Guess what they are called.

$$1^3 = 1 \times 1 \times 1 = 1$$
$$2^3 = 2 \times 2 \times 2 = 8$$
$$3^3 = 3 \times 3 \times 3 = \ldots$$
$$4^3 = \ldots \times \ldots \times \ldots = \ldots$$
$$5^3 = \ldots \times \ldots \times \ldots = \ldots$$
$$\ldots^3 = \ldots \times \ldots \times \ldots = \ldots$$
$$\ldots^3 = \ldots \times \ldots \times \ldots = \ldots$$
$$\ldots^3 = \ldots \times \ldots \times \ldots = \ldots$$
$$\ldots^3 = \ldots \times \ldots \times \ldots = \ldots$$
$$\ldots^3 = \ldots \times \ldots \times \ldots = \ldots$$

2   Mental maths

Ruth, Andrew and Allison have
£2 to spend on ice cream.
They need to know which
ice creams they can buy.

Sometimes we have to work things out in our heads.

Exercise 2:5   Adding

Work these out in your head.
Write down the answers.

1   **a** $4 + 7$ **b** $17 + 8$ **c** $23 + 8$ **d** $33 + 8$

       $8 + 8$ $13 + 9$ $25 + 4$ $7 + 36$

       $6 + 9$ $8 + 15$ $26 + 8$ $6 + 35$

       $5 + 6$ $17 + 9$ $7 + 24$ $42 + 8$

       $4 + 9$ $19 + 5$ $8 + 27$ $39 + 7$

       $5 + 7$ $7 + 16$ $29 + 5$ $46 + 4$

       $8 + 9$ $8 + 14$ $28 + 6$ $5 + 38$

       $7 + 8$ $12 + 9$ $7 + 26$ $37 + 8$

2   **a** $30 + 40$ **c** $80 + 70$ **e** $50 + 16$ **g** $27 + 40$

     b $50 + 20$ **d** $900 + 400$ **f** $70 + 19$ **h** $54 + 30$

3   **a** $34 + 7$ **b** $25 + 8$ **c** $37 + 4$ **d** $42 + 9$

       $34 + 17$ $25 + 18$ $37 + 14$ $42 + 19$

       $34 + 27$ $25 + 28$ $37 + 24$ $42 + 29$

Example   Work out $38 + 24$

                 $24 = 4 + 20$ Add 4 $38 + 4 = 42$

                                   Now add 20 $42 + 20 = 62$

---

4   Do these in your head in the same way as the example.
Write down the answers.

     a $35 + 23$ **c** $45 + 34$ **e** $57 + 34$ **g** $65 + 36$

     b $28 + 24$ **d** $36 + 17$ **f** $44 + 36$ **h** $73 + 28$

5 Ruth, Andrew and Allison have £2 to spend on ice cream. Work out all the different combinations of three ice creams that they could buy.

ICE CREAMS
SMALL 60p
MEDIUM 70p
LARGE 80p

Game   Run from six

This is a game for any number of players. You need a dice and a piece of paper and a pencil to keep the score.

Throw the dice. Add up the score as you go along. You can throw the dice as many times as you like. If you throw a six you lose the score for that go!

Sally is playing the game. She throws the dice and keeps a total in her head. Here are Sally's throws: $4 + 1 + 3 + 5 + 3 = 16$ If Sally throws a six she will score 0. Sally decides to stop. She writes down her score of 16.

It is Stewart's turn. He throws $5 + 2 + 6$. So Stewart scores 0.

The winner is the first person to get to 100.

Play this game with some friends.

Exercise 2:6 Subtracting

1 Work these out in your head. Write down the answers.

	a	b	c	d
	$11 - 4$	$20 - 2$	$16 - 7$	$27 - 13$
	$12 - 7$	$30 - 9$	$23 - 6$	$45 - 34$
	$14 - 8$	$50 - 4$	$45 - 7$	$36 - 25$
	$15 - 6$	$20 - 7$	$34 - 5$	$58 - 47$
	$12 - 4$	$70 - 6$	$17 - 8$	$29 - 17$
	$13 - 9$	$90 - 3$	$53 - 4$	$44 - 23$
	$14 - 6$	$40 - 8$	$68 - 7$	$56 - 34$
	$11 - 8$	$80 - 5$	$85 - 6$	$39 - 18$

2 Copy each number pattern. Write down its rule.
Use your rule to fill in the missing numbers.
   a 19, 16, 13, ..., ..., ...   **c** 29, 24, 19, ..., ..., ...
   b 23, 19, 15, ..., ..., ...   **d** 26, 22, 18, ..., ..., ...

3 Work these out in your head.
Write down the answers.
   a $90 - 50$ **c** $120 - 30$ **e** $60 - 51$ **g** $50 - 42$
   b $700 - 500$ **d** $200 - 60$ **f** $56 - 40$ **h** $64 - 50$

Example   Work out $53 - 27$

              $27 = 7 + 20$ Subtract 7 $53 - 7 = 46$
                                 Now subtract 20 $46 - 20 = 26$

---

4 Do these in your head in the same way as the example.
Write down the answers.
   a $45 - 17$ **c** $54 - 27$ **e** $51 - 28$ **g** $83 - 64$
   b $63 - 35$ **d** $72 - 43$ **f** $65 - 36$ **h** $74 - 55$

5 Copy these.
Fill in the missing numbers.
   a $18 - 9 = ...$ **b** $23 - 6 = ...$ **c** $42 - 28 = ...$
       $... + 9 = 18$ $... + 6 = 23$ $... + 28 = 42$

6 Write down the answers to these subtractions.
For each one, write down an addition sum using the same numbers.
   a $17 - 8$ **b** $34 - 16$ **c** $47 - 29$ **d** $96 - 78$

Game   Take away dice

This is a game for any number of players.
You will need a dice. (Try an 8 or 10 sided dice.)
Each player makes a score sheet like this.

One player throws the dice.
All the players write the number somewhere above
the line on their score sheet.
You cannot move a number once you have written
it down.

After 8 throws all the boxes will be filled up.

Game 1

6	2	5	4
4	3	4	2

Now do 4 subtraction sums.
Take the bottom number away from the top one.
If the top number is smaller than the bottom one,
leave the answer blank.

6	2	5	4
4	3	4	2
2̶		1	2̶

Score: 1

Cross out any answers that are the same.
Add the rest of the answers together to get
your score.

Game 2

5	6	4	6
3	2	1	6
2	4	3	

Score: 2 + 4 + 3 = 9

The player with the highest score wins.

Play this game with some friends.

Exercise 2:7 Multiplying

1 Copy this multiplication table on
to squared paper.
Make it go up to 12 × 12.
Fill it in.

×	1	2	3	4
1				
2				
3				
4				

2 Use your multiplication table to help you answer these.

a 6 × 5   **d** 7 × 8   **g** 6 × 7   **j** 8 × 9
b 7 × 4   **e** 9 × 12 **h** 9 × 5   **k** 7 × 7
c 8 × 6   **f** 6 × 9   **i** 12 × 7 **l** 5 × 8

3 **a** How many times is 40 written in your multiplication table?
b Write down all the pairs of numbers that multiply to give 40.

4 **a** How many times is 36 written in your multiplication table?
b Write down all the pairs of numbers that multiply to give 36.

5 Work these out in your head.
Write down the answers.

a 12 × 3   **b** 2 × 8   **c** 5 × 9   **d** 7 × 4
12 × 30   20 × 8   5 × 90   7 × 40
12 × 300   20 × 80   50 × 90   7 × 400

Example Work out **a** 7×500 **b** 40×60

a $500 = 5 \times 100$
Multiply by 5 $7 \times 5 = 35$
Multiply by 100 $35 \times 100 = 3500$

b $40 = 4 \times 10$ $60 = 6 \times 10$
$4 \times 6 = 24$
$40 \times 6 = 240$
$40 \times 60 = 2400$

6 Work these out in your head.
Write down the answers.
  a 6×30 **c** 40×70 **e** 8×300 **g** 4×9000
  b 7×300 **d** 60×70 **f** 400×8 **h** 50×40

7 Copy these.
Fill in the missing numbers.
  a $24 \times 6 = 12 \times 12$ **b** $14 \times 15 = 7 \times \dots$ **c** $24 \times 35 = \dots \times 70$
     $= \dots$ $= \dots$ $= \dots$

8 Do these in the same way as question 7.
  a 18×4 **b** 28×3 **c** 16×45 **d** 22×15

Month's choice

a What do you notice
about $7 + 15$ and $8 + 14$?

| 7 | 8 |
| 14 | 15 |

Try other four-number squares.
Is there a rule?

Try a larger square.
Does this square
follow your rule?

2	3	4
9	10	11
16	17	18

AUGUST

S	M	T	W	T	F	S
…	…	1	2	3	4	5
6	7	8	9	10	11	12
13	14	15	16	17	18	19
20	21	22	23	24	25	26
27	28	29	30	31	…	…

b What do you notice
about 7×15 and 8×14?

| 7 | 8 |
| 14 | 15 |

Try some other squares.

c Do the same rules work for rectangles?

Exercise 2:8 Dividing

Example

$5 \times 4 = 20$
We can write down two divisions using the same numbers.
$20 \div 5 = 4$ $20 \div 4 = 5$

1 Work these out in your head.
Write down the answers.
For each one, write down two divisions using the same numbers.
   a 8×5 **b** 7×9 **c** 12×8 **d** 7×6

Example

Use your multiplication table to answer this:
$24 \div 6 =$

×	1	2	3	4	5	6	7	8
1	1	2	3	4	5	6	7	8
2	2	4	6	8	10	12	14	15
3	3	6	9	12	15	18	21	24
4	4	8	12	16	20	24	28	32
5	5	10	15	20	25	30	35	40
6	6	12	18	24	30	36	42	48
7	7	14	21	28	35	42	49	56
8	8	16	24	32	40	48	56	64

Answer: $24 \div 6 = 4$

2 Use your multiplication table to answer these.
   a $35 \div 7$ **c** $36 \div 9$ **e** $56 : 8$ **g** $54 \div 6$
   b $48 \div 6$ **d** $42 \div 7$ **f** $64 \div 8$ **h** $72 \div 8$

3 Copy these.
Fill in the missing numbers.
   a $27 \div 3 = ...$ **b** $32 \div 8 = ...$ **c** $42 \div 6 = ...$
       $270 \div 3 = ...$ $320 \div 8 = ...$ $420 \div 6 = ...$
                                  $3200 \div 8 = ...$ $4200 \div 6 = ...$

Example

Work out $48 \div 24$

$24 = 4 \times 6$ Divide by 4 $48 \div 4 = 12$
                Divide by 6 $12 \div 6 = 2$

4 Work these out in your head.
Write down the answers.
   a $56 \div 28$ **b** $36 \div 18$ **c** $48 \div 16$ **d** $72 \div 24$

5 Work these out in your head.
Write down the answers.
   a $240 \div 48$ **b** $180 \div 36$ **c** $560 \div 28$ **d** $720 \div 48$

C O R E

3 Estimation

● ●

Susan is choosing the wallpaper for
her bedroom.
She knows that she needs 7 rolls.

The flowers pattern costs £6.30 a roll.
The teddy bears pattern costs £7.85 a roll.
Susan's mum has £50 to spend.

Susan estimates the cost of each type of paper.
She says that the flowers cost about £6 a roll,
        7 rolls cost about 7 × £6 = £42

She says that the teddy bears cost about £8 a roll,
        7 rolls cost about 7 × £8 = £56

Susan knows that she can only have the flowers.

◄◄ REPLAY ►

Rounding

Examples **1**   Round the number 5.7 to the nearest whole number.

5.7 is nearer to 6 than to 5. It is rounded to 6.

2   Round the number 3.5 to the nearest whole number.

3.5 is halfway between 3 and 4. It is rounded to 4.

3   Round the number 63 to the nearest 10.

63 is nearer to 60 than to 70.
So 63 is rounded to 60 to the nearest 10.

4   Round the number 633 to the nearest 100.

633 is nearer to 600 than to 700.
So 633 is rounded to 600 to the nearest 100.

Exercise 2:9

1 Round these numbers to the nearest whole number.

    a 4.6   **c** 5.9   **e** 8.1   **g** 13.6

    b 3.8   **d** 6.5   **f** 4.3   **h** 10.2

2 Round these numbers to the nearest 10.

    a 18   **c** 57   **e** 91   **g** 101

    b 46   **d** 55   **f** 52   **h** 247

3 Round these numbers to the nearest 100.

    a 127   **c** 757   **e** 411   **g** 1234

    b 426   **d** 650   **f** 635   **h** 8935

4 Round these numbers:

    a 27 to the nearest 10   **c** 243 to the nearest 100

    b 13.5 to the nearest whole number   **d** 3678 to the nearest 100

Significant figure	In any number the first **significant figure** is the first digit which is not a 0. For most numbers this is the first digit.
Examples	The first significant figure is the red digit: 21.4 312 45.78 0.81
Rounding to 1 significant figure (1 sf)	To **round to 1 significant figure (1 sf)**: **a** look at the first digit after the first significant one **b** use the normal rules of rounding **c** be careful to keep the number about the right size
Examples	21.4 to 1 sf is 20. It is *not* 2! 312 to 1 sf is 300 45.78 is 50 to 1 sf 0.81 is 0.8 to 1 sf

---

5 Round these numbers correct to one significant figure.

    a 22.7   **d** 780   **g** 0.64   **j** 6661

    b 346   **e** 672   **h** 0.78   **k** 4012

    c 75   **f** 6.5   **i** 0.375   **l** 99

Estimating

We often work things out on a calculator.
It is a good idea to check that your answer is about right.
It is very easy to hit the wrong key by accident!

To get an estimate, round each number to one significant figure.

Example

Work out 4.9×3.2

Calculation: **4** **·** **9** **×** **3** **·** **2** **=**
Answer: 15.68
Estimate: 4.9 is 5 to 1 sf
3.2 is 3 to 1 sf
4.9×3.2 is about $5 \times 3 = 15$

15 is near to 15.68. So the answer is probably right.

Exercise 2:10

1 Work these out.
Write down the answer and an estimate for each one.
  a 4.6×3.1 **c** 3.2×7.5 **e** 6×4.8 **g** 5×2.3
  b 2.4×4.7 **d** 2.9×7.3 **f** 3×6.5 **h** 8×4.12

Example

Work out 36×82

Calculation: **3** **6** **×** **8** **2** **=**
Answer: 2952
Estimate: 36 is 40 to 1 sf
82 is 80 to 1 sf
36×82 is about $40 \times 80 = 3200$

3200 is near to 2952. So the answer is probably right.

2 Work these out.
Write down the answer and an estimate for each one.
  a 54×36 **c** 58×23 **e** 40×23 **g** 60×56
  b 26×72 **d** 39×21 **f** 20×57 **h** 80×45

Example

Work out 352×286

Calculation: **3** **5** **2** **×** **2** **8** **6** **=**

Answer: 100 672

Estimate: 352 is 400 to 1 sf
286 is 300 to 1 sf
352×286 is about $400 \times 300 = 120\,000$

120 000 is near to 100 672. So the answer is probably right.

Work these out.
Write down the answer and an estimate for each one.

3 **a** 124×356 **c** 578×123 **e** 200×278 **g** 300×525
    b 278×312 **d** 234×652 **f** 400×897 **h** 800×233

4 **a** 231×34 **d** 25.3×768 **g** $234 + 567$ **j** $3.6 \div 1.2$
    b 1.9×435 **e** 256.1×22 **h** $315 - 189$ **k** $248 \div 49.6$
    c 345×85 **f** 201.3×350 **i** $535 - 95$ **l** $499.2 \div 9.6$

When you answer questions you should always make an estimate to
check your answer.

Exercise 2:11

In this exercise:
a work out the answers using a calculator
b write down an estimate to check that each answer is about right.

1 Four of the classes in Year 8 collect bottles for recycling.
The table shows how many bottles they collect.

8D	8F	8M	8P
246	624	335	479

How many bottles are collected altogether?

2 The height of the television and
the stand is 118 cm.
The height of the stand is 53 cm.
What is the height of the television?

118 cm

53 cm

3 Daniel runs the Year 8 snack bar.
A can of cola costs 38 p.
A packet of crisps costs 23 p.
He buys 180 of each.
How much does he spend?

4 This set of garden furniture costs
£137.50.
The table costs £39.50.
   a How much do the four chairs cost?
   b How much is it for one chair?

5 Veronica is having a party. Her mum
buys a jar containing 396 sweets.
18 people come to the party.
How many sweets does each
person get?

6 126 pupils from Year 8 go ten-pin
bowling.
Only six people can play in one lane.
How many lanes do they need?

7 54 pupils from Year 8 have a day
out at Alton Towers. It costs £375.30.
How much does each pupil have to pay?

At Alton Towers each pupil buys a can of drink.
If one can costs 58 p, how much does this cost altogether?

Exercise 2:12

1 **a** Copy this list of square numbers.
Fill in the gaps.

1^2	2^2	3^2	4^2	5^2	6^2	7^2	8^2	9^2	10^2
1	4	9	...	...	...	...	...	...	...

   b (1) Copy this.
Fill in the missing numbers.

Estimate of $\sqrt{13}$

$\sqrt{9} = 3$ $\sqrt{16} = 4$

$\sqrt{13}$ is between ... and ...

$\sqrt{13}$ is about ... (Guess an estimate here)

(2) Check with a calculator to see how close you are.

   c Estimate these in the same way.

     (1) $\sqrt{46}$ (2) $\sqrt{51}$ (3) $\sqrt{90}$ (4) $\sqrt{20}$

2 Estimate the value of $3.6^2 + \sqrt{47}$
You need to decide how to round the numbers in question.
Show all of your working.

Game   3 guesses

This is a game for two players.
One player has red counters. The other player has blue counters.

You need a game card like this:

13	19	26	35	46	57	69

and a table like this:

598	741	3174	665
3933	455	247	1083
1196	494	2622	874
1311	897	1482	338

Each number in the table comes from multiplying two of the numbers on the game card.

You can cover a number in the table with one of your counters if you can guess which two numbers it comes from.
Use estimation to guess which two numbers you need.
The winner is the first person to get 3 counters in a row: across, down or diagonally.

Play the game with a friend.

1 Jodie has a square of red paper. The length of a side is 8 cm.

   a Use to work out the area of the red square.

   b Jodie has a square of yellow card. The length of a side is 15 cm.

     Use x^2 to work out the area of the yellow card.

   c Jodie draws a pattern called a tangram on the red square.
She sticks all the pieces of the tangram on the yellow card to make a picture.
What is the area of yellow card left uncovered?

2 Use ⎷ to work these out.
Write your answers correct to 1 dp when you need to round.

   a $\sqrt{1764}$ **b** $\sqrt{1600}$ **c** $\sqrt{3.8}$ **d** $\sqrt{59}$ **e** $\sqrt{200}$

3 **a** Use ⎷ to find the length of a side of this square silk scarf.
The area of the scarf is 3721 cm².

   b The scarf has a narrow hem round its edge.
Use your answer to **a** to find the total length of the hem.

4 Copy these.
Fill in the missing numbers.

   a $34 + 28 = \ldots$
     $\ldots - 28 = 34$

   b $56 - 19 = \ldots$
     $\ldots + 19 = 56$

   c $32 \times 8 = \ldots$
     $\ldots \div 8 = 32$

   d $72 \div 18 = \ldots$
     $\ldots \times 18 = 72$

Do these the same way as **a** to **d**.
Work them out. Then write down a new question using the same numbers.

   e $56 + 25 =$ **f** $83 - 47 =$ **g** $58 \times 6 =$ **h** $80 \div 5 =$

5 Use y^x to work out:

   a 3^4 **c** 9^5 **e** 5.2^3 **g** 0.4^3

   b 5^3 **d** 8^6 **f** 1.8^7 **h** 0.2^4

6 Work these out in your head.
Write down the answers.

a 27 + 56   c 150 − 28   e 30 × 50   g 72 ÷ 18
b 45 + 38   d 84 − 65   f 4 × 7000   h 64 ÷ 16

7 Round these numbers:
a 5.5 to the nearest whole number   f 514 to the nearest 100
b 790 to the nearest 100   g 85 to the nearest 10
c 4.612 to 1 dp   h 3894 to 1 sf
d 17.45 to 1 sf   i 13.915 to 1 dp
e 23 to the nearest 10   j 12.1 to the nearest whole number

8 a Round these correct to 1 sf.
(1) £328   (2) £54   (3) £563   (4) £1150
b Use your answers to **a** to estimate the answers to these.
(1) £328 + £54   (4) £328 + £563 + £1150
(2) £563 − £328   (5) £563 ÷ 2
(3) £1150 − £563   (6) £54 × 3
c Work out the accurate answers to **b**.
Compare the answers with your estimates.

9 Mr and Mrs Davies want to
decorate the hall, stairs and
landing of their house.
They need 18 rolls of wallpaper
and three tins of white paint.
a Write down an estimate for
the cost of the wallpaper and
paint.
b Find the actual cost.

10 a Copy this pattern.
Use to fill in the missing numbers.
Write your answers correct to 1 dp
when you need to round.
Predict $\sqrt{10\,000}$
b Use your calculator to check your prediction.

$\sqrt{1}$ = ...
$\sqrt{10}$ = ...
$\sqrt{100}$ = ...
$\sqrt{1000}$ = ...

11 Give estimates for these.
a $\sqrt{48}$ b $\sqrt{90}$ c $\sqrt{18}$ d $\sqrt{57}$ e $\sqrt{44}$

1 a Use $\boxed{x^2}$ to work out the area of this square.
   b Copy this. Fill in the missing number.
      $1\,\text{m}^2 = \dots \text{cm}^2$

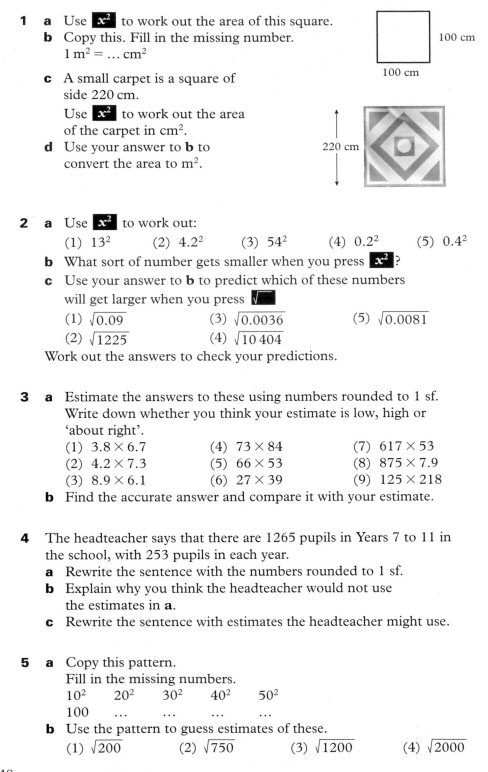

100 cm

100 cm

   c A small carpet is a square of side 220 cm.
      Use $\boxed{x^2}$ to work out the area of the carpet in cm^2.
   d Use your answer to **b** to convert the area to m^2.

220 cm

2 a Use $\boxed{x^2}$ to work out:
      (1) 13^2 (2) 4.2^2 (3) 54^2 (4) 0.2^2 (5) 0.4^2
   b What sort of number gets smaller when you press $\boxed{x^2}$?
   c Use your answer to **b** to predict which of these numbers will get larger when you press $\boxed{\sqrt{}}$
      (1) $\sqrt{0.09}$ (3) $\sqrt{0.0036}$ (5) $\sqrt{0.0081}$
      (2) $\sqrt{1225}$ (4) $\sqrt{10\,404}$
   Work out the answers to check your predictions.

3 a Estimate the answers to these using numbers rounded to 1 sf.
      Write down whether you think your estimate is low, high or 'about right'.
      (1) 3.8×6.7 (4) 73×84 (7) 617×53
      (2) 4.2×7.3 (5) 66×53 (8) 875×7.9
      (3) 8.9×6.1 (6) 27×39 (9) 125×218
   b Find the accurate answer and compare it with your estimate.

4 The headteacher says that there are 1265 pupils in Years 7 to 11 in the school, with 253 pupils in each year.
   a Rewrite the sentence with the numbers rounded to 1 sf.
   b Explain why you think the headteacher would not use the estimates in **a**.
   c Rewrite the sentence with estimates the headteacher might use.

5 a Copy this pattern.
      Fill in the missing numbers.
      10^2 20^2 30^2 40^2 50^2
      100   …   …   …   …
   b Use the pattern to guess estimates of these.
      (1) $\sqrt{200}$ (2) $\sqrt{750}$ (3) $\sqrt{1200}$ (4) $\sqrt{2000}$

- We can use the x^2 key on a calculator to work out square numbers.

  Example   Work out 6^2

      Key in: **6** x^2 **=**   Answer: 36

      You can use x^2 to find the areas of squares.

  Example   The area of this square is 4×4 or 4^2

      Key in: **4** x^2 **=**   Answer: $16\,cm^2$

  4 cm

  4 cm

- $\sqrt{}$ is the **square root** key.

  It will work out the sides of squares.

  Example   The length of a side of this square is $\sqrt{25}$

      Key in $\sqrt{}$ **2** **5** **=**

      Answer: 5 cm

  area $= 25\,cm^2$

- $\sqrt{7} = 2.645\,751\,3$

  $\sqrt{7}$ is 2.6
  correct to 1 dp

  2.6   2.7

  2.64 is nearer to 2.6 than to 2.7

- 4^3 means $4 \times 4 \times 4 = 64$. We can use y^x to work out powers.

  Example   Key in: **4** y^x **3** **=**   Answer: 64

- To work out questions in your head, do them a bit at a time.

  Examples   **1** $38 + 24$ Add the 4, then add the 20

                  2 $53 - 27$ Take away 7, then take away 20

                  3 7×500 Multiply by 5, then by 100

                  4 $48 \div 24$ Divide by 4, then by 6

- To round to one significant figure, look at the first unwanted digit. Then use the normal rules of rounding.

  Examples   21.4 to 1 sf is 20 not 2   312 to 1 sf is 300

                45.78 is 50 to 1 sf and 0.81 is 0.8 to 1 sf

- To make an estimate, round each number to 1 sf.

  Examples   **1** 2.8×34 **2** $589 - 128$

                  Estimate: $3 \times 30 = 90$ Estimate: $600 - 100 = 500$

                  Answer: 95.2   Answer: 461

- You can estimate square roots.

  Example $\sqrt{13}$ is between $\sqrt{9}$ and $\sqrt{16}$

                It is nearer to $\sqrt{16}$

                $\sqrt{13}$ is about 3.6

1 Use x^2 to work out:

   a 17^2 **b** 3.6^2 **c** 0.08^2

2 Use $\sqrt{}$ to work these out.

   Give your answer correct to 1 dp when you need to round.

   a $\sqrt{625}$ **b** $\sqrt{7.9}$ **c** $\sqrt{12\,345}$ **d** $\sqrt{45}$

3   **a**   Use x^2 to find the area of this square.

7.3 cm

   b   The area of this square is 250 cm².
      Use $\sqrt{}$ to find the length of a side.
      Give your answer correct to 1 dp.

area = 250 cm²

4 Use y^x to work out:

   a 7^5 **b** 13^4 **c** 8.4^3 **d** 0.2^6

5 Do these in your head.
   Write down the answers.

   a $37 + 56$ **c** $170 - 38$ **e** 80×8 **g** $108 \div 9$
   b $39 + 44$ **d** $38 - 19$ **f** 16×3 **h** $56 \div 14$

6   **a**   Round 5.6 to the nearest whole number.
   b   Round 65 to the nearest 10.
   c   Round 640 to the nearest 100.
   d   Round 1731 to the nearest 100.

7 Write these numbers correct to one significant figure.

   a 2.6   **b** 85   **c** 467   **d** 2370

8   **a**   Round the numbers correct to 1 sf to make estimates for these.
      (1) $327 + 589$ (3) 5.6×3.2
      (2) $1270 - 943$ (4) $504 \div 18$
   b   Work out the answers.
      Compare them with your estimates.

9 Make estimates for these.

   a $\sqrt{30}$ **b** $\sqrt{61}$ **c** $\sqrt{80}$ **d** $\sqrt{17}$

3 Statistics: questions and answers

The first opinion poll was done by **George Gallup** in **1935**.

Opinion polls are now often called Gallup polls. Gallup is one of the biggest survey companies in the world.

1 Diagrams and charts

◄◄ REPLAY ►

All of Year 8 have taken part in a survey.
The questions were about how much TV they watched.
They were also asked about their favourite type of programme and
their favourite channel.

Here are the results of the survey.

Number of hours watched per day

Hours per day	0	1	2	3	4	5	6
Number of pupils	20	45	75	60	10	5	5

Favourite type of TV programme

Type of programme	children's	soaps	sport	comedy	films	drama	news
Number of pupils	15	55	40	25	35	25	25

Favourite channel

Channel	BBC1	BBC2	ITV	C4	Sky	other
Number of pupils	73	22	66	19	24	16

Year 8 display this data.
Here is some of their work.

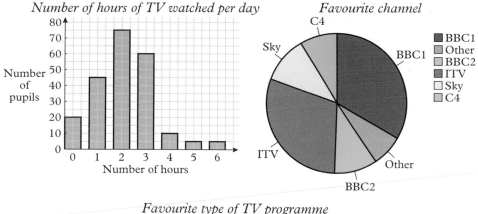

Number of hours of TV watched per day

Favourite channel

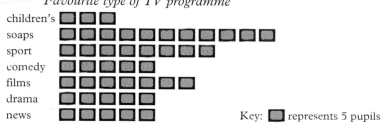

Favourite type of TV programme

children's
soaps
sport
comedy
films
drama
news

Key: ▢ represents 5 pupils

Exercise 3:1

1 Look at the bar-chart.
  a Add up the heights of all of the bars.
    How many pupils are there in Year 8?
  b Which is the highest bar?
    What does this tell you?
  c How many people watch TV for *more* than 3 hours a day?
  d There are 20 people in the 0 hours bar.
    Do you think they watch no TV at all?
    Explain your answer.

2 Look at the pictogram.
  a How many people does ▢ stand for?
  b How many more people liked soaps than liked news?
  c What is the least popular type of programme?
  d How could you show 3 people on this diagram?

3 Look at the pie-chart.
  a What is the most popular channel?
  b What is the least popular channel?
  c Can you tell how many people liked BBC2 the most?
    Explain your answer.

Exercise 3:2

1   Copy the axes on to squared paper.
Draw a bar-chart of the favourite types of programme.
Put a title on your diagram.

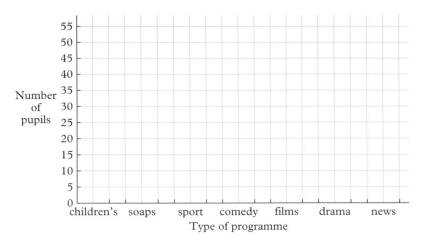

2   Draw a bar-chart to show the favourite channel.
Don't forget a title and labels.

3   Draw a pictogram of the number
of hours of TV watched.
Choose your own symbol.
Make sure that your diagram has a key.

Hours
0
1
2
3
4
5
6

4   Draw a pictogram of the favourite channels.
Choose a different symbol.
Don't forget the key.

● **5**   Compare each of your diagrams with the ones on page 53.
Write down which diagram you think is best for each set of data.
Explain your answer.

Year 8 were also asked how many videos they had hired in the last month.

Here are the answers from 8J and 8K.

8J

0	6	9	5	4	6	0	4	5	11
3	6	5	8	7	4	6	2	2	0
11	3	1	9	7	5	6	2	3	10

8K

2	5	4	9	6	8	2	3	4	0
1	8	5	3	10	5	9	4	2	6
4	5	8	9	6	3	5	10	2	0

Exercise 3:3

1 **a** Copy and finish off this tally-table for 8J.
Fill it in.

Number of videos	Tally	Total
0		
1		
2		
3		

b Draw a pictogram of these results.

2 **a** Make another tally-table for 8K.
b Draw a pictogram of these results.

• •

It is sometimes useful to collect data into groups.
This means that you have fewer categories.
It often makes diagrams easier to draw.

For the number of videos hired sensible groups might be:
0–2   3–5   6–8   9–11

Number of videos
0
1   this becomes group 0–2
2
3
4   this becomes group 3 –5
5

Exercise 3:4

1 **a** Copy this tally-table for 8J.
Fill it in.
You can use your chart from Exercise **3:3** to help you.
You do not have to start all over again!

Number of videos hired by 8J

Number of videos	Tally	Total
0–2 3–5 6–8 9–11		

b Copy the scales shown on to squared paper.

```
└───┴───┴───┴───┴───┴
  0–2  3–5  6–8  9–11
```

c Draw a bar-chart of your grouped data.
Remember that bar-charts of grouped data have their bars touching.

2 **a** Make a grouped tally-table for 8K.
Use the same groups.
b Draw a bar-chart for this data.
Use the same scale as in question **1**.

3 Here is the data for the videos hired by 8L.

5	1	9	0	0	6	7	10	5	9
8	3	5	6	8	9	0	0	1	4
5	10	1	7	3	6	7	7	5	4

a Make a grouped tally-table for this data.
b Draw a bar-chart for 8L.

2 Pie-charts

| Pie-chart | A **pie-chart** shows how something is divided up. The angle of the sector represents the number of items. |

Example

Class 8N were asked their favourite subject.

Out of the 28 pupils:
14 said Maths
 7 said PE
 7 said French

14 pupils is half the class.
Maths gets half of the pie.

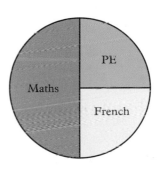

7 pupils is a quarter of the class.
PE and French both get one quarter of the pie.

Exercise 3:5

1 Class 8N were also asked where they had lunch.
One half used the canteen. One quarter went out of school and the other quarter brought sandwiches.
Draw a pie-chart to show this information.

2 100 people were asked to name a city in England.
Here are the results: London 50
                          Birmingham 25
                          York 25
  a Write down what fraction named each city.
  b Draw a pie-chart to show this information.

3 80 people were asked to name a city in Scotland.
Here are the results: Edinburgh 20
                       Aberdeen 20
                       Glasgow 20
                       Inverness 10
                       Dundee 10

a Draw a circle.
   Split it into 8 equal pieces.
   You could do this by cutting out
   the circle and then folding it.
b Use your circle to draw a pie-chart.

4 The same 80 people were asked to name an Irish city.

   40 people said Dublin
   30 people said Belfast
   10 people said Galway

a Split a circle into 8 equal pieces as you did in question **3**.
b Draw a pie-chart to show this information.

● **5** Finally the 80 people were asked to name a Welsh town.

   20 people said Cardiff
   30 people said Swansea
   25 people said Aberystwyth
    5 people said Aberdovey

Draw a pie-chart to show this information.

· ·

Sometimes the data does not work out into simple fractions.
When this happens you have to work out angles.

Remember: there are 360° in a full turn.
This means a pie-chart has 360° in the middle.
This 360° needs dividing up.

360°

Example
30 people were asked which national newspaper they read.
The results were: *The Guardian*   8   *The Times*   3   *Daily Express*   6
                    Daily Mirror   7   *The Sun*   6

Show these results in a pie-chart.

1 Divide up the 360°.

   There are 30 people in the survey so 360° ÷ 30 = 12°
   This means that each person gets 12° of the circle.

2 Work out the angle for each newspaper. This is easy to do in a table.

Newspaper	Number of people	Working	Angle
The Guardian	8	8 × 12° =	96°
Daily Mirror	7	7 × 12° =	84°
The Times	3	3 × 12° =	36°
The Sun	6	6 × 12° =	72°
Daily Express	6	6 × 12° =	72°
Total	30		360°

3 Check that the angles add up to 360°.
96° + 84° + 36° + 72° + 72° = 360°

4 a Draw a circle. Mark the centre.
Draw a line to the top of the circle.

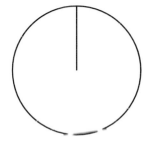

b Draw the first angle (96°).

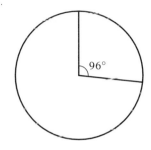

c Measure the next angle (84°) from the line that you have just drawn.

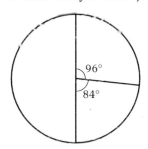

d Carry on until you have drawn all the angles.

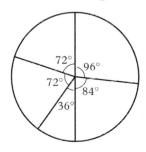

e Colour your pie-chart. Add a key.

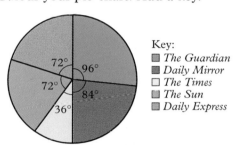

Key:
■ *The Guardian*
■ *Daily Mirror*
□ *The Times*
▨ *The Sun*
▨ *Daily Express*

Exercise 3:6

1 Class 8J were asked what they usually have for breakfast.
   a Copy this table.

Breakfast	Number of pupils	Working	Angle
cereal	9	9 ×	
toast	8	8 ×	
cooked	2	2 ×	
drink only	6	6 ×	
nothing	5	5 ×	
Total	30		360°

   b Copy and fill in:
      360° ÷ 30 pupils = ...° for each pupil.
   c Fill in the working and angle columns of the table.
   d Follow the instructions in the example to draw your pie-chart.

2 Class 8J were also asked how they travelled to school.
   a Copy this table.

Method of travel	Number of pupils	Working	Angle
walk	14		
bus	7		
car	6		
bike	3		
private jet	0		
Total	30		360°

   b Work out the angle for each pupil.
      360° ÷ 30 =
   c Fill in the rest of the table.
   d Draw a pie-chart to show this information.
      Don't forget the key.

3 Class 8P has 24 pupils.
Here are their answers to the travel survey.

Method of travel	Number of pupils	Working	Angle
walk	10		
bus	7		
car	6		
bike	1		

  a Copy the table.
  b Work out the angle for each pupil.
    $360° ÷ 24 =$
  c Fill in the rest of the table.
  d Draw a pie-chart to show this information.
    Don't forget the key.

4 90 people were asked which month
they were born in.

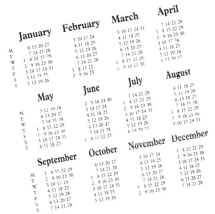

Here are the results.

Month	People	Month	People
January	7	July	6
February	4	August	8
March	9	September	11
April	8	October	7
May	7	November	10
June	6	December	7

  a Work out the angle for each person.
    $360° ÷ 90 =$
  b Work out the angle for each month.
  c Draw a pie-chart to show this information.
    Don't forget the key.

3   Designing a questionnaire

To get information, you need to ask questions.

You need to think carefully about the questions that you ask.
You must make sure that you get all the information that you need.
Your questions must be easy to answer.

Questionnaire   A **questionnaire** is a set of questions on a given topic.

There are two types of questionnaire.
Sometimes an interviewer asks the questions and fills in
the answers.
Sometimes you are given a form to fill in yourself.

There are some rules that you need to know when you write your own
questionnaire.

Rule 1   Questions should not be **biased**. They should not make you
think that a particular answer is right.
A question that does is called a **leading question**.

Example   Normal people like to watch football.
Do you watch football?

This question is biased.
The first sentence should not be there.
It makes you think that you aren't normal if you don't
watch football.

Exercise 3:7

Here is a list of questions.
- **a** Most people think that you should be able to learn to drive at 16. Do you agree?
- **b** Do you think you should eat less chocolate and more fruit?
- **c** How many weeks of school holiday should children get each year?
- **d** Most bright pupils watch the TV news. Do you watch the news?
- **e** Do you read a daily newspaper?

1 Which of these questions do you think are biased? Write down their letters.

2 Write down what makes each of these questions biased.

3 Write better questions to replace the ones that you thought were biased.

Rule 2   Questions should not upset people or embarrass them.

Exercise 3:8

Here is a list of questions.
- **a** How much do you weigh?
- **b** How much money have you got in your bank account?
- **c** How often do you have a shower?
- **d** Do you have any pets at home?
- **e** Most people use a deodorant. Do you?

1 Which of these questions do you think are upsetting or embarrassing? Write down their letters.

2 Write down what is wrong with each of the questions that you chose.

3 Write better questions to replace the ones that you didn't like.

Rule 3   Questions can give a choice of possible answers. This could be:
- **A** Yes, No or Don't know.
- **B** Agree, Disagree or Don't know.
- **C** A set of boxes with answers that you tick.
- **D** A scale where you circle your choice. This can be useful when you are asking for an opinion.

Exercise 3:9

Here is a list of questions.
Choose the style of answer that you would use for each one.
Write down **A**, **B**, **C** or **D**.

A ☐ Yes ☐ No ☐ Don't know

B ☐ Agree ☐ Disagree ☐ Don't know

C ☐ 0–2 ☐ 3–5 ☐ more than 5

D Strongly agree 1 2 3 4 5 Strongly disagree

1 How many chocolate biscuits do you eat each day?

2 The National Lottery is a good way of raising money for charity.

3 Do diesel cars cause less pollution than petrol cars?

4 Will you vote in the next general election?

5 How many brothers and sisters do you have?

Rule 4   Questions should be clear.
If people do not know what you mean you will not get the information that you need.

Rule 5   Don't ask questions that allow people to give lots of different answers.
This makes it very difficult to draw diagrams to show your results.

Rule 6   Don't ask questions that have nothing to do with your survey.

Rule 7   Questions should be in a sensible order.
Don't jump from one idea to another and back again.

Exercise 3:10

W   You need the **Fitness questionnaire worksheet** for this exercise.

1   Fill in the questionnaire.

2   For each question, write down the number of the rule that it has broken.

3   Rewrite the questionnaire using the rules that you have learned.

Exercise 3:11

You are now going to design your own questionnaire.
You can choose any topic that interests you.

You can't 'do' a wide topic like 'sport'. You need to focus on one
particular thing.
For example, you could find out how much sport pupils in Year 8 play.

When you have decided what you are going to do, you should guess what you
think you will discover.
For example, you might guess that Year 8 pupils spend less than 1 hour per
week doing sport.
This guess is called a hypothesis.
Then you design your questions to test whether your hypothesis is right or wrong.

You should plan your work like this:

1   Decide on your topic.
2   Guess what you think you will discover.
3   Decide who you will ask to fill in the
         questionnaire.
4   Write the questions for your questionnaire.
5   Try the questionnaire out on a friend.
6   Change the questions if you need to.

7   Do your survey!

8   Tally your results.
9   Decide which type of diagrams to use.
10   Draw your diagrams.
11   Work out some averages.
12   Write up your results.
13   Explain whether or not your hypothesis was right.

1 Class 8J were asked to name their favourite TV soap.
Their answers are shown in this table.

Soap	EastEnders	Coronation St	Brookside	Neighbours	Home and Away
Number of pupils	6	3	9	8	4

a How many pupils are there in Class 8J?

b Copy the axes on to squared paper.
Draw a bar-chart to show this information.
Don't forget a title and labels.

c Draw a pictogram to show the same information.
Don't forget to put a key and a title on your diagram.

2 Look at the pie-chart. It shows the results of a survey of 80 people.
They were asked how many cars their family had.

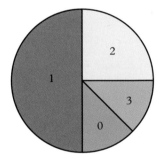

a How many families had 1 car?

b How many families had 2 cars?

c How many families did not have a car?

3 In a survey of 30 trains: 12 were on time, 10 were early and 8 were late.

a Copy this table. Fill it in.

	Number of trains	Working	Angle
on time	12	$12 \times 12° =$	
early	10		
late	8		

b Draw a pie-chart to show this information.

c Colour your chart. Add a key.

4   Class 8J were asked how long it took them to get to school.

The results are given correct to the nearest minute.

Time taken	Number of pupils
1–5	6
6–10	3
11–15	5
16–20	4
21–25	8
26–30	4

a   Copy the axes on to squared paper.

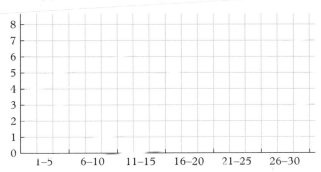

b   Draw a bar-chart to show this information.
Don't forget a title and labels.
c   How many pupils took 15 minutes or less to get to school?
d   How many pupils took more than 20 minutes to get to school?

5   A doctor recorded the length of time she spent with each patient.
Here are the times correct to the nearest minute.

10	5	9	20	14	3	8	6	9
4	23	16	11	15	17	8	6	3
9	5	6	8	19	21	6	10	11
5	9	29	3	6	14	18	17	8

a   How many patients did she see?
b   Copy this tally-table.
Add the extra rows that it needs.

Number of minutes	Tally	Total
1–5		
6–10		
11–15		

c   Fill in your tally-table.
d   Draw a bar-chart to show this information.

1 The 250 pupils in Year 8 chose the language that they would like to learn next.
The results are shown in this pie-chart.

50 pupils chose Italian.
  a How many pupils chose Spanish?
  b How many pupils chose Russian?
  c How many pupils chose German?

Russian 30%

Italian 20%

German 30%

Spanish 20%

2 Rajiv is planning a survey on smoking.
He has written some questions.
  a Which of Rajiv's questions do you think are biased?
    Say what makes them biased.
  b Which questions should have boxes to tick?
    Rewrite these questions showing the boxes.
  c Which questions are not clear enough?
    Rewrite these questions to make them clearer.

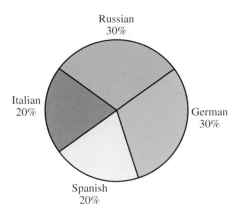

A. How often do you smoke?

B. Are cigarettes too expensive?

C. Do you think the unhealthy habit of smoking should be banned in public places?

D. Is it fair to take away people's right to smoke on aeroplanes?

E. Most sensible people do not smoke. Do you smoke?

3 Here is the most watched channel data from the beginning of the chapter.

Channel	BBC1	BBC2	ITV	C4	Sky	other
Number of pupils	73	22	66	19	24	16

There are 220 people in the survey.
  a Calculate the angle for each person.
  b Calculate the angle for each channel.
  c Round off the angles and then add them up.
    You will be 1° short. Add 1° to the biggest sector (BBC1).
  d Draw a pie-chart to show this data.
    Compare it with the one on page 53.

- **Pie-chart**

A **pie-chart** shows how something is divided up.

The angle of the slice represents the number of items.

Sometimes the data does not work out into simple fractions.

When this happens you have to work out angles.

A pie-chart has 360° in it.

This 360° needs dividing up.

Example

30 people were asked which national newspaper they read.

There are 30 people in the survey so $360° \div 30 = 12°$.

This means that each person gets 12° of the circle.

Work out the angle for each newspaper. This is easy to do in a table.

Newspaper	Number of people	Working	Angle
The Guardian	8	$8 \times 12° =$	96°
Daily Mirror	7	$7 \times 12° =$	84°
The Times	3	$3 \times 12° =$	36°
The Sun	6	$6 \times 12° =$	72°
Daily Express	6	$6 \times 12° =$	72°
Total	30		360°

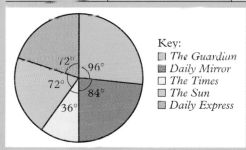

Key:
- The Guardian
- Daily Mirror
- The Times
- The Sun
- Daily Express

- **Questionnaire**

A **questionnaire** is a set of questions on a given topic.

There are two types of questionnaire.

Sometimes an interviewer asks the questions and fills in the answers.

Sometimes you are given a form to fill in yourself.

Remember:

1 Questions should not be biased.
2 Questions should not upset people or embarrass them.
3 Questions can give a choice of possible answers.
4 Questions should be clear.
5 Don't ask questions that allow lots of different answers.
6 Don't ask questions that have nothing to do with your survey.
7 Questions should be in a sensible order.

1   Phil is doing a survey into the time taken by Class 8J to get to school.
Here are the times correct to the nearest minute.

15	10	14	8	3	9	24	23	6	4
7	18	26	7	5	12	17	4	21	19
5	8	17	24	28	10	3	9	7	25

    a   Make a grouped tally-table for this data.
Use the groups 1–5, 6–10, 11–15, 16–20, 21–25, 26–30.
    b   Draw a bar-chart to show this information.

2   Year 8 were asked which was their favourite radio station.
200 answered the question.
100 said Radio 1, 25 said Radio 2, 25 said Atlantic 252 and
50 said Radio 5 Live.

    a   Work out what fraction chose each radio station.
    b   Draw a pie-chart to show this information.
Don't forget the key.

3   Pritti asked 8J to choose their favourite radio station.
Their answers were: Radio 1   10
                            Radio 2   4
                            Radio 5 Live   9
                            Atlantic 252   7
    a   Work out the angle for each pupil.
$360° \div 30 =$
    b   Copy this table. Fill it in.

	Number of pupils	Working	Angle
Radio 1	10		
Radio 2	4		
Radio 5 Live	9		
Atlantic 252	7		
Total	30		360°

    c   Use the table to help you draw a pie-chart of 8J's answers.
Don't forget the key.

4 Algebra

**Muhammed ibn Musa al-Khwarizmi
c780 – c850**

Al-Khwarizmi was a well known mathematician and astronomer who lived in Baghdad in the early 9th century. He wrote a book called *Kitab al-jabr wa al-nuqabalah*, which was about solving equations.

The word algebra comes from the word *al-jabr*.

1 Number patterns

Steve is making patterns with counters.
They are in the shapes of capital letters.

He wants to find the rules for his patterns.

1   2   3

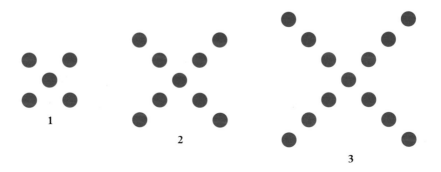

1   2   3

Exercise 4:1 Alphabet patterns

1 **a** Copy L shapes 1, 2 and 3 from the picture.
   b Draw L shapes 4 and 5.
   c Count the number of circles in each shape.
   d Copy this table.
     Fill it in.

L shape number	1	2	3	4	5
Number of circles	3	5			

   e Look at your table.
     How many circles are you adding each time?
   f Copy and fill in:
       The rule is add ... circles each time.

2 **a** Copy X shapes 1, 2 and 3 from the picture.
   b Draw X shapes 4 and 5.
   c Count the number of circles in each shape.
   d Copy this table.
     Fill it in.

X shape number	1	2	3	4	5
Number of circles	5	9			

   e Look at your table.
     How many circles are you adding each time?
   f Copy and fill in:
       The rule is add ... circles each time

3 Can you find some more letters that give patterns?
Draw your letters.
Fill in a table and find the rule.

Example   Lizzy is making triangles out of matchsticks.

    1   2   3

This table shows how many matchsticks she needs.

Number of triangles	1	2	3	4	5
Number of matchsticks	3	6	9	12	15

+3   +3   +3   +3

The rule is shown in red. It is $+3$.

Lizzy also finds a formula.
If she knows the number of triangles, she can work out the number of matchsticks.

Her formula is:
number of *m*atchsticks equals $3 \times$ number of *t*riangles.
In algebra this is $m = 3 \times t$

Exercise 4:2

1 Hitesh is making pentagons out of matchsticks.

1   2   3

a Copy this table.
Fill it in.

Number of pentagons	1	2	3	4	5
Number of matchsticks			15		

+?   +?   +?   +?

b Fill in the rule on your table.
c Copy and fill in:
The formula is:
number of *m*atchsticks $= \ldots \times$ number of *p*entagons
d Write this formula in algebra.

2 Apples are sold in trays of four.
   a Make a table to show the
      number of apples.
      Go up to 5 trays.
   b Write down the formula for
      finding the number of apples.
   c Write the formula in algebra.

Example

Computer disks are sold in boxes of 10.
The formula for the disks is:

   number of **d**isks = **10** × number of **b**oxes

In algebra this is: $d - 10 \times b$

We can use this formula to work out the number of disks in
any number of boxes.

Use your formula to find the number of disks in **20** boxes.

   number of **d**isks = 10 × **20**
                    = 200

---

3 Use the disks formula to find the number of disks in:
   a 6 boxes
   b 9 boxes
   c 100 boxes

4 The formula for the trays of apples in question 2 is: $a = 4 \times t$
   Use this formula to find the number of apples in:
   a 8 trays
   b 11 trays
   c 25 trays

5 Lucy is making **h**exagons out of **m**atchsticks.

   The formula is: $m = 6 \times h$

   Use this formula to find the number of matchsticks in:
   a 3 hexagons
   b 12 hexagons
   c 100 hexagons

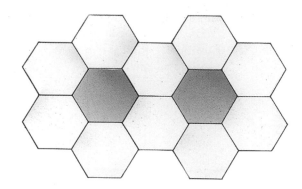

Rod is building a new patio.
He is using red and white slabs.
He wants to work out how many white slabs he needs for each red slab.

The formula is:
number of *w*hite slabs = **4 × number of *r*ed slabs + 2**
or $w = 4 \times r + 2$

Example   Use this formula to find the number of white slabs that Rod
needs for 5 red slabs.

number of *w*hite slabs = **4 × number of *r*ed slabs + 2**
$$= 4 \times 5 + 2$$
$$= 20 + 2$$
$$= 22$$

Exercise 4:3

1 Use the slabs formula to find the number of white slabs needed for:
   a 7 red slabs   **b** 10 red slabs   **c** 16 red slabs

2 Angela is tiling her bathroom.
She uses a formula to work out the number of tiles she needs.
The formula is:
$$t = 10 \times l + 8$$
(t = number of tiles, l = length of wall)
The wall is measured in metres.

Work out the number of tiles she needs if the length of the wall is:
   a 3 metres   **b** 5 metres   **c** 2.5 metres

3 This formula tells you how long to cook a turkey.
$$t = 10 \times w + 30$$

The weight (w) is in kilograms and the time (t) is in minutes.
How long does it take to cook a turkey which weighs:
a 3 kg **b** 6 kg **c** 7 kg

Aisha is working on an investigation into squares.

She has to find the formula for the number of matchsticks.

She has made a table.

Number of squares	1	2	3	4	5
Number of matchsticks	4	7	10	13	16

+3   +3   +3   +3

Aisha notices that the pattern goes up in 3s.
She knows that this means that the first part of the formula will be:
number of *m*atchsticks = 3 × number of *s*quares

She needs to work out the second part.
So far, her formula gives the green numbers in the table.

Number of squares	1	2	3	4	5
	3 +1	6 +1	9 +1	12 +1	15 +1
Number of matchsticks	4	7	10	13	16

Aisha needs to add 1 to get the right answers.

She writes the full formula:
number of *m*atchsticks = 3 × number of *s*quares + 1

Aisha uses her formula to work out how many matchsticks she will need to make 6 squares:
$$\text{number of } matchsticks = 3 \times 6 + 1$$
$$= 18 + 1$$
$$= 19$$

She makes 6 squares with matchsticks to check that her answer is right.

Exercise 4:4

1 These patterns are made from square tiles.

1   2   3

 a Look at the patterns
  Draw the next two.
 b Copy this table.
  Fill it in.

Number of blue tiles	1	2	3	4	5
Number of yellow tiles	8	13			

+?   +?   +?   +?

 c How many yellow tiles do you add each time?
 d Write down the first part of the formula.
 e Finish the row of green numbers.
  Use the first part of the formula.

Number of blue tiles	1	2	3	4	5
	5 +?	10 +?	+?	+?	+?
Number of yellow tiles	8	13			

 f What do you have to add to the green numbers to get the
  number of yellow tiles?
 g Copy and fill in the full formula:
   number of *yellow* tiles = ... × number of *blue* tiles + ...

Finding the first part of the formula

Look at your table of results.
See what you have to add each time.
This is the number that you multiply by in your formula.

2   Here are some diagrams of C shapes made out of squares.

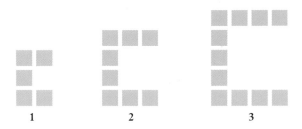

1   2   3

   a   Copy these diagrams.
      Draw the next two.
   b   Make a table to show the number of squares in each diagram.
   c   How many squares do you add each time?
   d   Write down the first part of the formula.
   e   What do you have to add to get the numbers in your table?
   f   Write down the full formula.
   g   Use your formula to work out the number of squares in the
      10th diagram.

3   **a**   Copy these dot diagrams.

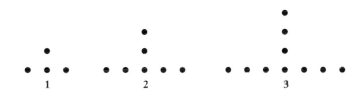

1   2   3

   b   Draw the next two diagrams.
      Count the dots in them.
   c   Make a table of your results.
   d   Write down the full formula.
   e   Check that your formula works with the next diagram.
   f   Use your formula to work out the number of dots in the
      20th diagram.

| | Number sequence | A **number sequence** is a pattern of numbers. |

Number sequence

Term

A **number sequence** is a pattern of numbers.

Each number in the sequence is called a **term**.
There is always a rule to work out the next term in
the sequence.

Example

Term number	1	2	3	4	5	6
Term	4	7	10	13	16	19

The rule to get the next term is $+3$.

Each term can also be worked out from a formula.
If you use the formula to work out the 20th term then you
do not have to work out all the previous 19 terms!

In this example the formula is: $t = 3 \times n + 1$
n is the term number and t is the term.

The 20th term is $t = 3 \times 20 + 1$
$= 60 + 1$
$= 61$

Exercise 4:5

1 For each of these sequences find:
  a the next three terms
  b the rule to get from one term to the next
  c the formula to work out each term from the term number
  (1) 7   9   11   13   ...   .
  (2) 5   8   11   14   ...   .
  (3) 6   10   14   18   ...   .
  (4) 20   30   40   50   ...   .
  (5) 18   36   54   72   ...   .
  • (6) 18   16   14   12   ...   .

2 For each of these sequences:
  a fill in the gaps
  b find the formula to work out each term from the term number
  (1) 5   8   ...   14
  (2) 7   ...   13   16
  (3) 4   9   ...   ...
  • (4) 12   33

2 Reversing rules

Rod has ordered 26 white slabs
for his patio.
He has forgotten how many
red slabs he needs.

Rod needs the inverse of his formula.
The formula is: $w = 4 \times r + 2$

First he writes his formula on robot screens.

$r \longrightarrow$ | $\times 4$ | $\longrightarrow$ | $+ 2$ | $\longrightarrow$ 26

The inverse machine is:

$6 \longleftarrow$ | $\div 4$ | $\xleftarrow{24}$ | $- 2$ | $\longleftarrow$ 26

He needs 6 red slabs.

Exercise 4:6

1 How many red slabs does Rod need for:
   a 34 white slabs   **b** 22 white slabs   **c** 42 white slabs

2 Zeta needs a new cycle helmet. The helmet costs £23.

   Zeta earns money delivering leaflets.
   Her wages are £2 for every packet of leaflets she delivers.
   She also gets £5 for lunch and bus fares.

   The formula is: $wages = 2 \times number\ of\ packets + 5$
   or: $w = 2 \times p + 5$

   a Write this formula on robot screens.
   b Draw the inverse machine.
   c How many packets does Zeta need to deliver to buy her cycle
          helmet?

3 George takes part in a sponsored silence.
His parents give him £5.
His friends sponsor him £2 per hour.

The formula is: *m*oney raised = 2 × number of *h*ours + 5
a Write George's formula in algebra.
b Draw the formula on robot screens.
c Draw the inverse machine.
d How long does George need to stay silent to raise:
  (1) £11   (2) £23   (3) £53

4 Some Year 8 pupils are going to Longleat.
The total cost (in £) is worked out using the formula:
  cost = 7 × number of *p*upils + 80
or: $c = 7 \times p + 80$

Work out the cost for:
a 20 pupils   **b** 36 pupils

· ·

You can also solve problems using equations.
To solve an equation you look to see what has been done to x.
You then find the inverse of this.

Examples   **1** Solve $x + 9 = 17$
The inverse of $+9$ is -9 so subtract 9 from both sides.

$$x + 9 - 9 = 17 - 9$$
$$x = 8$$

2 Solve $4r + 2 = 30$
$4r$ means $4 \times r$

This is the formula for the red and white slabs.
Solving this will answer the question
'How many red slabs does Rod need for 30 white slabs?'

The inverse of $+2$ is -2 so subtract 2 from both sides.

$$4r + 2 - 2 = 30 - 2$$
$$4r = 28$$

The inverse of $\times 4$ is $\div 4$ so divide both sides by 4.
$$\frac{4r}{4} = \frac{28}{4}$$
$$r = 7$$

◄◄ REPLAY ►

Exercise 4:7

Solve these equations.
You could write them using robot screens to help you.

1 $x + 4 = 10$

2 $x - 7 = 12$

3 $x + 15 = 23$

4 $3y = 12$

5 $4x = 24$

6 $\frac{1}{2}d = 5$

7 $2x + 1 = 9$

8 $7x - 3 = 46$

9 $2x - 5 = 15$

10 $3a - 2 = 8$

11 $6x + 7 = 19$

12 $\frac{b}{2} = 14$

13 $\frac{x}{3} = 5$

14 $\frac{x}{5} + 1 = 6$

15 $8 + 2y = 20$

● **16** $2z - 6 = 5$

Exercise 4:8

A cattle farmer wants to work out how many cows he can keep in each of his fields.
Each cow needs enough space to graze.

The formula for working out the area needed is: $A = 6c + 10$
c is the number of cows

This table gives the areas of the farmer's fields in square metres.
Work out how many cows he can keep in each field.

Field	A	B	C	D	E	F
Area of field	40	190	220	165	16	310

3 Substitution

Lots of equations used in maths and science have powers in them.

◀◀ **REPLAY** ▶

Exercise 4:9

The letters represent the numbers shown:

$$a = 2 \quad b = 5 \quad c = 3 \quad d = 4 \quad e = 10$$

Work these out.
(*Remember:* $3 \times a$ is written $3a$ in algebra and $a \times b$ is written ab.)

1 $b + 8$ **3** $d + e$ **5** $d + b - c$ **7** ab

2 $3a$ **4** $2c - a$ **6** $5d - 4b$ **8** $2cd - e$

9 A formula used in science is $F = ma$ where F is a force.
Find F if $m = 6$ and $a = 9$.

10 The formula $P = 2l + 2w$ gives the perimeter of a rectangle.
Find P when $l = 8$ and $w = 2$.

Power	a^2	The **power** '2' tells you how many a's are multiplied together.
		$a \times a = a^2$
		$a \times a \times a = a^3$

---

11 Write these as a power.
   a $d \times d \times d$ **c** $y \times y$
   b $a \times a \times a \times a \times a$ **d** $c \times c \times c \times c$

12 Find the value of:
   a 4^2 **b** 2^4 **c** 5^3

Kerry and Sapna are helping on a farm during their holiday.
The farmer asks them to find the area of these fields.

Kerry and Sapna work out the area in different ways.

Kerry's method
Area of 1 field $= 10 \times 10$
$= 100$
Area of 4 fields $= 4 \times 100$
$= 400$

Sapna's method
Area of big square $= 20 \times 20$
$= 400$

They both get the same answer.

They write a formula that gives the area of any size field.

Kerry's method
Area of 1 field $= y \times y$
$= y^2$
Area of 4 fields $= 4 \times y^2$
$= 4y^2$

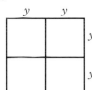

Sapna's method
Area of big square $= 2y \times 2y$
$= 2 \times y \times 2 \times y$
$= 4 \times y \times y$
$= 4y^2$

They both get the same answer again.

$y \times y$ is written y^2 so $2y \times 2y$ is written $(2y)^2$
      $(2y)^2$ is the same as $4y^2$

In algebra their formulas are:
    $A = 4y^2$ $A = (2y)^2$

Example

Use Kerry and Sapna's formulas to find the area of the fields when $y = 30$.

$$A = 4y^2$$
$$= 4 \times 30^2$$
$$= 4 \times 900$$
$$= 3600$$

$$A = (2y)^2$$
$$= (2 \times 30)^2$$
$$= (60)^2$$
$$= 60 \times 60$$
$$= 3600$$

Exercise 4:10

1 Use Kerry and Sapna's formulas to find the area of the fields when the value of y is:

a 20   **b** 35   **c** 40   **d** 25   **e** 33

2 John is using the formula $D = 3t^2$ in science.
Find the value of D when the value of t is:

a 2   **b** 5   **c** 9   **d** 10

3 The area of a shape is given by the formula $a = (4d)^2$
Find the value of a when the value of d is:

a 3   **b** 4   **c** 5   **d** 6

Example

$c = 2$ $d = 3$ $e = 5$ $f = 10$

Work out   **a** $3f^2$ **b** $4c^3$

a $3f^2 = 3 \times f^2$
$\qquad = 3 \times 10^2$
$\qquad = 3 \times 100$
$\qquad = 300$

b $4c^3 = 4 \times c^3$
$\qquad = 4 \times 2^3$
$\qquad = 4 \times 8$
$\qquad = 32$

Work these out.

4 d^3 **6** e^3 **8** $4e^2$ **10** $7f^4$

5 c^4 **7** $2d^2$ **9** $5c^3$ **11** $3e^2$

Example   Work out   **a** $(4d)^2$ **b** $(2e)^3$

a $(4d)^2 = (4 \times d)^2$ **b** $(2e)^3 = (2 \times e)^3$
$= (4 \times 3)^2$ $= (2 \times 5)^3$
$= 12^2$ $= 10^3$
$= 144$ $= 1000$

Exercise 4:11

$c = 2$ $d = 3$ $e = 5$ $f = 10$

Work these out.

1 $(2f)^2$ **4** $5d^2$ **7** $(4f)^3$

2 $(3d)^3$ **5** $(5d)^2$ **8** $3c^4$

3 $(4c)^2$ **6** $4f^3$ **9** $(3c)^4$

● **10**   Fill in the missing numbers.
  a $(y^2)^3 = y^?$ **b** $(m^4)^2 = m^?$ **c** $(s^3)^4 = s^?$

Exercise 4:12 Traffic light squares

Look at these patterns of coloured squares.

1

2

How many yellow and green squares would there be in the
50th traffic light square?
How many red squares would there be in the 50th traffic light square?

Design some square patterns of your own.
You could use more colours.
For each pattern, work out how many of each colour there would be in the
50th square.

1 The cost of having a car repaired is £10 plus £15 for each hour that the job takes.
  a Copy and fill in:
    The formula is:
        $cost = \ldots \times \text{number of } \boldsymbol{h}\text{ours} + 10$
  b Write the formula in algebra.
  c Find the cost of a repair that takes 3 hours.

2 Roundabouts are put at crossroads like this:

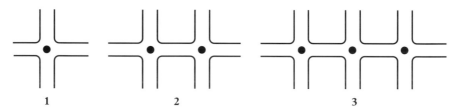

| 1 | 2 | 3 |

  a Draw the next two diagrams in this pattern.
  b Copy this table.
    Fill it in.

Number of roundabouts	1	2	3	4	5
Number of roads	4	7			

  c Look at the table.
    How many roads are you adding each time?
  d Copy and fill in:
    The formula is:
        number of $\boldsymbol{r}$oads $= \ldots \times \ldots \ldots \ldots \ldots + \ldots$
  e Write your formula in algebra.
        $\boldsymbol{r} = \ldots \times \ldots + \ldots$

3 Jane is having a party.
    The cost of the food is £15 plus £3 for each person.
  a Copy and fill in:
    The formula is:
        $cost = \ldots \times \text{number of } \boldsymbol{p}\text{eople} + \ldots$
  b Write the formula in algebra.
  c Work out the cost of food for 40 people.
  d Write the formula on robot screens.
  e Draw the inverse machine.
  f The food costs £78.
    How many people are coming to the party?

4   For each of these sequences find:
   a   the next three terms
   b   the rule to get from one term to the next
   c   the formula to work out each term from the term number

   (1)   1   3   5   7   ...   .
   (2)   7   11   15   19   ...   .
   (3)   1   6   11   16   ...   .
   (4)   9   12   15   18   ...   .
   (5)   4   14   24   34   ...   .

5   Solve these equations.
   a $x + 6 = 11$
   b $y - 9 = 15$
   c $7x = 21$
   d $2x + 3 = 15$
   e $5y - 8 = 12$
   f $8d + 11 = 35$
   g $\frac{x}{2} = 4$
   h $\frac{y}{3} = 12$
   i $\frac{t}{2} + 6 = 20$
   j $\frac{y}{2} - 7 = 11$

6   Write these as a power.
   a $t \times t$
   b $s \times s \times s \times s$
   c $y \times y \times y$

7   Find the value of:
   a 5^2
   b 4^3
   c 2^5
   d 3^4

8   $a = 5$ $b = 3$ $c = 2$ $d = 10$
   Work out:
   a $4 + b$
   b $c + d$
   c $3d$
   d $5 + 3c$
   e $2a + 3c$
   f $4d - 3a$
   g d^2
   h c^4
   i b^2
   j $a^2 + c^2$
   k $5c^2$
   l $(5c)^2$

1 The area of a rabbit run in square metres is worked out using the formula:

$$A = 4r + 3$$

r is the number of rabbits.

What area is needed for:

a 4 rabbits   **b** 7 rabbits

How many rabbits can you put in a run with area:

c $11\,\text{m}^2$ **d** $51\,\text{m}^2$

2 $V = IR$ is a formula used in science.
Find V when:

a $I = 8$ and $R = 5$ **b** $I = 12$ and $R = 2$

3 Peter is using the formula $D = 5t^2$ in maths.
Find the value of D when:

a $t = 7$ **b** $t = 12$

4 In science we use the formula Energy $= 8x^2$
Find the energy when:

a $x = 12$ **b** $x = 20$

5 Fill in the gaps in these sequences.

a 6.5   10   13.5   ...   .
b 8   7.8   ...   ...   7.2   ...
c 7   ...   10   ...   ...   14.5
d 6   ...   .   8.5

6 Find the formula for the sequence:

15   13   11   9   7   5

7 The formula for a sequence is $t = 8n - 7$
a Find the 26th term.
b Which term is equal to 65?

- **Number sequence**   A **number sequence** is a pattern of numbers
  Term   Each number in the sequence is called a **term**.

Example

Term number	1	2	3	4	5	6
Term	4	7	10	13	16	19

The rule to get to the next term is $+3$.

Each term can also be worked out from a formula.
In this example the formula is $t = 3 \times n + 1$
n is the term number and t is the term.

The 20th term is: $t = 3 \times 20 + 1$
$$= 61$$

- You can work backwards by reversing the formula.
  This is called **finding the inverse**.

If the formula is $w = r \times 4 + 2$
First write it on robot screens.

Then reverse it to find the **inverse**.

- **Solving equations**
  You can solve problems using equations.

Example   Solve $4r + 2 = 30$
$4r$ means $4 \times r$

The inverse of $+2$ is -2 so subtract 2 from both sides.

$$4r + 2 - 2 = 30 - 2$$
$$4r = 28$$

The inverse of $\times 4$ is $\div 4$ so divide both sides by 4.

$$\frac{4r}{4} = \frac{28}{4}$$
$$r = 7$$

- **Power** a^2 The **power** '2' tells you how many a's are multiplied together.
  $$a \times a = a^2 \qquad\qquad a \times a \times a = a^3$$

Be careful when substituting into powers.
Look at these when $d = 3$.
They give different answers.

$$4d^2 = 4 \times 3^2 \qquad\qquad (4d)^2 = (4 \times 3)^2$$
$$= 4 \times 9 \qquad\qquad\qquad\quad = 12^2$$
$$= 36 \qquad\qquad\qquad\qquad\quad = 144$$

1 Wesley is tiling his bathroom in a pattern like this:

       1   2   3

  a Draw the next two patterns.
  b Copy this table.
     Fill it in.

Number of blue tiles	1	2	3	4	5
Number of white tiles	5	8			

          +?   +?   +?   +?

  c How many white tiles do you add each time?
  d Write down the first part of the formula.
  e What do you have to add to get the numbers in your table?
  f Copy and fill in the full formula:
        number of **w**hite tiles = ... × number of **b**lue tiles + ...
  g Wesley uses 17 blue tiles.
     How many white tiles does he use?
  h Write your formula on robot screens.
  i Draw the inverse machine.
  j Wesley used 62 white tiles.
     How many blue tiles did he use?

2 The formula for a sequence is: $t = 4 \times n + 3$
   Work out the first 3 terms of the sequence.

3 $a = 2$ $b = 5$ $c = 7$
   Work out:
  a $2a + 10$ **c** c^2 **e** $2b^2$
  b $2b + c$ **d** b^3 **f** $(2b)^2$

5 Transformations

QUESTIONS

EXTENSION

SUMMARY

TEST YOURSELF

Mirror

Mirror   Objects

David Brewster invented the kaleidoscope in 1816. It is made with two mirrors in a tube. The angle between the mirrors can be 45° or 60°. When the end of the tube is rotated, coloured pieces of plastic between the two mirrors are reflected to make symmetrical patterns.

Which other angles would work? Why?

1 Reflections

The lake acts like a mirror.
The trees are reflected in it.
The mirror line is a line of symmetry.

◀◀ REPLAY ▶

Exercise 5:1

Copy these diagrams on to squared paper.
Draw their reflections in the mirror lines.

1

2
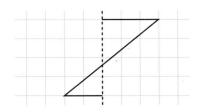

The object does not have to touch the mirror line.
The reflection is the same distance from the mirror line as the object.

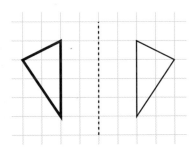

Put an object 2 squares
in front of a mirror line.

Its reflection is 2 squares
behind the mirror line.

Copy these diagrams on to squared paper.
Draw their reflections in the mirror lines.

3

5

4

6

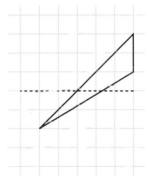

The mirror line is not always a line of the grid.

The reflection or image is still the same distance from the mirror line as the object.
Here the distance is diagonally across two squares.

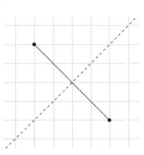

Image The **image** is how the object appears after reflection or rotation.

Copy these diagrams on to squared paper.
Draw their reflections in the mirror lines.

7

8

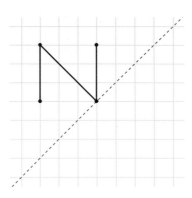

• **9** Trace these diagrams on to tracing paper.
Fold the tracing paper along the mirror line.
Trace the object again.
Open out the tracing paper and hold it up to the light.
You will see the object and its reflection.

a

b

c

Exercise 5:2

1 Copy these axes on to squared paper.
  a Plot these points:
    A (1, 2)   B (2, 4)   C (5, 1)
    Label each point with its letter.
    Join the points to get triangle ABC.
  b Reflect triangle ABC in the y axis to
    get a new triangle $A_1B_1C_1$.
    The reflection of A is A_1, etc.

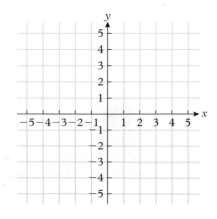

c Copy this table for the reflection.
Fill it in.

Co-ordinates of ABC		A(1, 2)	B(2, 4)	C(5, 1)
Co-ordinates of $A_1B_1C_1$		$A_1(-1, 2)$	B_1	C_1

d The reflection changes the co-ordinates.
Write down the rule for this change.
e Reflect the original triangle ABC in the x axis to get triangle $A_2B_2C_2$.
f Copy this table for the reflection.
Fill it in.

Co-ordinates of ABC		A(1, 2)	B(2, 4)	C(5, 1)
Co-ordinates of $A_2B_2C_2$		$A_2(1, ...)$	B_2	C_2

g The reflection changes the co-ordinates.
Write down the rule for this change.
h To complete the pattern triangle $A_3B_3C_3$ could be drawn in the third quadrant.
Use your rules from part **d** and part **g** to predict the co-ordinates of triangle $A_3B_3C_3$.
Draw $A_3B_3C_3$ to see if you are right.

2 Copy the axes from question **1** again.
  a This co-ordinate table is for the line $y = x$
  The y co-ordinate equals the x co-ordinate.
  Copy the table.
  Fill it in.

x		-5	-4	-3	-2	-1	0	1	2	3	4	5
y		-5			-2			1				

  b Plot the points. Join them with a ruler.
  Label your line $y = x$
  c Plot these points: A(-2, 1)   B(-2, 5)   C(3, 5)   D(2, 3)
  Label each point with its letter.
  Join the points to get quadrilateral ABCD.
  d Reflect ABCD in the line $y = x$
  Label the reflected shape $A_1B_1C_1D_1$.

This shape made from cubes
is reflected in a mirror.

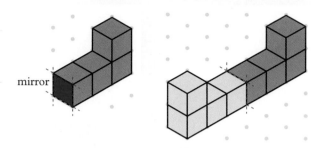

mirror

Exercise 5:3

You will need some cubes and some dotty isometric paper for
this exercise.

1 Make these shapes from cubes.
Make their reflections.

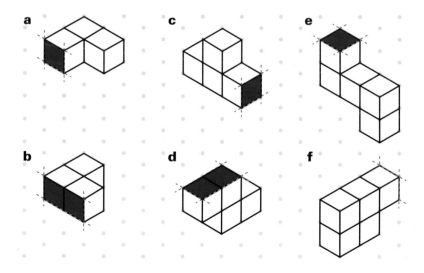

a

c

e

b

d

f

2 a Make this shape and its reflection.
b Draw your shape on isometric paper.

3 Make some shapes and their reflections of your own.

2 Movement – translations

There are different rides at the fair.
You can go straight down the field on the train.
You can go round and round on a roundabout.

Translation	A **translation** is a movement in a straight line.
Rotation	A **rotation** is a movement round in a circle.

Exercise 5:4

1 Write down whether these movements are translations or rotations.
  a opening an ordinary door
  b running 100 metres
  c going up in a lift
  d opening a book
  e swimming a length
  f unscrewing the top of a bottle

2 Give two examples of your own of translations.

3 Give two examples of your own of rotations.

5

Translations

Example

Translate the L shape 4 squares to the right.

Choose one point.
Move the point 4 squares to the right.
Move the other points in the same way.

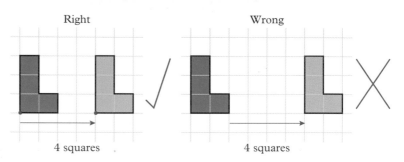

Exercise 5:5

You will need squared paper for this exercise.

1 Copy this L shape on to squared paper.
You will need a new copy for each part of the question.
Label each copy with the question number.

Translate your L:
a 5 squares to the right
b 4 squares down
c 3 squares to the left
d 5 squares up
e 6 squares down
f 5 squares to the left

2 The dark blue L has moved
4 squares to the right and
3 squares up.
a Copy the diagram on to
squared paper.
b Draw a new L on the same
piece of paper.
Translate it 2 squares to the
left and 4 squares down.

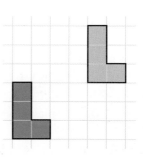

3 Write down the number of squares that the dark blue L has moved.
Write down if it went left, right, up or down.

a

c

e

b

d

4 Draw an *x* axis and a *y* axis from 0 to 10.
  a Plot these points:
    A (1, 1)   B (4, 1)   C (3, 3)
    Join the points to make a triangle.
  b Translate triangle ABC 5 units to the right and 2 units up.
    Label the image triangle $A_1B_1C_1$
  c Translate triangle ABC 2 units to the right and 6 units up.
    Label the image triangle $A_2B_2C_2$.
  d Write down the translation that takes $A_1B_1C_1$ to $A_2B_2C_2$.
  e Write down the translation that takes $A_2B_2C_2$ to $A_1B_1C_1$.

Game Translate a cube

This is a game for two players.
You need a board like this,
a red dice and a blue dice, and
a small cube.
Put the cube on 'start'.

The first player rolls both dice.

The red dice gives the number of squares to move the cube across.
You can move left or right.
The blue dice gives the number of squares to move the cube
up or down.
The first player moves the cube.

The second player now rolls both dice and moves the cube.

You score points if you land on a coloured square.

= 1 point   = 3 points

The first person to score 5 points or more wins.

3 Rotation

When the traffic is on the roundabout it goes in circles. The centre of the circles is the middle of the roundabout.

◄◄ **REPLAY** ►

A rotation or turning can be clockwise or anti-clockwise.
The amount of turning can vary.

Quarter turn clockwise

Half turn anti-clockwise

Exercise 5:6

1 Are these rotations clockwise or anti-clockwise?
How much have they turned?

a **b** **c** **d**

2 Start with this arrow each time.
Draw the arrow after each rotation:
   a a quarter turn anti-clockwise
   b a half turn clockwise
   c a three-quarter turn clockwise

Centre of rotation

When an object rotates it turns about a **centre of rotation**.

The centre of rotation can be in different places.

The arrow has moved a quarter turn clockwise about different centres.

In this exercise centres of rotation are shown in red.

Start by copying an arrow into your book.
Use tracing paper to trace the arrow.
Put your pencil point on the centre. Rotate the tracing paper.
The tracing paper shows you the new position of the arrow.
Draw the new position of the arrow in your book.

Rotate the tracing paper

3 Give the arrow a quarter turn anti-clockwise about the centre.
The centre each time is marked with ●

a ●——▶   b ——▶●   c ——●—▶

4 Give the arrow a half turn clockwise about the centre.

a   b   c

The centre of rotation does not have to be on the arrow.

The arrow has moved a quarter turn clockwise about different centres.
The arc showing the turn has not been drawn.

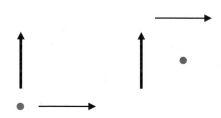

5 Give the arrow a quarter turn anti-clockwise about the centre.
Use tracing paper to help you.
Do not draw the arc showing the turn.

a

b

6 Give the arrow a half turn clockwise about the centre.

a

b

◄◄ **REPLAY** ►

Rotational symmetry	A shape has **rotational symmetry** if it fits on top of itself more than once as it makes a complete turn.
Order of rotational symmetry	The **order of rotational symmetry** is the number of times that the shape fits on top of itself. This must be 2 or more.

These shapes have rotational symmetry.

order 2

order 3

order 4

Exercise 5:8

C marks the centre of rotation.

1 a Copy the diagram on to squared paper.
b Give the flag a half turn about C.
Draw the new position.
c Write down the order of rotational symmetry of your diagram.

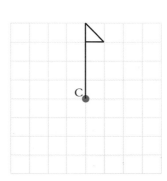

2 a Copy the diagram for question **1** on to squared paper.
  b Give the flag a quarter turn clockwise about C.
    Draw the new position.
  c Give the flag another quarter turn clockwise about C.
    Draw the new position.
  d Give the flag another quarter turn clockwise about C.
    Draw the new position.
  e Write down the order of rotational symmetry of your diagram.

Exercise 5:9

1 Copy these. Fill in the missing numbers.
      a full turn $= 360°$ a half turn $= ...°$
      a quarter turn $= ...°$ a three-quarter turn $= ...°$

2 Copy each diagram on to squared paper.
    Rotate the triangle about C each time.

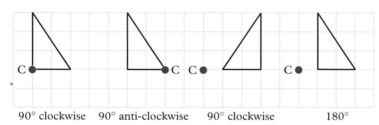

      90° clockwise   90° anti-clockwise   90° clockwise   180°

3 Copy these axes on to squared paper.
  a Plot these points:
    A(2, 1) B(6, 1) C(6, 3) D(4, 3)
    Join the points to make a
    trapezium.
  b Rotate ABCD 90° clockwise about
    the origin.
    Label the image $A_1B_1C_1D_1$.
  c Rotate ABCD 180° about the
    origin.
    Label the image $A_2B_2C_2D_2$.
  d Rotate ABCD 90° anti-clockwise
    about the origin.
    Label the image $A_3B_3C_3D_3$.
  e How many degrees do you turn
    clockwise to rotate ABCD to
    $A_3B_3C_3D_3$?

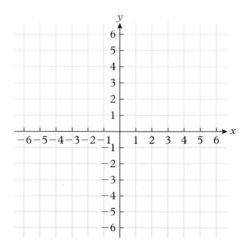

Patterns with reflections, translations and rotations

You need some large squared paper.
Cut out a 4 × 4 grid of squares.

Draw a pattern in the top left-hand corner.

Translate the pattern to
each square to get this.

Reflect the pattern in each
line of the grid to get this.

This pattern has
been rotated through
a quarter turn clockwise
each time.

Try some patterns of your own.

4 Enlargement

The photographs of the school play at Stanthorne High are ready.

There is a standard size or an enlargement.
The enlargement is twice as wide and twice as long as the standard size.

Enlargement An **enlargement** changes the size of an object.
The change is the same in all directions

Scale factor The **scale factor** tells us how many times bigger the enlargement is.

Example Enlarge the rectangle by a scale factor of **2**.

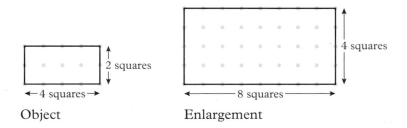

Object   Enlargement

The enlargement is **2** times as long and **2** times as wide as the object.

Exercise 5:10

1 Copy these shapes on to squared paper.
Enlarge each shape by a scale factor of 2.

a **b** **c** **d**

2 Enlarge the shapes in question **1** by a scale factor of 3.

· ·

Exercise 5:11

1 Draw an x axis from 0 to 9 and a y axis from 0 to 12.
  a Plot these points in order.
     Join them as you go.
     $(2, 2)$ $(2, 4)$ $(1, 6)$ $(3, 6)$ $(3, 2)$ $(2, 2)$
  b Copy this table.
     Fill it in.

Co-ordinates of object	$(2, 2)$	$(2, 4)$	$(1, 6)$	$(3, 6)$	$(3, 2)$	$(2, 2)$
Co-ordinates × 2	$(4, 4)$	$(4, 8)$	...			

  c Plot the new co-ordinates in order.
     Join them as you go.
  d Write down the scale factor of the enlargement.

2 Draw an x axis from 0 to 9 and a y axis from 0 to 12.
  a Plot these points in order.
     Join them as you go.
     $(1, 1)$ $(1, 4)$ $(2, 4)$ $(3, 2)$ $(3, 1)$ $(1, 1)$
  b Copy this table.
     Fill it in.

Co-ordinates of object	$(1, 1)$	$(1, 4)$	$(2, 4)$	$(3, 2)$	$(3, 1)$	$(1, 1)$
Co-ordinates × 3	...					

  c Plot the new co-ordinates in order.
     Join them as you go.
  d Write down the scale factor of the enlargement.

| Centre of enlargement | An enlargement can be done from a **centre**.

Measure the distances of points on the object from the centre. Multiply these distances by the scale factor. This gives the distances of points on the image from the centre. |

| *Example* | Enlarge the triangles by a scale factor of 2. Use C as the centre of enlargement. |

  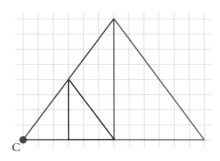

Exercise 5:12

1 Copy these diagrams on to squared paper. Use C as the centre of enlargement. Enlarge the triangle by a scale factor of 2.

a   **b**   **c**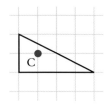

2 Copy these diagrams on to squared paper. Use C as the centre of enlargement. Enlarge the quadrilateral by a scale factor of 3.

a   **b**   **c**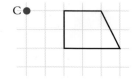

1 Copy these diagrams on to squared paper.
Draw their reflections in the mirror lines.

a

b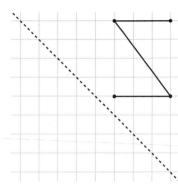

2 Trace this diagram on to
tracing paper.
Fold the tracing paper along the
mirror line.
Trace the object again.

Open out the tracing paper and
hold it up to the light.
You will see the object and its
reflection.

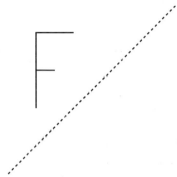

3 Draw an x axis from 0 to 10 and a y axis from 0 to 16.
  a Plot these points:
     $(4, 1)$ $(9, 1)$ $(9, 3)$ $(4, 3)$
     Join the points to make a rectangle.
     Translate the rectangle 5 units up.
  b Plot these points:
     $(2, 13)$ $(4, 13)$ $(4, 16)$
     Join the points to make a triangle.
     Translate the triangle 5 units down.
  c Plot these points: $(0, 8)$ $(1, 10)$
     Join the points to make a line.
     Translate the line 9 units to the right.
  d Plot these points: $(0, 5)$ $(0, 6)$ $(1, 6)$
     Join the points to make a triangle.
     Translate the triangle 4 squares to the right.
     Translate the triangle another 4 squares to the right.
  e Plot the point $(1, 4)$.
     Translate the point 2 units to the right and 5 units up.

4 **a** Make these arrangements of cubes.
Imagine a mirror to the right of each shape.
Make a reflection of each shape in the mirror.
The first one has been done for you.

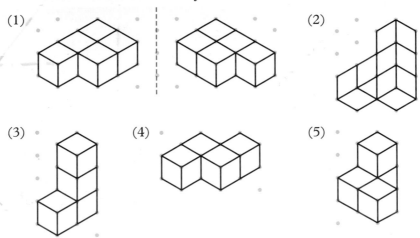

(1)   (2)

(3)   (4)   (5)

b Choose one shape and its reflection.
Draw them on isometric paper.

5 Copy the diagram on to squared paper.
  a Give the arrow a quarter turn
anti-clockwise about C.
Draw the new position.
  b Give the arrow two more
quarter turns anti-clockwise.
Draw each one.
  c Write down the order of
rotational symmetry of the
finished diagram.

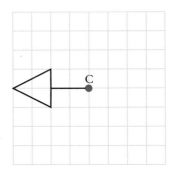

6 Copy these shapes on to squared paper.
Enlarge them by a scale factor of 3.

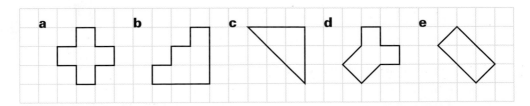

a   b   c   d   e

1   Traditional Islamic patterns are made like this.

Make a pattern   Reflect the pattern across   Colour the pattern.
in a square.   and down.

Make your own pattern like this.

2   Start with a simple shape that tessellates.
You can make a more interesting shape with rotations and translations.

Cut a semicircle from the shape.
Give the semicircle a half turn.

   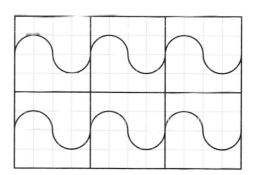

Cut a triangle from the shape.
Translate the triangle to the opposite side.

   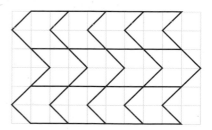

Try some patterns of your own.

3 This triangle has been given a
half turn about the midpoint of
one of its sides.
The triangle and its rotation make
a parallelogram.

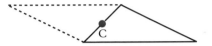

a Copy each diagram.
Use tracing paper to give each triangle a half turn about C.
Write down the name of each quadrilateral that you get.

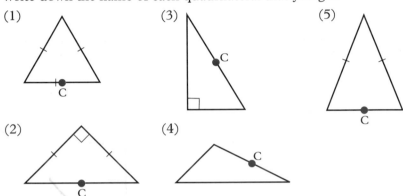

(1)

(2)

(3)

(4)

(5)

b It is impossible to make a kite or a trapezium this way.
Explain why.

4 The diagram shows different transformations of an L shape.
For example, A to G is a reflection in the *y* axis.
Write down full descriptions of these transformations:

a A to D   **f** G to H
b D to F   **g** F to G
c A to F   **h** G to D
d A to B   **i** B to C
e B to A   **j** B to E

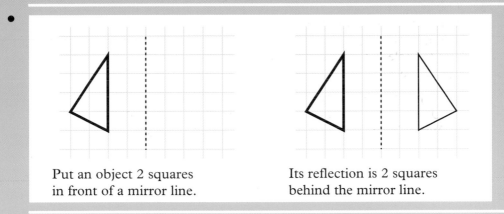

Put an object 2 squares
in front of a mirror line.

Its reflection is 2 squares
behind the mirror line.

Translation   A **translation** is a movement in a straight line.
Rotation   A **rotation** is a movement round in a circle.

Example   Translate the L shape 4 squares
                 to the right.

                 Choose one point.
                 Move the point 4 squares to
                 the right.
                 Move the other points in the
                 same way.

4 squares

The centre of rotation can be in
different places.

The arrow has been moved a
quarter turn clockwise about
different centres.

Enlargement   An **enlargement** changes the size of an object.
Scale factor The **scale factor** tells us how many times bigger the
                  enlargement is.

Example
Enlarge the rectangle by a
scale factor of 2.

The enlargement is 2 times
as long and 2 times as wide
as the object.

Object   Enlargement

1 Copy these diagrams on to squared paper.
Draw their reflections in the mirror lines.

a **b**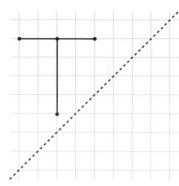

2 For each part start with a new copy of
this L shape drawn on squared paper.
Label each copy with the question number.

Translate your L:
a 3 squares to the right
b 5 squares down
c 2 squares to the left and 4 squares up

3 a Copy the diagram.
Give the flag a
quarter turn anti-clockwise
about C.

b Copy the diagram
Give the flag a
half turn clockwise
about C.

4 Copy the diagram on to squared paper.
Rotate this shape about C a quarter turn at
a time.
Make a new shape with rotational symmetry
of order 4.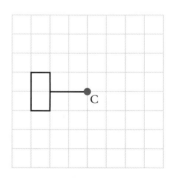

5 a Copy this shape on to
squared paper.
Enlarge it by a scale factor of 2.

b Copy this shape on to squared paper.
Enlarge it by a scale factor of 3.
Use C as the centre of enlargement.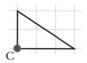

6 | Don't be negative!

QUESTIONS

EXTENSION

SUMMARY

TEST YOURSELF

The coldest place in the world is the Pole of Inaccessibility in Antarctica. Its annual mean temperature is –58°C.

Braemar, in Scotland, is the coldest weather station in the UK. Its annual mean temperature is 6.3°C. On cold nights, Braemar has had temperatures down to –27°C.

The lowest temperature possible is absolute zero, 0 K on the Kelvin scale or –273.15°C. The lowest temperature reached on Earth is 0.000 000 000 28 K. This was at the Low Temperature Laboratory of Helsinki University, Finland, in February 1993.

1 ◄◄REPLAY►

You have already met negative numbers.

Negative numbers	Numbers with minus signs in front are called **negative** numbers.
Positive numbers	Other numbers except nought are **positive**. Positive numbers are sometimes written with a plus sign in front. Nought is not positive or negative.
Number line	We can show positive and negative numbers on a **number line**.

Negative direction
numbers are getting
smaller

Positive direction
numbers are getting
larger

Examples	1 is smaller than 4	−2 is smaller than 1	−4 is smaller than −1
	3 is larger than 2	1 is larger than −2	−1 is larger than −3

Exercise 6:1

1 Which number is smaller?
   a   −2 or 4   **b**   0 or −5   **c**   −2 or −5

2 Which number is larger?
   a   −6 or 1   **b**   −1 or 0   **c**   −3 or −4

3 Put these numbers in order, smallest first.
    a −4, 5, −2, 3   **b** 5, −3, 0, −2, 7 **c** −6, 1, −1, −3, 0, 4

4 Put these numbers in order, largest first.
    a −1, 2, −3   **b** −2, 5, 1, −1, 2 **c** −11, 8, −5, −9, 2, −1

5 Write down the next two terms in these number patterns.
    a 4, 2, 0, −2, −4, ..., ...   **d** 30, 20, 10, 0, ..., ...
    b 8, 5, 2, −1, −4, ..., ...   **e** 7, 1, −5, ..., ...
    c 10, 5, 0, −5, −10, ..., ...   **f** 6, 5, 3, 0, −4, −9, ..., ...

6 Copy these number patterns.
Fill in the missing numbers.
    a 5, 3, 1, ..., −3, ..., −7
    b 9, 6, 3, ..., −3, ..., −9
    c 100, 50, ..., −50, ..., −150

| **Less than <** | We often use the signs < and > with numbers. |
| **Greater than >** | < means **'less than'**   > means **'greater than'** |

Examples   −5 < −2 means −5 is less than −2
                 2 > −4 means 2 is greater than −4

Exercise 6:2

1 Copy the pairs of numbers.
Write in < or >
    a 4 2   **d** 6 −6
    b 0 −3   **e** −2 1
    c −5 −1   **f** −3 −8

2 The normal height of a river is
marked as zero on the scale.
At the beginning of the month the
level was at 4 metres.
    a What is the level of the river
       now?
    b How much has the water level
       fallen?

3 What is the difference between these day and night temperatures?

a	b	c	d	e	f
day 8 °C	day 4 °C	day 6 °C	day 9 °C	day 10 °C	day 7 °C
night −1 °C	night −7 °C	night 0 °C	night −3 °C	night 2 °C	night −9 °C

4 How many degrees difference is there between these night and day temperatures?

  a 6 °C and 11 °C

  b −2 °C and 14 °C

  c −5 °C and 0 °C

  d −1 °C and 10 °C

  e −5 °C and −1 °C

  f −10 °C and 20 °C

5 The temperature in a freezer is −18 °C.
  A frozen pizza is thawed to room temperature.
  Room temperature is 21 °C.
  How many degrees does the temperature of the pizza rise?

We can use calculators for questions with negative numbers.
We can use the **+/−** key.

Example   One night the temperature is −4 °C. The following day the
                temperature rises to 9 °C.
                How many degrees difference is there between the day and
                night temperatures?

                Key in: **9** **−** **4** **+/−** **=**

                Answer: 13 °C

---

6 Here are some night and day temperatures.
Use your calculator to find the difference between each pair.

   a −3 °C and 7 °C   **d** 2 °C and 17 °C

   b −1 °C and 13 °C   **e** −9 °C and −1 °C

   c −5 °C and 10 °C   **f** −9 °C and 0 °C

7 Jane is standing on a cliff.
This picture shows what is above
and below sea level.

   a What is at about +60 m?

   b How far below the fish is the
top of the wreck?

   c How far above the fish is the
seagull?

   d Estimate the distance of the
seabed below sea level.

8 On a quiz show contestants score 2 points for a correct answer.
They lose a point for a wrong answer.
What is the final score for:

   a 9 correct and 2 wrong answers?

   b 4 correct and 8 wrong answers?

   c 2 correct and 11 wrong answers?

In the same quiz these contestants all scored 11 points.

   d Mark gave 5 wrong answers.
How many questions did he answer correctly?

   e Jamila gave 7 correct answers.
How many questions did she get wrong?

   f Luke got the same number of correct and wrong answers.
How many questions did he answer?

2 The rules for directed numbers

Sally and Peter enjoy scuba diving.
They are talking about their dives.
They call sea level 0.
Sally says she dived to $-5\,\text{m}$.
Peter says he dived 4 m further down.
Sally knows how to work this out:
$-5 - 4 = -9$
Peter dived to $-9\,\text{m}$.

Directed numbers	**Directed numbers** are numbers with signs in front of them, for example $-3, +5, -7$

Adding and subtracting directed numbers

Example

Use the number ladder to answer these:
a $7 - 4$ **b** $3 - 6$ **c** $-5 - 2$

Always start at 0.
Count up for positive numbers.
Count down for negative numbers.

a $7 - 4$
Start at 0 on the line.
Count 7 spaces up.
Count 4 spaces down.
Answer: 3

b $3 - 6$
Start at 0 on the line.
Count 3 spaces up.
Count 6 spaces down.
Answer: -3

c $-5 - 2$
Start at 0 on the line.
Count 5 spaces down.
Count 2 spaces down.
Answer: -7

```
10
 9
 8
 7
 6
 5
 4
 3
 2
 1
 0
-1
-2
-3
-4
-5
-6
-7
-8
-9
-10
```

Exercise 6:3

1 Copy the number ladder from the example into your book.
Put it down the side of your page.
Use your number ladder to answer these:

a	$6 - 4$	**g**	$-6 + 7$	**m**	$9 - 10$
b	$3 - 5$	**h**	$-5 + 8$	**n**	$-1 + 3 - 4$
c	$5 - 7$	**i**	$-3 - 4$	**o**	$5 - 6 + 3$
d	$2 - 8$	**j**	$-5 + 5$	**p**	$-2 - 3 - 1$
e	$6 - 10$	**k**	$-3 - 3$	**q**	$-2 + 6 - 8$
f	$-3 + 4$	**l**	$-6 - 2$	**r**	$-1 - 5 - 3$

2 **a** Copy this addition table into your book.
b Fill in the boxes that are shaded blue.
Work from the right hand side.
The first one has been done for you.
c Look at the pattern of numbers in the blue boxes.
What number do you think should go in the green box?
d Fill in the rest of the row.
Follow the pattern.
e Fill in the second row of the table.
Start at the right hand side.
$3 + 2 = 5$.
f Fill in the rest of the table.

second number

+	-3	-2	-1	0	1	2	3
3							6
2							
1							
0							
-1							
-2							
-3							

first number (labels the rows)

Adding a negative number is the same as taking the number away.
This means that $6 + -3$ is the same as $6 - 3$

Example   Work out   **a** $5 + -2$ **b** $3 + -5$ **c** $-3 + -2$

a	$5 + -2$	**b**	$3 + -5$	**c**	$-3 + -2$
	$= 5 - 2$		$= 3 - 5$		$= -3 - 2$
	$= 3$		$= -2$		$= -5$

---

3 Use the rule for adding negative numbers to answer these:

a	$4 + -2 = 4 - 2 = \ldots$	**d**	$-5 + -2$	**g**	$9 + -7$
b	$5 + -4 = 5 \ldots 4 = \ldots$	**e**	$-6 + 3$	**h**	$-8 + 1$
c	$2 + -7 = 2 \ldots 7 = \ldots$	**f**	$-3 + -4$	**i**	$-5 + -5$

4 a Copy this subtraction table into your book.

b Fill in the boxes that are shaded blue.
Work from the right hand side. The first one has been done for you.

c Look at the pattern of numbers in the blue boxes. What number do you think should go in the green box?

d Fill in the rest of the row. Follow the pattern.

e Fill in the second row of the table.
Start at the right hand side.

f Fill in the rest of the table.

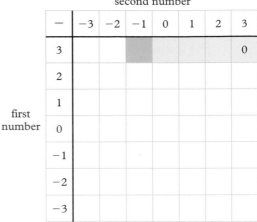

second number

−	−3	−2	−1	0	1	2	3
3							0
2							
1							
0							
−1							
−2							
−3							

first number

Subtracting a negative number is the same as adding the number.
This means that $6 - -3$ is the same as $6 + 3$

Example   Work out   **a** $5 - -2$ **b** $-3 - -5$ **c** $-3 - -2$

a $5 - -2$
$= 5 + 2$
$= 7$

b $-3 - -5$
$= -3 + 5$
$= 2$

c $-3 - -2$
$= -3 + 2$
$= -1$

---

5 Use the rule for subtracting negative numbers to answer these:

a $6 - -4 = 6 + 4 = \ldots$ **d** $-5 - -7$ **g** $-7 - -2$

b $3 - -7 = 3 \ldots 7 = \ldots$ **e** $1 - -6$ **h** $-6 - -3$

c $-9 - -8 = -9 \ldots 8 = \ldots$ **f** $8 - -2$ **i** $-1 - -5$

6 Use both the rules you have learnt to answer these:

a $5 - -4$ **c** $3 + -5$ **e** $-5 + 4$ **g** $-3 + 7$

b $4 + -2$ **d** $7 - -1$ **f** $-3 - -6$ **h** $-3 - 4$

You can think about negative numbers as moving left on a number line and positive numbers as moving right.

Negative direction   ⟸   ⟹   Positive direction
Minus −   + Plus

$-5 \quad -4 \quad -3 \quad -2 \quad -1 \quad 0 \quad 1 \quad 2 \quad 3 \quad 4 \quad 5$

You can use this idea to help you do questions.

Example   Work these out.

    a $4 - 3 + 2$ **b** $-4 + -1 + 6$

    a Start at 4. Move 3 to the left to get to 1

Now move 2 to the right to get to 3

So $4 - 3 + 2 = 3$

    b Use the rules that you already know first. $+ -1$ is the same as -1 so $-4 + -1 + 6$ is the same as $-4 - 1 + 6$.

Start at -4. Move 1 to the left to get to -5

Now move 6 to the right to get to 1

So $-4 + -1 + 6 = 1$

---

7 Use a number line to help you to work these out.

    a $5 + 2 - 3$ **e** $-5 - 4 + 1$ **i** $-6 + -3 + 4$

    b $4 - 7 + 1$ **f** $-7 + 3 - 5$ **j** $-6 + 3 - -5$

    c $6 - 8 + 5$ **g** $-4 - 2 + 4$ **k** $-4 - -6 + -5$

    d $-3 + 4 - 5$ **h** $5 + -4 + 3$ **l** $-5 - -7 + -3$

· ·

Multiplying and dividing directed numbers

Exercise 6:4

1 Copy these number patterns.
Fill in the missing numbers.

    a $-3, \ldots, -1, 0, \ldots, 2, 3$

    b $-6, -4, \ldots, 0, 2, \ldots, 6$

    c $\ldots, -6, -3, 0, 3, 6, \ldots$

2 a Copy this multiplication table into your book.

b Fill in the boxes that are shaded blue.
Work from the right hand side.
The first one has been done for you.

c Look at the pattern of numbers in the blue boxes.
What number do you think should go in the green box?

d Fill in the rest of the row.
Follow the pattern.

e Fill in the second row of the table.
Start at the right hand side.

f Fill in the rest of the table.

second number

×	−3	−2	−1	0	1	2	3
3							9
2							
1							
0							
−1							
−2							
−3							

first number

If you multiply a positive number by a negative number the answer is a negative number.
If you multiply two negative numbers together the answer is a positive number.
The same rules are true for division.

Example Work out **a** 5×-2 **b** -3×-5 **c** $-12 \div -3$

a 5×-2 **b** -3×-5 **c** $-12 \div -3$
$= -10$ $= 15$ $= 4$

---

3 Use the rules for multiplying negative numbers to answer these:

a -2×5 **e** 6×-4 **i** -7×-6
b -3×-6 **f** -10×-9 **j** -6×-9
c 4×-7 **g** -5×8 **k** -7×5
d -5×-5 **h** 9×9 **l** -12×-12

Look at the multiplication: $-3 \times 4 = -12$
We can write two divisions using the same numbers: $-12 \div -3 = 4$
$-12 \div 4 = -3$

---

4 Write two divisions for each of these.

a $-5 \times 3 = -15$ **c** $-3 \times -6 = 18$ **e** $-5 \times -10 = 50$
b $4 \times -5 = -20$ **d** $3 \times 11 = 33$ **f** $5 \times -6 = -30$

You can also use your calculator to help you with directed numbers.

Questions with negative numbers are easy with a calculator.
There is only one very important fact to remember.

You **must** use the [+/−] key to enter negative numbers and not the [−] key.

You still use the [−] key when you want to subtract.

Example Work these out using a calculator.

  a $12 - 4 + -3$ **c** 15×-14
  b $-3 - 4 + -5$ **d** $-276 \div -12$

  a This is 12 subtract 4 add negative 3.

   Use the [+/−] key to enter the -3.

   Key in: [1] [2] [−] [4] [+] [+/−] [3] [=]
   Answer: 5

  b Key in: [+/−] [3] [−] [4] [+] [+/−] [5] [=]
   Answer: -12

  c Key in: [1] [5] [×] [+/−] [1] [4] [=]
   Answer: -210

  d Key in: [+/−] [2] [7] [6] [÷] [+/−] [1] [2] [=]
   Answer: 23

Exercise 6:5

1 Use a calculator to answer these.
  a $17 + -14$ **g** $-37 - -14$
  b $35 - -16$ **h** $-54 + -28$
  c $24 - 38$ **i** $-36 + -43$
  d $27 + -42$ **j** $-57 - 44$
  e $-21 - 28$ **k** $56 - 97$
  f $-19 - -26$ **l** $-45 - -174$

2 Use a calculator to answer these.
  a 17×-12 **g** -43×-12
  b -13×23 **h** $-279 \div 9$
  c 27×-28 **i** 17×-26
  d $-165 \div -15$ **j** $-322 \div -23$
  e -24×-6 **k** 43×-13
  f $1700 \div 25$ **l** $-306 \div 18$

3 Using negative numbers

8M are having a science lesson.
They are learning about the
Kelvin scale for measuring
temperature.
The coldest temperature possible
is 0 K.
This is about $-273\,°C$.
The formula for converting K to
$°C$ is:

$$C = K - 273$$

Exercise 6:6

1 Use the formula $C = K - 273$ to convert these temperatures to $°C$.
    a 273 K   **b** 373 K   **c** 1000 K   **d** 0 K   **e** 100 K

The formula for converting $°C$ to K is $K = C + 273$

Example   Use the formula $K = C + 273$ to convert $-50\,°C$ to K.

Substitute for C $K = -50 + 273$

Key in: **5**   **0**   **+/−**   **+**   **2**   **7**   **3**   **=**

Answer: 223 K

---

2 Use the formula $K = C + 273$ to convert these temperatures.
    a $-20\,°C$ **b** $-100\,°C$ **c** $200\,°C$ **d** $-15\,°C$ **e** $-200\,°C$

3 Use the formula $p = q + 10$ to find p for these values of q.
    a -5 **b** -10 **c** -30 **d** 18   **e** -2

4 Use the formula $r = s - 25$ to find r for these values of s.
    a -15 **b** 25   **c** 0   **d** -6 **e** -10

5 Use the formula $w = 50 + v$ to find w for these values of v.
    a 25   **b** -30 **c** -85 **d** -5 **e** -100

6 Use the formula $b = 75 - c$ to find b for these values of c.
    a 50   **b** -40 **c** -10 **d** -25 **e** -100

Example 1   Use the formula $g = 3h$ to find g when $h = -5$

Substitute for h $g = 3 \times -5$
Answer: -15

Example 2   Use the formula $n = \dfrac{m}{2}$ to find n when $m = -8$

Substitute for m $n = -8 \div 2$
Answer: -4

Exercise 6:7

1 Use the formula $g = 3h$ to find g for these values of h.
    a -7 **b** -2 **c** 0 **d** 5 **e** -20

2 Use the formula $n = \dfrac{m}{2}$ to find n for these values of m.
    a -6 **b** -3 **c** 16 **d** 0 **e** -50

3 Use the formula $y = 4x$ to find y for these values of x.
    a -1 **b** 0 **c** 5 **d** -0.5 **e** -6

4 Use the formula $d = \dfrac{c}{10}$ to find d for these values of c.
    a -20 **b** -15 **c** -35 **d** 5 **e** -150

5 Use the formula $y = \dfrac{12}{x}$ to find y for these values of x.
    a -6 **b** -2 **c** -3 **d** 10 **e** -4

It is a very cold day. Gary hears on the radio that the temperature is $-6\,°C$.
Gary's grandmother is old-fashioned. She likes to use the Fahrenheit scale for temperature. Gary knows a formula for converting Celsius to Fahrenheit:
$$F = 1.8 \times C + 32$$

Gary works out the temperature on his calculator like this:
Substitute for C $F = 1.8 \times -6 + 32$
Key in:

$\boxed{1}\ \boxed{.}\ \boxed{8}\ \boxed{\times}\ \boxed{6}\ \boxed{+/-}\ \boxed{+}\ \boxed{3}\ \boxed{2}\ \boxed{=}$

Answer: $21.2\,°F$

Exercise 6:8

1 Use Gary's formula F = 1.8C + 32 to convert these temperatures to Fahrenheit.
   a −10 °C   **b** −5 °C   **c** 15 °C   **d** −8 °C   **e** −20 °C

2 Use the formula $v = 5t + 20$ to find v for these values of t.
   a 7   **b** −4   **c** −10   **d** −6   **e** −2.5

3 Use the formula $p = 3q - 15$ to find p for these values of q.
   a −4   **b** −12   **c** 0   **d** 5   **e** −1

4 Use the formula $s = 4t - 6$ to find s for these values of t.
   a −2   **b** −6   **c** −20   **d** 0   **e** 1.5

5 a Write the formula F = 1.8C + 32 on robot screens.
     Copy and fill in:

   b Draw the inverse machine for F = 1.8C + 32.
   c Use your inverse machine to convert these temperatures to Celsius.
     Round your answers correct to one decimal place if necessary.
     (1) 50 °F   (2) −4 °F   (3) −40 °F   (4) 0 °F   (5) 212 °F

Example   Find the value of $3t^2$ when $t = -4$

             Substitute for t $3 \times (-4)^2$

             Without a calculator: $3 \times -4 \times -4 = 48$
                                       No sign as $3 \times 4 \times 4 = 48$
                                       − × − = +

             With a calculator:
             Key in:

             Answer: 48

Exercise 6:9

1 Find the value of these when $t = -4$.
   a t^2 **b** $2t^2$ **c** $5t^2$ **d** $10t^2$ **e** $6t^2$

2 Find the value of these when $s = -3$.

   a s^2 **b** $4s^2$ **c** $5s^2$ **d** $2s^2$ **e** $9s^2$

3 **a** Copy this table.
     Fill it in.

$y = x^2$

x	-3	-2	-1	-0.5	0	0.5	1	2	3
x^2	9	...	...	...	...	...	...	4	...

  b Copy the axes on to squared paper.

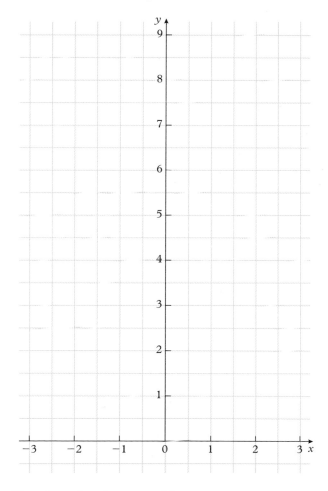

  c Plot the points in your table.
     Join the points with a smooth curve.
  d Label your graph $y = x^2$.
  e What line is the line of symmetry of the curve?

1   Use your rules to answer these.

   a $6 - -2$ **c** $-6 + -2$ **e** $-4 - -4$ **g** $-5 - 4$

   b $4 + -5$ **d** $-2 - 4$ **f** $-2 + -3$ **h** $0 - -5$

2   Use your rules to answer these.

   a -6×-4 **c** -7×7 **e** -9×-2 **g** -4×-4

   b -3×5 **d** 4×-8 **f** -10×-8 **h** -11×-6

3   Use your rules to answer these.

   a $-20 \div 4$ **c** $-55 \div 11$ **e** $-56 \div 7$ **g** $27 \div -9$

   b $-32 \div -4$ **d** $-36 \div -9$ **f** $-42 \div 6$ **h** $-35 \div -7$

4   Use a calculator to answer these.

   a 14×-17 **d** -45×-13 **g** $-570 \div -19$

   b $-37 + -16$ **e** $-55 - 34$ **h** 23×-16

   c $-1288 \div -56$ **f** $67 - 86$ **i** $-25 - -30$

5   **a**   Use the formula $e = 25 + f$ to find e for these values of f.

      (1) $f = 15$ (2) $f = -16$ (3) $f = -25$ (4) $f = -40$

   b   Use the formula $g = 80 - h$ to find g for these values of h.

      (1) $h = 55$ (2) $h = 85$ (3) $h = -20$ (4) $h = -35$

6   **a**   Use the formula $r = 6s$ to find r for these values of s.

      (1) $s = 5$ (2) $s = -4$ (3) $s = -10$ (4) $s = -50$

   b   Use the formula $m = \dfrac{n}{5}$ to find m for these values of n.

      (1) $n = 5$ (2) $n = -10$ (3) $n = -30$ (4) $n = -50$

7   **a**   Use the formula $p = 15 - 3q$ to find p for these values of q.

      (1) $q = 4$ (2) $q = -2$ (3) $q = -5$ (4) $q = -7$

   b   Use the formula $a = 3b + 12$ to find a for these values of b.

      (1) $b = -4$ (2) $b = -3$ (3) $b = 0$ (4) $b = -7$

8   Find the value of $10t^2$ for these values of t.

   a $t = 1$ **b** $t = 0$ **c** $t = -2$ **d** $t = -6$

9   Find the value of these when $y = -5$.

   a y^2 **b** $2y^2$ **c** $5y^2$ **d** $3y^2$

Game Make it to zero

This game is for two or more players.
You need a dice and a coin.

Megan and Andrew are playing
'Make it to zero'.
Megan tosses the coin and rolls the dice.
The coin decides the sign of the number:
heads is positive, tails is negative.
Megan gets a tail and a 3. Both players
write down the number -3.

Megan tosses the coin and rolls the dice five more times.
She gets these numbers: $-3, 2, -5, -1, 4, 3$

Megan and Andrew each put the numbers into pairs.
Then they multiply each pair.
Megan adds her answers and Andrew adds his answers.
The winner is the one who gets a total closest to zero.

Here are Megan's and Andrew's results:

Andrew is closest to zero, so he wins.

Play this game with some friends.

1 Malcolm has a remote controlled car.
He moves the car backwards and forwards and makes it accelerate at a
constant rate.

Here are two equations which describe the way the car moves:
$v = u + at$ u = the speed at the start of a journey in m/s
$s = ut + \frac{1}{2}at^2$ v = the speed at the finish of a journey in m/s
a = the acceleration in m/s^2
s = the distance travelled in metres
t = the time taken in seconds

a The car makes a journey where $u = 0$, $t = 4$ s, $a = 0.5$ m/s^2.
(1) Use the equation $v = u + at$ to find the speed at the end of
the journey.
(2) Use the equation $s = ut + \frac{1}{2}at^2$ to find the distance travelled.
b The car makes a second journey where $u = 1$ m/s, $t = 2.5$ s,
$a = -0.4$ m/s^2.
(1) Use the equation $v = u + at$ to find the speed at the end of
the journey.
(2) Use the equation $s = ut + \frac{1}{2}at^2$ to find the distance travelled.

2 The formula for a sequence is $10 - 2n$.
  a Write down the first three terms of the sequence.
  b Which term is 0?
  c Write down the 10th term.

3 Copy these sequences.
Fill in the missing terms.
  a $-12, -7, \dots, 3, 8, 13$ **c** $17, 8, -1, -10, \dots, -28$
  b $9, 5, 1, -3, \dots, -11$ **d** $\dots, -31, -25, -19, -13, -7$

4 Solve these equations.
  a $4x = -12$ **c** $5p = -10$ **e** $x - 5 = -6$
  b $\frac{y}{2} = -5$ **d** $x + 7 = 4$ **f** $-3y = 21$

5 **a** Copy and fill in:
    $-1 \times 12 = -12$ $\dots \times 6 = -12$ $-3 \times \dots = -12$
    $1 \times -12 = -12$ $\dots \times -6 = -12$ $3 \times \dots = -12$
  b Write down all the factors of -12.

6 **a** Copy and fill in:
    $-1 \times 20 = -20$ $\dots \times 2 = -20$ $\dots \times 4 = -20$
    $1 \times -20 = -20$ $\dots \times -2 = -20$ $\dots \times -4 = -20$
  b Write down all the factors of -20.

7 Work out the answers to these.
  a $-2 \times -4 \times 5$ **b** $-3 \times 4 \times -10$ **c** $-4 \times -4 \times -4$

8 Work out the answers to these.
  a $(-2)^2$ **b** $(-5)^2$ **c** $(-8)^2$ **d** $(-10)^2$

9 Copy these and fill them in.
Use the answers to question **8** to help you.
  a $(-?)^2 = 9$ **b** $(-?)^2 = 36$ **c** $(-?)^2 = 100$ **d** $(-?)^2 = 49$

10 **a** Write the formula $v = 50 + 10a$ on robot screens.

  b Draw the inverse machine for $v = 50 + 10a$
  c Use your inverse machine to find a when v takes these values.
    (1) $v = 0$ (2) $v = -10$ (3) $v = 25$ (4) $v = 50$

- **Negative** numbers

  Numbers with minus signs in front are called **negative** numbers.

  Positive numbers

  Other numbers except nought are **positive**. Positive numbers are sometimes written with a plus sign in front. Nought is not positive or negative.

Negative direction
numbers are getting
smaller

Positive direction
numbers are getting
larger

- **Less than <**
  Greater than >

  We often use the signs < and > with numbers.
  $-5 < -2$ means -5 is less than -2
  $2 > -4$ means 2 is greater than -4

- **Directed numbers**

  Directed numbers are numbers with signs in front of them, for example -3, $+5$, -7.

- **Adding and subtracting directed numbers**

  Example

  Use the number ladder to answer $3 - 5$

  Always start at 0
  Count up for positive numbers.
  Count down for negative numbers.

  $3 - 5$
  Start at 0 on the line.
  Count 3 spaces up.
  Count 5 spaces down.
  Answer: -2

- **Rules for directed numbers**

  $+ \times -$ and $- \times +$ are the same as $-$ $+ -$ is the same as $-$
  $+ \div -$ and $- \div +$ are the same as $-$ $- -$ is the same as $+$

- **Multiplying and dividing directed numbers**

  Examples

  $5 \times -4 = -20$ $-10 \div 2 = -5$
  $-3 \times -2 = 6$ $-6 \div -2 = 3$

- *Example*

  1   Use the formula $g = 3h$ to find g when $h = -5$

       Substitute for h $g = 3 \times -5$
                               Answer: -15

  2   Use the formula $n = \dfrac{m}{2}$ to find n when $m = -8$

       Substitute for m $n = -8 \div 2$
                               Answer: -4

1   Put these temperatures in order, lowest first.
    6 °C,   −5 °C,   −3 °C,   2 °C,   1 °C,   −1 °C,   0 °C

2   Copy the pairs of temperatures.
    Write in < or >
    a 5 °C   3 °C   **b** −6 °C   −8 °C   **c** −4 °C   0 °C

3   The temperature in the desert at night is −9 °C.
    During the day it reaches 43 °C.
    How many degrees does the temperature rise?

4   Use a number ladder to answer these.
    a 8 − 2   **b** 3 − 9   **c** −4 − 5   **d** 3 − 5 + 4 − 1

5   Work these out.
    a 4 − −6   **c** −7 − −3   **e** −3 × 5   **g** 6 × −10
    b −5 + −2   **d** −5 − 3   **f** −4 × −2   **h** −10 ÷ −2

6   Use a calculator to answer these.
    a 31 × −56   **c** 19 + −36   **e** −280 ÷ −14
    b 175 ÷ −25   **d** −25 − −48   **f** −45 × −23

7   Use the formula $r = s - 25$ to find r for these values of s.
    a 68   **b** 12   **c** −35

8   Use the formula $v = 5t - 12$ to find v for these values of t.
    a 6   **b** 2   **c** −4

9   Find the value of these when $t = -2$.
    a t^2 **b** $5t^2$ **c** $8t^2$

10 Use the formula $E = 5v^2$ to find E for these values of v.
    a 3   **b** 1   **c** −5

7 Angles

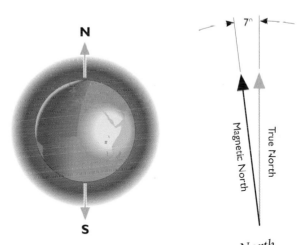

Compass needles point to *magnetic North*. This is slightly different from true North. Maps often have two arrows for North. One arrow is for true North and one is for magnetic North. Magnetic North should have a date by it because it varies from year to year! The angle between true North and magnetic North is around 7°.

1 ◀◀REPLAY▶

40°

The cable car takes tourists up and down the mountain.
The cable is at an angle of 40° with the horizontal. It is dangerous for
this angle to be too large.

| **Degree** | We use degrees (written °) to measure angles. |

Right angle
90°

Straight line
180°

Full turn
360°

| **Acute Obtuse Reflex** | **Acute** angle | **Obtuse** angle | **Reflex** angle |

less than 90°   between 90° and 180°   between 180° and 360°

Exercise 7:1

1 Write down the angle that is:
   a acute   **b** obtuse   **c** reflex   **d** a right angle

A pair of scissors

A pair of glasses

2 Write down the name of each of these angles.
Choose from:
straight line, acute angle, reflex angle, right angle, obtuse angle.

   a 30°   **c** 270°   **e** 45°   **g** 320°   **i** 116°
   b 125°   **d** 180°   **f** 90°   **h** 170°   **j** 6°

Exercise 7:2

1 Take a piece of rough paper.
   a Fold it to make a straight line.
   b Fold it again to make a
      right angle.
Keep your right angle to use in
the next question.

Example   Estimate the sizes of these angles.

Fold 90° in half
to get 45°

2 Estimate the size in degrees of each of these angles.
Use your folded right angle to help you.
Copy this table and fill in your estimates.
You will need the 'Actual' column for question **3**.

	Estimate	Actual
a		
b		
c		
...		

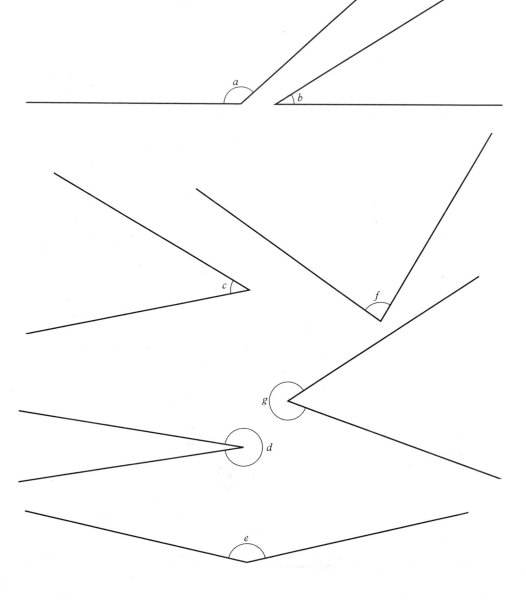

3 Measure the angles in question **2**.
If you have a 180° protractor, measure the smaller angle for reflex angles.
Then take the answer away from 360°.
Write your answers in the 'Actual' column in your table.

4 Draw and label these angles.
a 67°   **c** 113°   **e** 165°   **g** 96°   **i** 198°
b 42°   **d** 270°   **f** 18°   **h** 154°   **j** 315°

Examples   Calculate the angles marked with letters.

1 **Angles on a straight line**
add up to 180°
$a = 180° - 55° - 30°$
$a = 95°$

2 **Angles at a point** add up
to 360°
$b = 360° - 140° - 135°$
$b = 85°$

3 **Opposite angles** are equal.
p is opposite 120° and
q is opposite 60°.
$p = 120°$ $q = 60°$
(p and q add up to 180°)

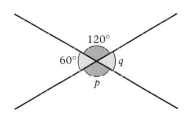

Exercise 7:3

Calculate the angles marked with letters.

1

2

3

7

4

8

5

9

6

● **10**
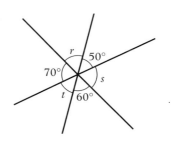

Example   Calculate angle *c*.

The angles of a triangle
add up to 180°
c = 180° − 30° − 40°
c = 110°

Exercise 7:4

Calculate the angles marked with letters.

1

2

3

A **scalene triangle** has no equal angles and no equal sides.

An **isosceles triangle** has two equal angles and two equal sides.

An **equilateral triangle** has three equal angles and three equal sides.

Calculate the angles marked with letters.

4

35°

5

6

65°

7

20°

8 Copy and fill in:

$2k = 180° - 30°$

$2k = ...$

$k = ...$

30°

9 Copy and fill in:

$2l - 180° - 50°$

$2l = ...$

$l = ...$

50°

10

46°

2 Parallel lines

Pairs of railway lines are parallel. The two tracks on a railway line never meet. They always stay the same distance apart.

Different pairs of railway lines can cross.
Sometimes a train can change from one pair of lines to another. A system of moveable parts of lines is used. These are called points.

Exercise 7:5

1 **a** Draw a pair of parallel lines. Mark them with arrows.
   b Draw a line intersecting both of your parallel lines.
   c Measure and label all eight angles.

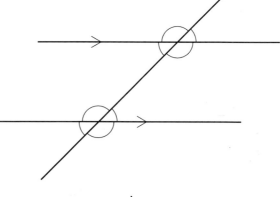

2 **a** Draw another pair of parallel lines.
      Mark them with arrows.
   b Draw a line intersecting both of your parallel lines at a different angle.
   c Measure and label all eight angles.

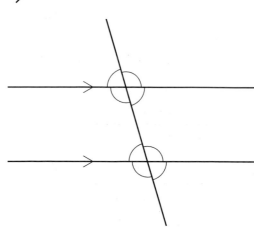

3 a Look at the angles you have
measured in questions **1** and **2**.
What do you notice?

  b Copy this diagram.
Colour the four equal obtuse angles red.
Colour the four equal acute angles blue.

4 Copy the diagram.
Colour the four equal obtuse angles orange.
Colour the four equal acute angles green.

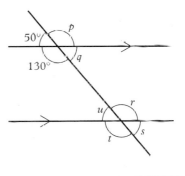

Example

Find the angles marked with
letters.

p is opposite 130°
q is opposite 50°
p = 130°   *q* = 50°

The 'bottom' set of four angles
is the same as the 'top' set.
r = 130° and *t* = 130°
s = 50° and *u* = 50°

Exercise 7:6

Find the angles marked with letters.

1

2

3

5

4

6

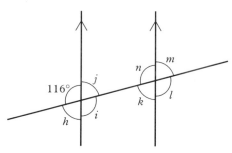

Alternate angles	Angles on opposite sides of the intersecting line are called **alternate angles**. They are found in **Z** shapes. **Alternate angles are equal**.	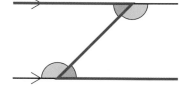
Corresponding angles	Angles in the same place in 'top' and 'bottom' sets of angles are called **corresponding angles**. They are found in **F** shapes. **Corresponding angles are equal**.	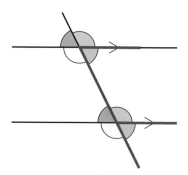
Interior angles	Angles between parallel lines are called **interior angles**. **Interior angles add up to 180°**	

Exercise 7:7

1 **a** Copy the diagram.
   b Colour one pair of alternate angles red.
       Colour the other pair blue.
   c Label your diagram 'Alternate angles'.

2 **a** Make another copy of the diagram.
   b Choose four colours.
       Colour each pair of corresponding angles in a different colour.
   c Label your diagram 'Corresponding angles'.

3 **a** Copy the diagram.
   b Calculate the missing angles.
   c Label your diagram 'Interior angles'.

4 Find the angles marked with letters.
   Write down whether each pair of angles is alternate, corresponding or interior.

a

d

b

e

c

f

Example Find the angles marked with letters.

p and 130° are interior angles
(using the parallel lines with
one arrow)
p = 180° − 130°   *p* = 50°

r and 130° are interior angles
(using the parallel lines with
two arrows)
r = 180° − 130°   *r* = 50°

p and *q* are interior angles
(using the parallel lines with two arrows)
q = 180° − 50°   *q* = 130°

Exercise 7:8

Find the angles marked with letters.

1

6

2

7

3

8

4

9

5

● 10

3 Polygons

Most buildings are rectangular.
Sometimes buildings use a
different polygon in their shape.
Can you see why this building is
called the Octagon?

◀◀ REPLAY ▶

Polygon

A **polygon** is a shape with straight sides.

Number of sides	Name of polygon
3	triangle
4	quadrilateral
5	pentagon
6	hexagon
7	heptagon
8	octagon

6 sides: hexagon

Exercise 7:9

1 Write down the sum of the angles of a triangle.

2 **a** Draw any quadrilateral.
  b Divide the quadrilateral into
    two triangles with a diagonal.
  c Copy and fill in:
    A quadrilateral can be divided into ... triangles.
    The angles of two triangles add up to $2 \times ...° = ...°$
    The angles of the quadrilateral add up to ...°

3 **a** Draw any pentagon.
  b Draw diagonals from one vertex
    to each of the other vertices.
  c Copy and fill in:
    A pentagon can be divided into ... triangles.
    The angles of ... triangles add up to ... $\times 180° = ...°$
    The angles of the pentagon add up to ...°

4 Repeat question **3** for a hexagon.

5 a Copy this table.

Number of sides	Name of polygon	Number of triangles	Sum of angles of polygon
3	triangle	1	180°
4	quadrilateral	...	...
...			

b Use your answers to questions **1–4** to fill in the table up to hexagons.
c (1) Look at the patterns of the numbers in your table.
Use the patterns to fill in the table up to octagons.
(2) Draw a heptagon and an octagon.
Divide them into triangles.
Check that you have filled in your table correctly.

6 a (1) How many triangles can a 20-sided polygon be divided into?
(2) What is the angle sum of a 20-sided polygon?
b Repeat part **a** for a 100-sided polygon.
c (1) Copy and fill in:
The number of triangles a polygon can be divided into is
the same as the number of .... of the polygon take
away ...
The angles of the polygon add up to the number of
.... multiplied by ...°
(2) Write your rule for finding the angles of a polygon in algebra.
Use *n* for the *n*umber of sides of the polygon.

Regular polygon

Regular polygons have all their sides the same length.
Also all their angles are equal.

Equilateral triangles and squares are regular polygons.

Example

Calculate an angle of a regular pentagon.

A regular pentagon can be divided
into three triangles.
Sum of angles of pentagon
$3 \times 180° = 540°$
One angle of pentagon
$540° \div 5 = 108°$
Answer: 108°

Exercise 7:10

1 Calculate the angles of regular polygons with these numbers of sides.
  a 6   **b** 7   **c** 8   **d** 10   **e** 12   **f** 20

2 a (1) Draw a triangle with
        extended sides like this.
    (2) Measure each of the
        marked angles.
    (3) Add your three angles
        together.
  b Draw a quadrilateral with its
     sides extended in the same way.
     Repeat part **a** (2) and (3).
  c Draw a pentagon with extended sides.
     Repeat part **a** (2) and (3).
  d The angles you have measured are called **exterior angles**.
     The exterior angles of any polygon always add up to the
     same number.
     What do they add up to?

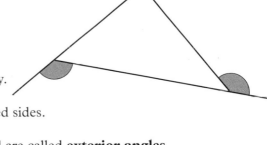

◄◄ REPLAY ►

Tessellation	A **tessellation** is a pattern

A **tessellation** is a pattern
made by repeating the
same shape over and over
again.
There are no gaps in a
tessellation.

A tessellation of trapeziums

An investigation into tessellating shapes

You need a set of tiles in the shapes of regular polygons.
Use the tiles to see which regular polygons tessellate.
What is special about the angles of the regular polygons that tessellate?
Can you find any irregular polygons that tessellate?
Are their angles special in any way?

McT

4 Bearings

Simon is orienteering. He has an orienteering map with checkpoints marked on it.
Simon is using a compass to find the direction or bearing of the next checkpoint.

| **Bearing** | A compass gives the **bearing** of an object. This is the direction you travel in to go straight to the object. |

A compass gives the **bearing** of an object. This is the direction you travel in to go straight to the object.
Bearings are measured clockwise from north in degrees.
Bearings always have three figures.

Examples

Find the bearing of B from A in each case.

1

N

65°

A

B

Bearing of B from A
is 065°

2

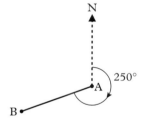

N

250°

A

B

Bearing of B from A
is 250°

Exercise 7:11

Find the bearing of B from A in each case.

1

N

B

37°

A

2

N

126°

A

B

3

N

B

80°

A

4

5

6

Simon stands on the path. He needs to find an orienteering control point.

Simon uses his compass to find the control point.
It is on a bearing of 070°

Simon then wants to return to the path from the control point.
He makes a half turn to face the way he came.
Simon needs to know the bearing for his return.

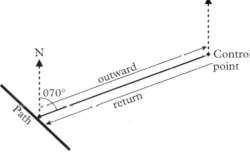

Exercise 7:12

1 Here is a diagram of Simon's run.
  a Write down the colour of the outward bearing of 070°
  b Write down the colour of Simon's return bearing.
  c Copy and fill in:
      Return bearing is 070° + 180° = ...°

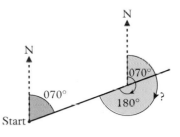

2 The diagram shows Simon's run to another control point on a bearing of 120°.
  a Sketch the diagram.
  b Colour the outward bearing red. Colour the return bearing blue.
  c Copy and fill in:
      Return bearing is
      120° + ...° = ...°

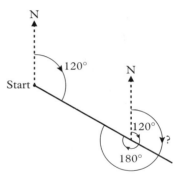

3 Neena leaves the path on a bearing
of 240°
  a Sketch this diagram of Neena's
   run.
  b Colour the outward bearing of
   240° red.
   Colour the return bearing blue.
  c Copy and fill in:
   Return bearing is
   240° − 180° = ...°

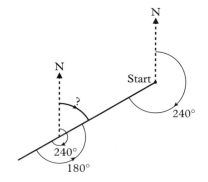

4 Joel runs on a bearing of 305°
  a Sketch this diagram of Joel's run.
  b Colour the outward bearing red.
   Colour the return bearing blue.
  c Copy and fill in:
   Return bearing is
   305° − ...° = ...°

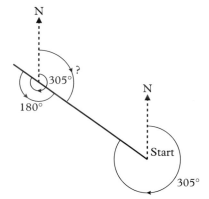

Find the return bearings for these.

5   **6**   **7**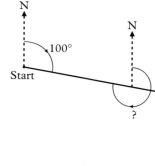

There is always a difference of 180° between outward bearings and return bearings.

Size of outward bearing	Rule for finding return bearing
less than 180°	outward bearing + 180°
more than 180°	outward bearing − 180°

The diagrams give the bearings of point B from point A.
Find the bearing of A from B (the return bearing).

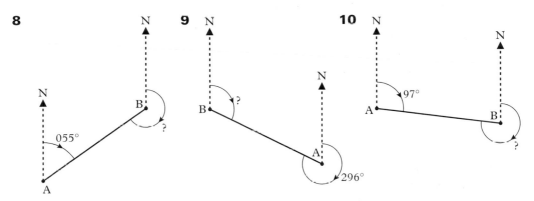

8

9

10

055°

?

296°

97°

?

• **11**   The diagram is a scale drawing of a piece of coastline.

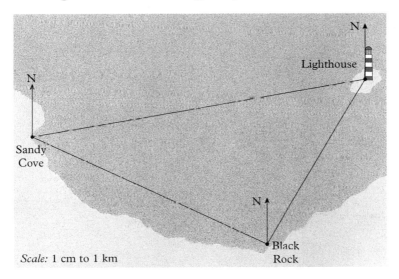

Lighthouse

Sandy
Cove

Black
Rock

Scale: 1 cm to 1 km

Find these answers by accurate measurement.
a   A boat sails from Sandy Cove to Black Rock.
  Find the bearing and the distance the boat sails.
b   The boat then sails from Black Rock to the lighthouse.
  Find the bearing and the distance the boat sails.
c   The boat then sails directly from the lighthouse to Sandy Cove.
  Find the bearing for this journey and the distance the boat sails.
d   The boat makes a second trip to the lighthouse. This time it goes
  straight there.
  Explain how you can calculate the bearing of the lighthouse from
  Sandy Cove using the bearing you found in part **c**.

1 Find the angles marked with letters.

a

c

b

d

2 Find the angles marked with letters.

a

b

3 Find the angles marked with letters.

a

b

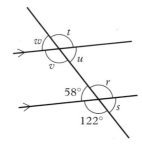

4 Find the angles marked with letters.
Write down whether the angles are alternate, corresponding or interior.

a

b

c

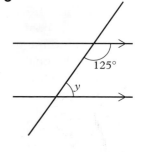

5 Find the angles marked with letters.

a

b

6 **a** Calculate the angle sum of a 9-sided polygon.
   b Calculate an angle of a regular 9-sided polygon.

7 Find the bearing of B from A in each case.

a

b

c

8 We use the points of the compass
to describe direction.
This method is not very accurate.
We use it to describe the direction
of winds, for example.

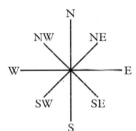

Write these points of the compass as bearings in degrees.
a E	**c** S	**e** NW	**g** SW
b W	**d** SE	**f** NE	**h** N

9 Find the bearing of A from B in each case.

a **b** **c**

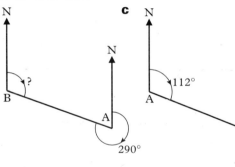

1 Find the angles marked with letters.

a

b

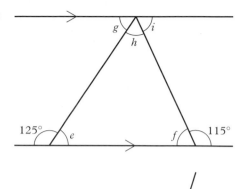

2 **a** Write down the angle sum of the **exterior** angles of any polygon.
   b A regular polygon has an exterior angle of 36°
      (1) How many times does 36° divide into 360°?
      (2) How many sides must the polygon have?
   c Use 180° − 36° to calculate an interior angle of this polygon.
   d Repeat parts **b** and **c** for these exterior angles.
      (1) 30°   (2) 24°   (3) 20°   (4) 18°

3 **a** A boat sails from Red Pier to Whitesands Bay.
      Find the bearing and the distance the boat sails.
   b The boat then sails from Whitesands Bay to Cave Point.
      Find the bearing and the distance the boat sails.
   c On the return journey the boat sails directly from Cave Point to Red Pier.
      Find the bearing for the return journey, and the distance the boat sails.

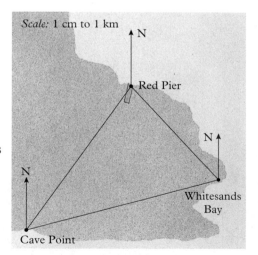

Scale: 1 cm to 1 km

● *Example*

Find the angles marked with letters.

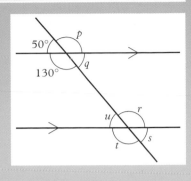

p is opposite 130°
q is opposite 50°
$p = 130°$ $q = 50°$

The 'bottom' set of four angles is equal to the 'top' set.
$r = 130°$ and $t = 130°$
$s = 50°$ and $u = 50°$

Alternate angles

Angles on opposite sides of the intersecting line, like q and u, are called **alternate angles**.
Alternate angles are equal.

Corresponding angles

Angles in the same place in 'top' and 'bottom' sets of angles, like p and r, are called **corresponding angles**.
Corresponding angles are equal.

Interior angles

Angles between the parallel lines, like q and r, are **interior angles**. Interior angles add up to 180°

● *Example*

Calculate an interior angle of a regular pentagon.

A regular pentagon can be divided into three triangles.
Sum of angles of pentagon $3 \times 180° = 540°$
One angle of pentagon $540° \div 5 = 108°$
Answer: 108°

● **Exterior angles**

The **exterior angles** of any polygon add up to 360°

●

Regular polygons which tessellate are equilateral triangles, squares and regular hexagons.

● **Bearing**

A compass gives the **bearing** of an object. This is the direction you travel in to go straight to the object.
Bearings are measured clockwise from north in degrees.
Bearings always have three figures.

1   Find the angles marked with letters.

a

c

b

d

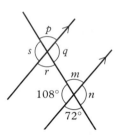

2   Find the angles marked with letters.

a

b

3   Find the angles marked with letters.
Write down whether the angles are alternate, corresponding or interior.

a

b

c

4   **a**   Calculate the angle sum of the interior angles of an octagon.
    b   Calculate an interior angle of a regular octagon.

5   Find the bearing of A from B in each case.

a

b

c

8 Probability

MCT

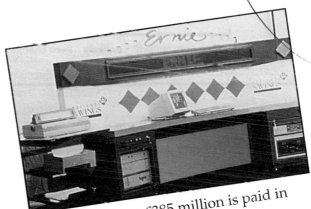

Every year about £385 million is paid in prizes by ERNIE.

ERNIE stands for Electronic Random Number Indicating Equipment.

ERNIE picks the numbers of the winning Premium Bonds each month.

Each Premium Bond costs £1 and every Bond has a 1 in 19 000 chance of winning a prize. Most prizes are £50 or £100 but there is a monthly prize of £1 million.

The chance of any Bond winning the £1 million prize in any month is about 1 in 8 billion!

1 ◄◄REPLAY►

Last year you used probability to help you decide what to say in the card game Higher or Lower.

Probability

Probability tells us how likely something is to happen.

We can show it on a probability scale:

impossible　very unlikely　unlikely　even chance　likely　very likely　certain

---

Exercise 8:1

1　Draw a probability scale.
　　Mark on it points **a**, **b** and **c** to show how likely you think each one is.
　a　The next person you see will be over 2 metres tall.
　b　There will be at least one sunny day in June in London.
　c　You will pass your driving test before you are 18 years old.

Probability is written as a number.
We write 0 for impossible and 1 for certain.

We can draw our probability scale like this:

0　　　　　　$\frac{1}{2}$　　　　　　1
impossible　　even chance　　certain

All probabilities must be between 0 and 1.

2 Draw a probability scale like this one:

Mark on it points **a**, **b** and **c** to show how likely you think each one is.

a The next person you meet will be older than you.

b The next person you meet will have a twin.

c The next person you meet will be right-handed.

3 For each letter that you marked in question **2**, give an estimate of the probability.

Write your answer as a decimal or a fraction.

Probability is usually written as a fraction.

Sally bought 3 raffle tickets.
100 tickets were sold.

The probability that Sally wins the raffle is $\frac{3}{100}$.

Exercise 8:2

1 A card is picked at random from an ordinary pack of 52 playing cards.

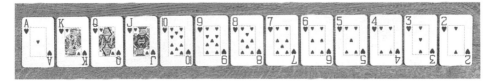

What is the probability that it will be

a red

b a spade

c a 9

d a picture card?

Remember: the picture cards are jack, queen, king and ace.

2 A bag contains 6 yellow counters and 5 green counters.
One counter is taken out at random.
Write down the probability that the counter is

a yellow   **b** green   **c** blue

3 Pat's piggy bank contains four £1 coins, three 50 p coins and five 20 p coins.

She shakes out a coin at random.

Write down the probability that the coin will be

a 50 p   **b** £1   ● **c** worth less than £1

● **4** The table shows the membership of a youth club.

	Under 13 years old	13 years old and over
boys	20	15
girls	18	22

a How many members are there in the club?

A person is chosen at random from the club.

Write down the probability that the person chosen is

b a boy

c a teenager (13 or older)

d a girl who is under 13 years old

- -

A box contains 12 counters.
There are 8 red and 4 blue.

Rolf picks a counter from the box without looking.
He writes down the colour and puts it back in the box.

He does this 12 times.

Rolf *expects* to get 8 reds and 4 blues.

Exercise 8:3

1 Rolf picks a counter 24 times.
  a How many reds does he expect to get?
  b How many blues does he expect to get?

2 This spinner has 3 equal sections.

How many times would you expect to get a 2 if you spin it
  a 3 times
  b 6 times
  c 30 times?

3 A bag contains 5 blue balls, 4 yellow balls and 1 black ball.
  Malcolm takes a ball at random and writes down the colour.
  He then puts the ball back in the bag.
  a He does this 10 times.
    Write down how many balls he would expect to be
    (1) blue   (2) black   (3) yellow
  b He does this 50 times.
    Write down how many balls he would expect to be
    (1) blue   (2) black   (3) yellow

4 A fair dice is thrown 300 times.
  Write down the number of times you would expect to get
  a a 6
  b a 2 or a 3
  c an odd number

5 In a survey of pupils at Stanthorne High, Sunita discovered that
  1 in every 10 pupils is left-handed.
  Write down the number of left-handed pupils you would expect in
  a a group of 10 pupils
  b a form of 30 pupils

6 A factory making calculators expects 1 in every 100 calculators to be faulty.

   a How many faulty calculators would you expect to find in a batch of 1000?

   b In a batch of 3420 calculators, 41 are found to be faulty. Is this more or less than the number of faulty calculators you would expect?

Game   *Holder of the box*

You will need a box and
3 different colours of counters.
This is a game for 3–5 players.

One player is the 'Holder of the box'.
This player chooses 12 counters
of three different colours and puts
them in the box.
There must be at least one counter of each colour.
The other players must not see the counters.

The other players take turns to choose a counter at random from the box, note the colour and return it to the box.
When a player returns a counter to the box he or she can guess how many counters of each colour there are in the box.

You can only guess when you have just had your turn.
You will probably not want to guess until everyone has had a couple of turns.

The first person to guess correctly wins.
The winner becomes the 'Holder of the box' for the next game.

Once you have played this game a few times you might like to make up a new game of your own.
Write down the rules and explain how to play your game.

2   It always adds up to 1

Peter and Jane are going to the fair. The weather forecast says that the probability of rain is 60%.

Peter does not want to get wet. Jane is more cheerful. She says that the probability of it not raining is 40%.

We usually write probabilities as fractions.
60% is $\frac{60}{100}$ and 40% is $\frac{40}{100}$.
$\frac{60}{100} + \frac{40}{100} = \frac{100}{100} = 1$

Probabilities always add up to 1.
We can show this on a probability scale.

Exercise 8:4

1   The scale shows the probability that Siobahn will take her dog for a walk after school.

Draw a scale to show the probability that Siobahn will not take her dog for a walk.

2   The scale shows the probability that Manzoor will be on time for school.

Draw a scale to show the probability that Manzoor will be late for school.

3 The probability that Liam cooks the tea is $\frac{5}{8}$.
What is the probability that he doesn't cook the tea?
Draw a probability scale to help you.

4 Gemma likes to talk to her friend Sadie on the phone.
Gemma can only use the phone if her Dad is in a good mood.
The probability that he is in a good mood is $\frac{4}{11}$.

What is the probability that Gemma will not be able to ring Sadie tonight?

Example A box contains red, blue and green counters.
One counter is picked at random.
The probability that it is red is $\frac{5}{10}$ and
the probability that it is blue is $\frac{3}{10}$.
What is the probability that it is green?

This time we split the probability scale into tenths.
We have to colour 3 different sections to show
the probabilities of the 3 colours.

The part left over shows the probability of green.
The probability of green is $\frac{2}{10}$.

---

5 Emma gets the bus to school each morning.
The probability that the bus is early is $\frac{3}{10}$.
The probability that the bus is exactly on time is $\frac{1}{10}$.
  a Draw a scale to show the probabilities of the bus being early and on time.
  b What is the probability that the bus is late?
Show this probability on your scale.

6 A box contains yellow, green and red counters.
One counter is picked at random.
The probability that it is yellow is $\frac{7}{20}$ and
the probability that it is green is $\frac{11}{20}$.
  a Draw a scale to show the probabilities of yellow and green.
  b What is the probability that the counter is red?
Show this probability on your scale.

3 Probability: how to make it look difficult

. . . .

We often talk about an important
event happening in sport.
We use the word event in
probability too.

Event

An **event** is something that can happen in a probability question.

When you roll a dice, there are lots of events.
One event is 'getting a 6'.
Another event is 'getting an odd number'.

We sometimes call an event by a letter.
The event 'getting a 6' might be called event A.
We write $P(A)$ for the probability of A happening.

Probability

The **probability** of an event A is the number of ways that the event A can happen divided by the total number of things that can happen.

Example

One card is chosen from an ordinary pack of playing cards.
Let A be the event 'getting a heart'.

There are 13 ways that event A can happen because there are 13 hearts in a pack.
There are 52 things that can happen altogether because there are 52 cards in a pack.

So $P(A) = \frac{13}{52}$

Exercise 8:5

1 Find $P(A)$ if the event A is getting
   a a 1 on a fair dice
   b a red card from an ordinary pack of cards
   c a king from an ordinary pack of cards
   d a blue sock from a drawer containing 6 blue socks and 4 grey socks
   e an even number on a 20-sided dice numbered 1–20

◀◀ REPLAY ▶

Cancelling fractions	When we write probabilities as fractions, we should **cancel the fractions** to their simplest form. We can do this using the $a\frac{b}{c}$ button on the calculator.
Example	To cancel the fraction $\frac{13}{52}$ we press:

1 **3** $a\frac{b}{c}$ **5** **2** **=**

The display shows ⌐⌐. This means $\frac{1}{4}$.

In the rest of this exercise give all probabilities as fractions in their simplest form.

2 Scott has a bag containing 15 sweets. 8 of them are toffees,
4 are fruit drops and 3 are chocolates.
He takes a sweet out at random.
Find the probability that the sweet he gets is
   a a toffee   **b** a fruit drop   **c** a chocolate

● Scott actually takes out a fruit drop, which he eats.
He then offers the bag to Natalie and she takes a sweet at random.
Find the probability that Natalie gets
   d a toffee   **e** a fruit drop   **f** a chocolate

3 Sinead is not a tidy girl. She has
all of her exercise books in a heap
in her room.
When she does her homework she
picks them up at random until
she gets the right one.
In her pile of books are 3 Maths,
4 English, 4 Science, 3 French,
2 History, 2 Geography and
2 Music.

What is the probability that the book she chooses first will be
   a Maths
   b English
   c Music?

Probability of something not happening	The **probability of something not happening** is 1 minus the probability that it does happen. For an event A, $$P(\text{not A}) = 1 - P(A)$$
Example	The probability of getting a 6 on a dice is $\frac{1}{6}$. The probability of not getting a 6 is $\frac{5}{6}$. We know this because there are 5 ways of not getting a 6. If A is the event 'getting a 6' $$P(\text{not A}) = 1 - P(A) = 1 - \tfrac{1}{6} = \tfrac{5}{6}$$

4 Find $P(\text{not A})$ for the events given in question **1**.

5 The probability that Janice will go round to see her friend on any night is $\frac{7}{12}$.
Find the probability that Janice won't see her friend tonight.

● **6** A bag contains a full set of 22 snooker balls.
There are 15 reds, and 1 each of white, yellow, green, brown, blue, pink and black.
One ball is chosen at random.
Write down the probability that it is

   a black
   b red
   c grey
   d not black
   e not red
   f not grey

4 Sample space diagrams

Sarah and Gavin are choosing their meal.

Sarah wants to know how many different meals she can choose.
She can have soup and fish fingers, soup and sausages,
soup and veggie burger, juice and fish fingers, juice and sausages or
juice and veggie burger.

There are 6 possibilities.
These can be shown in a table like this:

Starter	Main course
soup	fish fingers
soup	sausages
soup	veggie burger
juice	fish fingers
juice	sausages
juice	veggie burger

Exercise 8:6

1 Draw a table to show all of the possible meals from this menu.

2 Philippa is on an adventure holiday.
In the morning she can choose from Sailing, Windsurfing and Canoeing.
In the afternoon she can choose from Climbing, Horse-riding and Archery.

Draw a table to show all the ways that Philippa can spend her day.

● **3** Write down the different breakfasts that you can choose from this menu.

Bill, Rudi and Keith decide to toss a coin to see who does the washing up.

As there are 3 of them they need 3 possible outcomes.
They decide to use 2 coins.

If the outcome is 2 heads Bill will wash up.

If the outcome is 2 tails Keith will wash up.

If the outcome is 1 head and 1 tail Rudi will wash up.

Is this fair?

Here are the possible outcomes. There are four.

We can use a table to show these.

		20 p coin	
		H	T
2 p coin	H	H, H	H, T
	T	T, H	T, T

1 outcome gives 2 heads.
1 outcome gives 2 tails.
2 outcomes give 1 head and 1 tail.

Probability of 2 heads = $\frac{1}{4}$
Probability of 2 tails = $\frac{1}{4}$
Probability of 1 head and 1 tail = $\frac{2}{4}$

So this is not fair. 1 head and 1 tail will happen the most.

Exercise 8:7

1 David tosses the coin at the same time as Kelly spins the spinner.

a Copy the table to show the possible outcomes.
Fill it in.

		Spinner		
		1	2	3
Coin	H	H, 1		
	T			T, 3

b Write down the number of possible outcomes.
c How many ways can you get a tail on the coin and a 3 on the spinner?
d What is the probability of getting a tail on the coin and a 3 on the spinner?
e What is the probability of getting an odd number and a head?

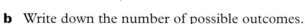

Sample space	A **sample space** is a list of all the possible outcomes.
Sample space diagram	A table which shows all of the possible outcomes is called a **sample space diagram**.

2 Saleem throws a coin and rolls a dice.
   a Copy this sample space diagram.
   Fill it in.

		Dice					
		1	2	3	4	5	6
Coin	H						
	T						

   b What is the total number of possible outcomes?
   c What is the probability of getting a head and a 6?
   d What is the probability of getting a tail and a number less than 3?
   e What is the probability of getting a tail and a multiple of 3?
   f What is the probability of getting a head and a prime number?

3 The picture shows two tetrahedral dice.

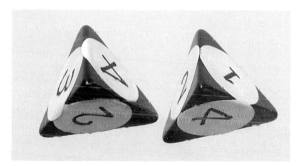

They both have four faces.
The faces are numbered 1, 2, 3 and 4.
The score is on the face that the dice lands on.

Copy this sample space diagram.
Fill it in.

		Second dice			
		1	2	3	4
First dice	1			1, 3	
	2				
	3		3, 2		
	4				

   a What is the total number of possible outcomes?
   b What is the probability of getting a 1 on both dice?
   c What is the probability of getting the same number on both dice?

Surrinder decides to add the two numbers that the dice land on.
He calls this the score.
In the picture above the score is $1 + 3 = 4$

d Copy the sample space diagram to show the score.
Fill it in.

		Second dice			
		1	2	3	4
First dice	1	2			
	2		4	5	
	3			6	
	4		6		8

e How many ways can you score 2?
f What is the probability of scoring 2?
g How many ways can you score 5?
h What is the probability of scoring 5?

4 Each form in Stanthorne High has a quiz team.
The best teams in Year 8 are 8S and 8H.

8S has a team of 3 boys and 1 girl.
8H has a team of 2 boys and 2 girls.
One person is chosen from each team to represent the year.

Copy the sample space diagram to show the possible pairs of pupils.
Fill it in.

		8S Team			
		B	B	B	G
8H Team	B				
	B				
	G				
	G				

Write down the probability that the pair chosen is
a a boy and a girl
b two pupils of the same sex

Game   It's not fair

This is a game for two players
A and B.
Take turns to roll the dice.
Multiply the two numbers scored.
In this picture the score is
    $4 \times 3 = 12$

For each roll:
player A gets a point if the product is even
player B gets a point if the product is odd

The first player to 10 points wins.

Play the game with a partner.
Who should win? Explain your answer using a sample space diagram.
Can you change the rules of the game to make it fair?

Chinese dice

For this investigation, you need 3 dice.

Dice A has faces labelled	2	2	2	2	6	6
Dice B has faces labelled	1	1	5	5	5	5
Dice C has faces labelled	3	3	3	4	4	4

Two players play like this.

The first player chooses a dice.
The second player chooses a dice from the remaining two.

Each player rolls their dice and the player with the higher number scores
1 point.

This is done 12 times. The player with the most points wins.

Using these rules it is possible for one player to win nearly all the time.
How should they choose? Investigate.

1   Jenny takes one card at random from the 13 hearts from a pack of cards.
What is the probability that she gets
   a   a 4   **b**   a picture card   **c**   a heart   **d**   a spade?

2   A 12-sided dice has the numbers 1 to 12 on its faces.
Hiten rolls the dice once.
Write down the probability that he gets
   a   a 6   **c**   a prime number
   b   an even number   **d**   a number which is greater than 7

3   A farmer supplies a shop with baking potatoes.
6 out of every 10 potatoes are large.
   a   How many large potatoes would you expect in a bag of 30 potatoes?
   b   In a bag of 25 potatoes, 12 are large.
      Is this more or less than you would expect?

4   A letter is chosen at random from the word ASSESSMENT.
What is the probability that the letter is
   a   T   **b**   S   **c**   A or E?

5   One hundred tickets numbered 1 to 100 are sold for a raffle.
One winning ticket is chosen at random.
Write down the probability that the winning ticket is
   a   43   **b**   a 2-digit number   **c**   a multiple of 10

6   The bar-chart shows the favourite flavour of crisps of 48 pupils.
One of the 48 pupils is chosen at random.

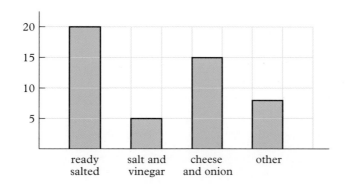

What is the probability that the favourite flavour of the person chosen is
   a   ready salted
   b   not salt and vinegar
   c   ready salted or salt and vinegar?

7 The probability that Tanya hands her homework in on time is $\frac{7}{10}$.
The probability that she hands it in late is $\frac{2}{10}$.
What is the probability that she hands it in early?

8 A game uses 2 spinners.
The two numbers that they land
on are added together to give
the score.

a Copy this table to show the score.
Fill it in.

		Blue spinner			
		0	1	2	3
Green	2	2			
spinner	3			5	
	4				

Find the probability that the score is
b 4   **c** less than 6   **d** 6 or more

9 Michael wants to buy a pack of sandwiches and a drink for his lunch.
He has to choose from this selection.

Sandwiches	Drinks
cheese	cola
tuna	lemonade
egg	milk

Write down all the possible lunches that he can have.

10 **a** Draw a sample space diagram to show all the possible outcomes
when two ordinary dice are rolled together.
b What is the probability of rolling double 6?

1 200 tickets are sold for a raffle.
The probability that John wins first prize is $\frac{7}{100}$.
How many raffle tickets has John bought?

2 500 light bulbs are tested to see
how long they last.
The results are shown on
the bar-chart.

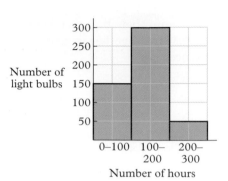

Kevin buys one of this type of
light bulb.
Write down the probability that it
will last
 a less than 100 hours
 b between 100 and 200 hours
 c at least 100 hours

3 Michelle and Leila are playing a
game with this spinner.
They spin it twice and write down
the colour of each spin.

Draw a sample space diagram to show the possible outcomes.
Write down the probability of getting
 a 2 reds
 b a red followed by a yellow
 c a red and a yellow

4 Copy this table to show the possible outcomes when
three coins are thrown.
Fill it in.

First coin	Second coin	Third coin
H	H	H
H	H	T
H	T	
H	T	
T		
T		
T		
T		

What is the probability of getting
 a 3 heads
 b head head tail in this order
 c two heads and one tail?

- Probability tells us how likely something is to happen.
  We write it as a number.
  We write 0 for impossible and 1 for certain.

  We can show it on a probability scale:

  All probabilities must be between 0 and 1.

- Probability is usually written as a fraction.

  Example   Sally bought 3 raffle tickets.
  100 tickets were sold.
  The probability that Sally wins the raffle is $\frac{3}{100}$.

- Probabilities always add up to 1.
  We can show this on a probability scale.

  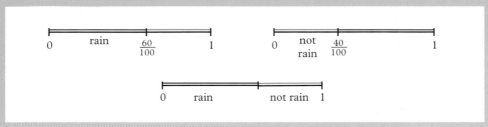

- An **event** is something that can happen in a probability question.
  We sometimes call an event by a letter.
  The event 'getting a 6' might be called event A.
  We write $P(A)$ for the probability of A happening.

- The **probability of something not happening** is
  1 minus the probability that it does happen.
  For an event A,
  $P(\text{not } A) = 1 - P(A)$

  Example   The probability of getting a 6 on a dice is $\frac{1}{6}$
  The probability of not getting a 6 is $1 - \frac{1}{6} = \frac{5}{6}$

- A **sample space** is a list of all the possible outcomes.
  A table which shows all of the possible outcomes is called
  a **sample space diagram**.

1 A bag of sweets contains 4 toffees and 10 fruit drops.
Francis takes 1 sweet at random from the bag.
Write down the probability that the sweet is
a a toffee **b** a fruit drop

2 Penny has 3 red, 5 green and 7 black pencils in her pencil case.
She takes 1 pencil out at random.
She writes down the colour and puts the pencil back in the case.
a She does this 30 times.
Write down how many pencils she expects to be
(1) red (2) green (3) black
b She does this 90 times.
Write down how many pencils she expects to be
(1) red (2) green (3) black

3 The probability that Kirk gets all his homework right is $\frac{2}{5}$.
What is the probability that he gets something wrong?

4 Barbara rings her friend Renie.
The probability that the phone call will last for less than 10 minutes is $\frac{1}{6}$.
The probability that it will last between 10 and 20 minutes is $\frac{3}{6}$.
What is the probability that the call will last for more than 20 minutes?

5 The event A is 'getting an odd number' on an ordinary dice.
Write down
a $P(A)$ **b** $P(\text{not } A)$

6 David throws a coin and rolls this dice.
Copy this sample space diagram.
Fill it in.

		Dice			
		1	2	3	4
Coin	H	H, 1			
	T			T, 3	

a What is the total number of possible outcomes?
b Ring the outcomes that give a tail and an even number.
c What is the probability of getting a tail and an even number?

Percentages and fractions

Emily owns shares worth £200.
The share value rises by 10%.
Then the value falls by 10%.

True or False?
Emily's shares are now worth £200.

1 Simple percentages

82 out of these 100 children have blue eyes.

This is the same as saying that 82% have blue eyes.

16 out of these 100 children are left-handed.

This is the same as saying that 16% of them are left-handed.

Exercise 9:1

1 Pupils who are right-handed are shaded blue.
What percentage are right-handed?

2 Pupils who stay at school for lunch are shaded red.
What percentage stay for lunch?

3 Pupils who did not do their homework are shaded green.

   a What percentage did not do their homework?

   b What percentage *did* do their homework?

4 Pupils who play in a school sports team are shaded pink.

   a What percentage of the pupils play for a school team?

   b What percentage do *not* play for a school team?

5 Pupils who own a computer are shaded yellow.

   What percentage of the pupils do *not* own a computer?

You can also work out percentages when there are not 100 children.

82 out of 100 is 82%   41 out of 50 is still 82%

is the same as

41 out of 50
↓ ×2   ↓ ×2
82 out of 100

Exercise 9:2

1 Pupils who have a part-time job are shaded red.
   a How many of the 50 have a part-time job?
   b What percentage have a part-time job?

2 Pupils who read a daily newspaper are shaded green.
   a How many of the 50 read a newspaper?
   b What percentage read a newspaper?

3 Pupils who own a cat are shaded brown.
   a How many of the 50 own a cat?
   b What percentage own a cat?

4 Pupils who go swimming regularly are shaded blue.
   a How many pupils out of the 25 are shaded blue?
   b What percentage go swimming?
   c What percentage do *not* go swimming?

5 Pupils who support Manchester United are shaded orange.
   a How many of the 25 are shaded orange?
   b What percentage support Manchester United?
   c What percentage do *not* support Manchester United?

Shops often have special sale days.
They mark some items with a blue cross.
This means that there is 10% off the price.

They do not change the price on the ticket because the sale only lasts a few days.

You have to work out the sale price for yourself.

10% means 10 in every 100.

This is the same as 10 p in every £1

This is the same as 1 p in every 10 p

This makes it easy to find 10% of an amount of money.
You divide the amount by 10.

To divide by 10, move all the numbers one place to the right.

Example   A T-shirt costing £6.50 is in the blue cross sale.
Work out how much you would save.

10% of £6.50 = £6 . 5 0 ÷ 10
                    ÷10 ÷10

            = £0 . 6 5
            = 65 p

You would save 65 p

Exercise 9:3

All these items are in the blue cross sale.
This means take 10% off.

BLUE CROSS SALE

10% OFF
ALL MARKED ITEMS

1 Work out how much you would save
on each of these.
a A T-shirt costing £7.50
b Shorts costing £9.50
c Socks costing £3.50
d A sweatshirt costing £8.50

2 Work out how much these would *cost*
in the blue cross sale.
a A T-shirt costing £5.20
b A board game costing £7.40
c A pen costing £1.20
d A diary costing £4.90

3 Work out the sale price of these.
a Jeans costing £22.50
b A jacket costing £35.90
c A jumper costing £12.80
d Trainers costing £89.90

4 A personal stereo costs £24.90
How much would the stereo cost in
the sale?

5 A pair of jeans costs £35.50
How much would the jeans cost in
the sale?

6 A computer game costs £26.90
Work out its new price in the sale.

7 A pair of shoes costs exactly £25
Work out how much they would cost in
the sale.

● **8** A CD costs £12.99
How much would it cost in the sale?

Once you have worked out 10% it is quite easy to work out other percentages.

On the last day of the blue cross sale the discount is increased to 20%.

Everything marked with a blue cross now has 20% off.
To work out 20% of an amount:
First work out 10% of the amount.
Then multiply by 2.
$$10\% \times 2 = 20\%$$

Example

A pair of jeans costs £35.90
Work out the new price with 20% off.

10% of £35.90 = £3.59
20% of £35.90 = £3.59 × 2 = £7.18

The jeans would cost £35.90 − £7.18 = £28.72

Exercise 9:4

1 A pair of jeans costs £27.90
The price is reduced by 20%.
  a Work out 20% of £27.90
  b Work out the cost of the jeans.

2 A portable TV costs £90
  a Work out 20% of £90
  b Work out the cost of the TV if it is reduced by 20%.

3 A box of computer disks costs £8.50
The price is reduced by 20% in the sale.
  a Find 20% of £8.50
  b How much does the box of disks cost in the sale?

4 A ski jacket costs £120
The price is reduced by 20% in the sale.
Work out the cost of the jacket in the sale.

You can make up other percentages from 10%.

If you want to work out 40%, find 10% and then multiply by 4.
70% is 10% multiplied by 7.

Examples

1   Find 40% of £24

10% of £24 = £2.40
40% of £24 = £2.40 × 4 = £9.60

2   Find 60% of £50

10% of £50 = £5
60% of £50 = £5 × 6 = £30

Exercise 9:5

1   Find these percentages. You will need to work out 10% first.
   a   30% of £24   **c**   40% of £45
   b   40% of £30   **d**   60% of £150

2   A pair of jeans is reduced by 30%
in a sale.
They normally cost £33
   a   Work out 30% of £33
   b   How much do the jeans cost
in the sale?

3   There are 220 pupils in Year 8.
20% have brown eyes.
How many pupils have brown eyes?

4   In an election 22 000 people voted.
35% of them voted Conservative.
   a   Find 10% of 22 000
   b   Use your answer to **a** to find 5% of 22 000.
   c   Find 35% of 22 000.
      This is the number of people who voted Conservative.
   d   How many people did not vote Conservative?

5   In a trial of 2300 dogs, 65% preferred Dogidins.
   a   Find 10% and 5% of 2300.
   b   How many dogs preferred Dogidins?
   c   What percentage preferred another brand?
   d   How many dogs preferred another brand?

50% of something is half of it. You can divide by 2 to find 50%.
This is easier than finding 10% and then multiplying by 5.

You can find 25% by finding 50% and then dividing this by 2.

Examples

1 Find 50% of £70

50% of £70 = £70 ÷ 2 = £35

2 Find 25% of £130

50% of £130 = £130 ÷ 2 = £65
25% of £130 = £65 ÷ 2 = £32.50

---

6 Find:
  a 50% of £60   **b** 50% of £46

7 Work out these percentages. Find 50% first.
  a 25% of £40
  b 25% of £180
  c 25% of £170

8 There are 760 pupils at St Giles School.
55% have school meals.
25% take a packed lunch.
20% go home.
  a How many pupils have school meals?
  b How many pupils take a packed lunch?

9 Here are 6 question cards and 6 answer cards.
Work out each question.
Match it with its answer.
Write the questions and answers in your book.

20% of 300	**50% of 450**	**65% of 800**
35% of 400	**60**	**25% of 160**
40% of 700	**140**	**225**
40	**520**	**280**

2 Calculating percentages

These opinion poll results are given as percentages.
We can work them out with a calculator.

To work out a percentage on a calculator:

(1) Turn the percentage into a decimal.
To do this, divide it by 100.

(2) Multiply the amount by the decimal.

Examples

1 Find 38% of 1200 people.

$$38\% = \frac{38}{100} = 38 \div 100 = 0.38$$

38% of 1200 = 0.38 × 1200 = 456 people

2 Find 47% of 1200 people.

$$47\% = \frac{47}{100} = 47 \div 100 = 0.47$$

47% of 1200 = 0.47 × 1200 = 564 people

Exercise 9:6

1 Copy and fill in:

    a $56\% = \dfrac{?}{100} = 0.56$ **d** $98\% = \dfrac{?}{100} = \ldots$

    b $76\% = \dfrac{76}{100} = \ldots$ **e** $9\% = \dfrac{?}{100} = 0.09$

    c $32\% = \dfrac{?}{100} = \ldots$ ● **f** $\ldots\% = \dfrac{8}{100} = \ldots$

2 1200 people take part in a survey about banks.
They are asked which bank they use.

        23% say Nat West   15% say Midland
        17% say Lloyds   9% say Yorkshire
        18% say Barclays   18% say another bank

    a Copy and fill in:
       (1) 23% of $1200 = 0.23 \times 1200 = \ldots$
       (2) 17% of $1200 = 0.17 \times 1200 = \ldots$
       (3) 18% of $1200 = \quad \ldots \times 1200 = \ldots$
       (4) 15% of $1200 = \quad \ldots \times 1200 = \ldots$
       (5) 9% of $1200 = \quad \ldots \times 1200 = \ldots$
       (6) 18% of $1200 = \quad \ldots \times 1200 = \ldots$
    b Add up your answers to part **a**.
       Write down the total.

3 Class 8J have a Maths test. The total mark is 40.
The teacher gives them their marks as percentages.
       Terry 35%   Sian 65%   Lindsey 95%
They want to know how many marks they got.
Work out the marks for each person.

4 Look at this advertisement.
    a Pritesh buys a Chart CD. It normally costs £13
       How much does the CD cost in the sale?
    b Glenn also buys a Chart CD. It normally
       costs £13.80
       How much does the CD cost in the sale?
    c Michelle buys a Rock CD. It normally costs £11
       There is 26% off in the sale.
       How much does the CD cost?
    d Anne buys a Classical CD. It normally costs £15
       How much does the CD cost in the sale?

> *Rob's Records*
>
> **CD Sale**
>
> 15% off Chart CDs
> Up to 33% off Rock CDs
> 12% off all Classical CDs

5 Ben works part-time in a shop. He earns £2.50 per hour.
  a Ben gets a rise of 8%.
    How much extra will he get per hour?
  b How much will he earn per hour after his rise?

6 VAT stands for Value Added Tax. You pay it on lots of things you buy.
  VAT is charged at $17\frac{1}{2}$% on most things.
  $17\frac{1}{2}$% is 0.175 as a decimal.
  Work out the VAT on each of these items.
  a Jeans costing £30 without VAT.
  b A stereo costing £290 without VAT.
  c A car costing £9950 without VAT.

7 Hayley earns £3.20 per hour as a waitress.
  She gets a rise of $12\frac{1}{2}$%.
  Find her new hourly rate.

· ·

Exercise 9:7 Four in a row

This is a game for two players.
You will need two colours of counters.
Each player uses a different colour.
You need one calculator between you.

Underneath the number 650 you can see a list of 36 percentages.
If you work out these percentages of 650 you get the answers shown in
the board underneath.

Player 1:
(1) Choose a square on the board.
(2) One percentage from the list will give the answer in the square.
    Choose the percentage that you think is correct.
(3) Calculate the percentage.
(4) Cover up the calculator answer on the board with a counter.

Player 2:
You do the same thing using your counters.

The winner is the first person to get four counters in a straight line.
The line can be in any direction.
The better you are at predicting the answers, the more likely you are
to win!

650

23%	57%	68%	24%	12%	45%	97%	81%	27%
39%	42%	17%	15%	47%	25%	84%	71%	55%
66%	10%	13%	54%	93%	61%	49%	60%	80%
22%	43%	74%	99%	24%	33%	58%	17%	75%

149.5	110.5	305.5	214.5	357.5	442
390	162.5	156	292.5	110.5	396.5
526.5	643.5	604.5	461.5	175.5	520
97.5	429	370.5	143	318.5	630.5
78	481	253.5	65	487.5	546
84.5	396.5	279.5	273	377	351

To work out what percentage one number is of another:

(1) Write the numbers as a fraction.

(2) Change the fraction to a decimal.

(3) Change the decimal to a percentage.

Examples

1 Michael gets £80 for his birthday. He saves £15
What percentage does he save?
We need 15 as a percentage of 80.

$$\frac{15}{80} = 15 \div 80 = 0.1875$$

To change a decimal to a percentage, multiply by 100.

$$0.1875 = 18.75\%$$

2 Nick scores 33 in a test. The test is out of 40.
What percentage is this?

$$\frac{33}{40} = 33 \div 40 = 0.825 = 82.5\%$$

Exercise 9:8

1 Copy this table. It shows the marks in a test out of 40.
Fill in the rest of the table.

Pupil	Mark	Fraction	Decimal	Percentage
Sean	34	$\frac{34}{40}$	0.85	
Gavla	19			
Shellene	27		0.675	
Jamie	37			
Emma	21			

2 Jonathan runs a record shop.
He keeps a note of how many CDs, tapes and records he sells each day.

Here are his results for Monday.
  a How many items did he sell on Monday?
  b What percentage of these were CDs?
  c What percentage were tapes?

	Mon
CDs	34
tapes	35
records	11
Total	80

3 Here are the CD sales figures for the whole week.

	Mon	Tues	Wed	Fri	Sat	Total
CDs	34	38	42	41	95	250

   a What percentage of the CDs did he sell on Saturday?
   b What percentage of the CDs did he sell on Friday?

4 Here are all the figures for the week.

	Mon	Tues	Wed	Fri	Sat	Total
CDs	34	38	42	41	95	250
tapes	35	29	20	48	68	200
records	11	3	18	21	27	80
Total	80	70	80	110	190	530

   a Look at the Wednesday column.
      What percentage of Wednesday's sales were CDs?
   b What percentage of total tape sales did he make on Friday?
   c Round your answers to parts (1)–(3) to 2 dp.
      Look at the last column.
      (1) What percentage of the week's sales were CDs?
      (2) What percentage of the week's sales were tapes?
      (3) What percentage of the week's sales were records?

5 This table shows the number of people living in Australia who were not born there.
The figures are in thousands.

Year	Number born overseas	Total population
1947	744.2	7518.6
1954	1286.5	8900.3
1966	2130.9	11 500.6
1976	2718.8	14 033.1
1986	3427.4	16 018.4

   a Work out the percentage of the population who were born overseas in each year. Round your answers to 1 dp.
   b Has emigrating to Australia become more or less popular?

3 Fractions

Bill is ordering some new stock.
Three-quarters of the ice creams that he sells are cornets.
One-quarter are lollies.

Bill has sold 1200 ice creams this week.
He wants to work out how many of each he has sold.

Example

Find one-quarter of 1200.

$1200 \div 4 = 300$
He has sold 300 lollies.

Find three-quarters of 1200.

$1200 \div 4 \times 3 = 900$
He has sold 900 cornets.

To find $\frac{3}{4}$ you divide by 4 and then
multiply by 3.

Exercise 9:9

1 Find:
  a $\frac{1}{4}$ of 240
  b $\frac{3}{4}$ of 240

2 Find:
  a $\frac{1}{5}$ of 240
  b $\frac{2}{5}$ of 240
  c $\frac{3}{5}$ of 240

3 Find:
  a $\frac{1}{7}$ of 168
  b $\frac{2}{7}$ of 168
  c $\frac{5}{7}$ of 168

4 Find:
  a $\frac{1}{8}$ of 192
  b $\frac{3}{8}$ of 192
  c $\frac{7}{8}$ of 192

5 In a box of apples, $\frac{2}{7}$ have gone bad.
There are 35 apples in the box.
How many apples have gone bad?

6 $\frac{2}{5}$ of the cars sold by a garage are hatchbacks.
The garage sells 45 cars in August.
a How many hatchbacks do they sell?
b How many other cars do they sell?

You can do fractions questions on your calculator.
You use the button $\boxed{a^b/_c}$ to enter a fraction.

To enter $\frac{3}{4}$ press $\quad \boxed{3} \; \boxed{a^b/_c} \; \boxed{4}$

To find $\frac{3}{4}$ of 240 press $\quad \boxed{3} \; \boxed{a^b/_c} \; \boxed{4} \; \boxed{\times} \; \boxed{2} \; \boxed{4} \; \boxed{0} \; \boxed{=}$

You should get 180

Exercise 9:10

1 Copy this diagram.
Join each question to the correct answer with an arrow.
One has been done for you.

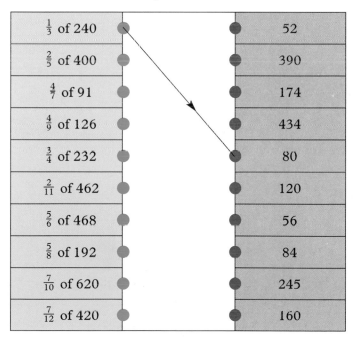

$\frac{1}{3}$ of 240	52
$\frac{2}{5}$ of 400	390
$\frac{4}{7}$ of 91	174
$\frac{4}{9}$ of 126	434
$\frac{3}{4}$ of 232	80
$\frac{2}{11}$ of 462	120
$\frac{5}{6}$ of 468	56
$\frac{5}{8}$ of 192	84
$\frac{7}{10}$ of 620	245
$\frac{7}{12}$ of 420	160

Examples

1 Change $\frac{3}{5}$ to a decimal and a percentage.

$\frac{3}{5} = 3 \div 5 = 0.6$

$0.6 = 60\%$

2 Change 80% to a fraction.

$80\% = \dfrac{80}{100}$

Cancel this fraction to its simplest form

| 8 | 0 | $a^b\!/_c$ | 1 | 0 | 0 | = | ⁴⌐⁵ |

Answer: $\frac{4}{5}$

Exercise 9:11

You will need a set of Cuisenaire rods.
Each picture shows a pair of Cuisenaire rods. The table shows what fraction the smaller rod is of the bigger one.

1 Copy this table.
Fill it in.

Picture		Fraction	Decimal	Percentage
a		$\frac{1}{2}$		
b			0.25	
c		$\frac{1}{3}$		

Picture	Fraction	Decimal	Percentage
d			20%
e		0.4	
f	$\frac{3}{4}$		
• **g**			$66\frac{2}{3}\%$

2 Now choose pairs of rods for yourself.
Make a table like the one in question **1** to show the rods you choose.
Work out the fraction, decimal and percentage columns for each pair.

Some pairs will give you the same answers you saw in question **1**.
You do not have to do these again.

How many different sets of results can you find?

1 There are 25 pupils in 8N.
12 of them come to school by bus.
What percentage of the pupils in 8N come to school by bus?

2 A computer game usually costs £38
In a sale the cost is reduced by 20%.
How much does the game cost in the sale?

3 Freda asked 50 pupils in Year 8 for their favourite sport.
Here are her results:
Football 34   Swimming 5   Running 4   Hockey 4   Netball 3
What percentage of pupils like each sport?

4 Work out how much you would
save on each of these in the sale.
  a A shirt costing £15
  b A coat costing £25
  c A book costing £9.50
  d A CD costing £13.50
  e A watch costing £14.80

5 Mr Hussein can earn £3500 before he pays tax.
Then he pays 25% on the rest of his earnings.
In one year Mr Hussein earns £12 500
Copy and fill in:
  a Mr Hussein pays tax on £12 500 − £3500 = £...
  b Amount of tax = 25% of £... = £...
  c Mr Hussein keeps £12 500 − £... = £...

6 There are 220 pupils in Year 9 at Stanthorne High.
  a 65% of them have chips every day.
       How many pupils have chips every day?
  b 35% have a brother.
       How many pupils have a brother?
  c 40% have a sister.
       How many pupils have a sister?
  d 45% walk to school each day.
       How many pupils walk to school each day?
  e What percentage of pupils *do not* walk to school each day?

7 Work these out.
  a 25% of £500   **c** 35% of 340 girls   **e** 75% of 5 metres
  b 45% of £600   **d** 65% of 8 hours   **f** 85% of 15 kilograms

8 Find:
  a 64% of 3800 people
  b 29% of £4600
  c 52% of 450 grams
  d 37% of £2479

9 Work out the VAT at $17\frac{1}{2}$% on these.
  a A video costing £10 without VAT.
  b A picture frame costing £30 without VAT.
  c Training shoes costing £40 without VAT.

10 1400 people take part in a shopping survey.
  They are asked if they use a supermarket for all of their shopping.
  47.5% say that they do use a supermarket.
  a How many people use a supermarket for all of their shopping?
  b What percentage of people *do not* use a supermarket for all of their shopping?

11 Khalid shares his 140 sweets with his friends.
  He gives $\frac{1}{7}$ to Rebecca and $\frac{3}{7}$ to Harry.
  He keeps the rest himself.
  a How many sweets does Khalid give to Rebecca?
  b How many sweets does Khalid give to Harry?
  c What fraction of the sweets does Khalid keep for himself?

12 Work these out.
  a $\frac{4}{7}$ of 350
  b $\frac{5}{8}$ of 640
  c $\frac{7}{12}$ of 2448
  d $\frac{5}{11}$ of 286

13 Camille does a survey about favourite flavours of ice cream.
  She writes a report of her results.
  This is part of her report.

Favourite flavours of ice cream
of 200 people
Vanilla   57.5%
Chocolate   23%
Strawberry   12.5%
Other   7%

How many people like each flavour of ice cream the best?

1 School bus fares are increased by $3\frac{1}{2}\%$ due to increased fuel costs.
Find the new prices to the nearest penny for:
  a Jan who normally pays £1.30
  b Clive who normally pays 95 p
  c Ian who normally pays £1.25

2 Mrs Barton can earn £4500 before she pays tax.
Then she pays 20% on the next £3200 and 25% on the rest of
her earnings.
In one year Mrs Barton earns £12 500
Copy and fill in:
  a Mrs Barton pays tax on £12 500 − £4500 = £...
  b Mrs Barton pays 20% tax on £...
  c Mrs Barton pays 25% tax on £... − £... = £...
  d Amount of tax
      20% of £... = £...
      25% of £... = £...
      Total tax   = £...
  e Mrs Barton keeps £12 500 − £... = £...

3 A trade warehouse shows all of its
prices without VAT.
Manesh buys:
a CD costing £9.99
a jumper costing £19.99
a pair of shoes costing £24.99

  a Work out the VAT at $17\frac{1}{2}\%$ on each item.
    Give your answers correct to the nearest penny.
  b How much does Manesh spend altogether?

4 A bag contains 36 beads.
$\frac{1}{12}$ of them are orange, $\frac{2}{9}$ are black and the rest are white.
  a How many beads of each colour are in the bag?
  b What fraction of the beads are white?

5 There are 32 teeth in a full adult set.
$\frac{1}{8}$ are canines, $\frac{3}{8}$ are molars and $\frac{1}{4}$ are incisors.
The rest are called pre-molars.
  a How many canines are there?
  b How many molars are there?
  c What percentage of the teeth are pre-molars?

● To find 10% of an amount divide the amount by 10.

Example   10% of £6.50 = £6 . 5   0 ÷ 10

$$= £0 . 6 \quad 5$$
$$= 65\,p$$

● You can make up other percentages from 10%.

If you want to work out 40%, find 10% and then multiply by 4.
70% is 10% multiplied by 7.

50% of something is half of it. You can divide by 2 to find 50%.
This is easier than finding 10% and then multiplying by 5.

You can find 25% by finding 50% and then dividing this by 2.

Example   Find 40% of £24

10% of £24 = £2.40
40% of £24 = £2.40 × 4 = £9.60

● To work out a percentage on a calculator:

(1) Turn the percentage into a decimal.
    To do this, divide it by 100.

(2) Multiply by the decimal.

Example   Find 38% of 1200 people.

$$38\% = \frac{38}{100} = 38 \div 100 = 0.38$$

38% of 1200 = 0.38 × 1200 = 456 people

● To work out what percentage one number is of another:

(1) Write the numbers as a fraction.

(2) Change the fraction to a decimal.

(3) Change the decimal to a percentage.

Example   What percentage is 15 of 80?

$$\frac{15}{80} = 15 \div 80 = 0.1875 = 18.75\%$$

● You can do fractions questions on your calculator.
You use the button $a^b\!/_c$ to enter a fraction.

To enter $\frac{3}{4}$ press $\boxed{3}$ $\boxed{a^b\!/_c}$ $\boxed{4}$

To find $\frac{3}{4}$ of 240 press $\boxed{3}$ $\boxed{a^b\!/_c}$ $\boxed{4}$ $\boxed{\times}$ $\boxed{2}$ $\boxed{4}$ $\boxed{0}$ $\boxed{=}$

You should get ¦80

1   There are 50 bananas on a supermarket shelf.
     12 of them are very ripe.
     What percentage of the bananas are very ripe?

2   In a sale everything is reduced by 10%.
     Work out how much you could save on each of these in the sale.
     a   A tape costing £9.50
     b   A CD costing £12.50
     c   A book costing £14.80

3   Work these out.
     a   10% of £400
     b   40% of £400
     c   25% of £340

4   Work these out.
     a   48% of 6700 people   **c**   7% of £1327
     b   38% of 1200 metres   **d** $67\frac{1}{2}$% of 750 grams

5   Work out the VAT at $17\frac{1}{2}$% on these items.
     a   A computer game costing £30 without VAT.
     b   A tracksuit costing £40 without VAT.

6   Tanya scores 26 out of 40 in a test.
     What percentage is this?

7   A garage sells 2400 cars in August.
     In the rest of the year they sell 3600 cars.
     a   How many cars do they sell altogether in the year?
     b   What percentage of their cars do they sell in August?

8   Paul eats a lot of sweets. He has fillings in $\frac{2}{7}$ of his 28 teeth.
     a   How many fillings has Paul got?
     b   What fraction of his teeth are *not* filled?

9   The table shows how many cakes Ahsan sells in one week.

Monday	Tuesday	Wednesday	Thursday	Friday
24	28	28	36	44

     a   What fraction of the cakes did he sell on Friday?
     b   What percentage of the cakes did he sell on Monday?

10 Straight lines

The co-ordinates we use to draw graphs are called Cartesian co-ordinates. They were named after a Frenchman called René Descartes (1596–1650). In 1619 he had a dream in which he realised that all the sciences were connected and that physics could be expressed using the language of geometry. One of Descartes' famous sayings was: '*Cogito ergo sum*' which is Latin for '*Je pense, donc je suis*'.

1   Lines of the grid

Bill is on holiday in New York.
He wants to visit the World Trade Center Building.
It is at the intersection of Liberty Street with West Street.

◄◄ REPLAY ►

Exercise 10:1

1   Look at the red line.
The co-ordinates of the point P
are $(2, 3)$.

Write down the co-ordinates of
the points A, B, C, D and E.

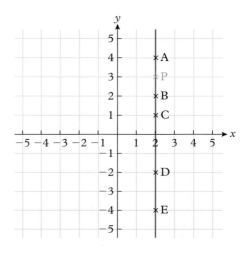

All these points have **x** co-ordinate = **2**
In algebra this is   **x = 2**
The rule for the line is **x = 2**

2 Write down the rules for
these lines.
Copy and fill in:
a The rule is x = ...
b The rule is x = ...
c The rule is ... = ...
d The rule is ... = ...

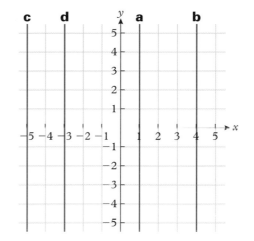

3 Look at the red line.
Write down the co-ordinates of
the points A, B, C, D and E.

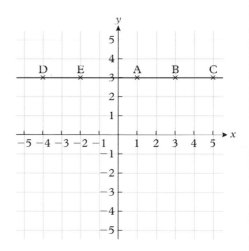

All these points have **y** co-ordinate = **3**
In algebra this is   **y = 3**
The rule for the line is **y = 3**

4 Write down the rules for these lines.
Copy and fill in:
  a The rule is $y = ...$
  b The rule is $y = ...$
  c The rule is $... = ...$
  d The rule is $... = ...$

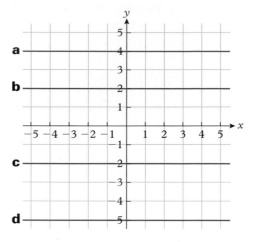

5 Write down the rules for these lines.

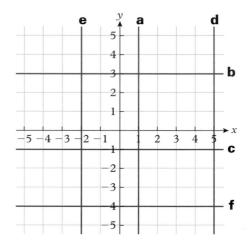

6 **a** Copy the diagram on to squared paper.
  b Label each line with its rule.
  c The lines cross at a point.
Write down the co-ordinates of this point.
Remember to use brackets $(..., ...)$

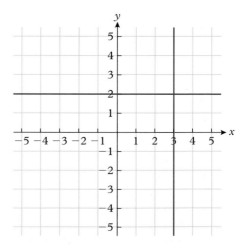

7   **a** Draw a new set of axes like the ones in question **6**.
    b Draw the line $x = 4$
       Label the line.
    c Draw the line $y = -1$
       Label the line.
    d Write down the co-ordinates of the point where the lines cross.

8   **a** Draw a new set of axes like the ones in question **6**.
    b Draw a vertical line and a horizontal line.
       They must cross at the point $(2, 5)$
    c Copy and fill in the rules for these two lines.
         $x = \ldots$ $y = \ldots$

9   Which vertical and horizontal lines cross at each point?
    a $(3, 6)$ **b** $(2, 5)$ **c** $(6, 1)$

Point of intersection	The point where two lines cross is called a **point of intersection**.

Exercise 10:2

1   Write down the co-ordinates of the point of intersection of these lines.
    a $x = 1$ and $y = 6$ **c** $x = 5$ and $y = -7$
    b $x = -4$ and $y = 3$ **d** $x = 0$ and $y = 1$

2   Which vertical and horizontal lines have the point of intersection:
    a $(8, 0)$ **c** $(-3, -4)$ **e** $(5, 0)$
    b $(-2, 1)$ **d** $(5, -1)$ **f** $(0, 3)$

3   Write down the rule for:
    a the x axis
    b the y axis
    c Write down the co-ordinates of the point of intersection of these two lines.
    d What do we call this point?

4 The diagram shows a square. Write down the rule for each side of the square.

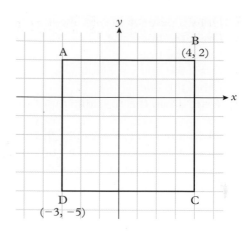

5 a Copy the axes on to squared paper.
 b Draw the rectangle whose sides have the rules
 $x = -1$, $y = 3$, $x = 4$, $y = 7$
 c Draw the line $y = 1$
 d Reflect the rectangle in $y = 1$
 e Write down the rules of the sides of the new rectangle.

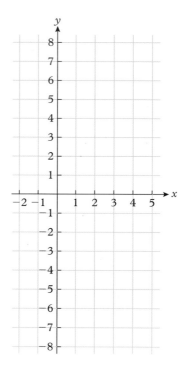

2 Patterns of lines

Matthew and Katy are looking for patterns on a grid.

Exercise 10:3

You will need some counters and a grid.

1 a Copy the axes on to the grid. Use it for all the questions in this Exercise.

b Matthew has put counters on points of the grid. He wants the y co-ordinate to be the same as the x co-ordinate. Katy sees that they are in a straight line.

Mark the points on your grid where the y co-ordinate = the x co-ordinate In algebra this is $y = x$ Join the points with a straight line. The rule for the line is $y = x$

c Label the line with its rule $y = x$

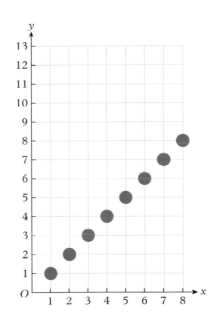

Equation	

The rule of a line is called the **equation** of the line. The equation of this line is $y = x$

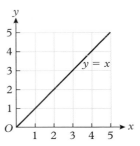

2 Katy puts counters on the grid where
the **y** co-ordinate = **2** × the **x** co-ordinate
She marks the points on her grid.
She joins the points with a straight line.
  a Mark the points on your grid.
     Join them with a straight line.
  b Copy:
        The equation of the line is **y = 2 × x**
        In algebra this is   **y = 2x**
  c Label the line with its equation.

3 **a** Put counters on your grid where the
        y co-ordinate is **3** × the **x** co-ordinate
  b Mark the points.
     Join them with a straight line.
  c Copy and fill in the equation of the line.
        $y = \dots x$
  d Label the line with its equation.

4 You have drawn the lines $y = x$
                                 $y = 2x$
                                 $y = 3x$
  a Which line is the steepest?
  b Which line is the least steep?
  c Which part of the equation tells you how steep the line is?

. . . .

We can use robots to help us draw lines.
To draw the line $y = 3x$ we use the
'×3' robot.

                    0 ↘   0 ↗
                    1 ↘   ↗ 3
Put the x co-ordinates in. 2 → ×3 → 6 You get the y co-ordinate out.
                    3 ↗   ↖ 9

We now plot the points
(0, 0) (1, 3) (2, 6) (3, 9)
Join the points with a straight line.
Label the line with its equation $y = 3x$

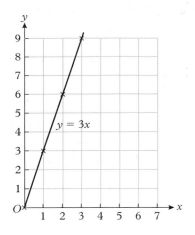

5 a Which line do you think will be steeper:
$y = 3x$ or $y = 4x$
  b Copy these axes on to squared paper.
  c Draw and label the line $y = 3x$
  d Draw and label the line $y = 4x$
Use this robot to help you.
Copy and fill in:

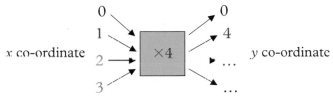

The points to plot are (0, 0) (1, 4) (2, ...) (3, ...)
Join them with a straight line.
Label the line with its equation $y = 4x$
  e Was your answer to **a** correct?

6 Which line is the steeper in each of these pairs?
  a $y = x$ or $y = 4x$
  b $y = 2x$ or $y = 6x$
  c $y = 5x$ or $y = 4x$
  d $y = 3x$ or $y = 7x$
  e $y = 8x$ or $y = 5x$

7 Which line is the steeper in each of these pairs?

   a $y = x$ or $y = 2\frac{1}{2}x$

   b $y = 5x$ or $y = 3\frac{1}{2}x$

   c $y = 4\frac{1}{2}x$ or $y = 7\frac{1}{2}x$

   d $y = 3\frac{1}{2}x$ or $y = 3\frac{1}{4}x$

8 The diagram shows three graphs.
Write down the equation of each graph.
Choose from these equations:

   $y = 3x$ $y = \frac{1}{2}x$ $y = 5x$

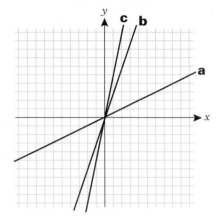

Marcus is looking at some
patterns on a grid.
He has put his counters on the
grid where
y co-ordinate = x co-ordinate + 1
The equation is:
    $y = x$ + 1

Exercise 10:4

You will need some counters.

1 a Make a new grid like the one that you used in Exercise 10.3.
Use it for all the questions in this Exercise.

  b Use counters on your grid to help you draw the line $y = x$
Label the line with its equation.

  c Now put the counters on the grid like Matthew did.
Remember: **y co-ordinate = x co-ordinate** + 1
Your counters should be in a straight line.

  d Mark the points.
Join them with a straight line.

  e Copy and fill in the equation of the line.
    $y = \dots + \dots$

  f Label the line with its equation.

2　**a**　Put counters on your grid where
　　　　y co-ordinate = **x** co-ordinate + 2
　　b　Mark the points.
　　　　Join them with a straight line.
　　c　Copy and fill in the equation of the line.
　　　　　$y = \ldots + \ldots$
　　d　Label the line with its equation.

3　You have drawn the lines　$y = x$
　　　　　　　　　　　　　　　$y = x + 1$
　　　　　　　　　　　　　　　$y = x + 2$
　　a　Copy and fill in:
　　　　The lines are all p..................
　　b　Which line is highest up the grid?
　　c　Where do you think the line $y = x + 3$ will go?
　　d　Use counters to help you draw the line $y = x + 3$ on your grid.
　　　　Label the line with its equation.
　　e　Was you answer to **c** correct?

4　Look at your grid. You have drawn four lines on it.
　　a　Copy and fill in these sentences.
　　　　The line $y = x$ crosses the y axis at 0.
　　　　The line $y = x + 1$ crosses the y axis at 1.
　　　　The line $y = x + 2$ crosses the y axis at ...
　　　　The line $y = x + 3$ crosses the y axis at ...
　　b　Where will the line $y = x + 4$ cross the y axis?
　　c　Use counters to help you draw the line $y = x + 4$ on your grid.
　　　　Label the line with its equation.
　　d　Was your answer to **b** correct?

5　Where will these lines cross the y axis?
　　a　$y = x + 5$
　　b　$y = x + 7$
　　c　$y = x + 8$
　　d　$y = x + 12$

6　Where will these lines cross the y axis?
　　a　$y = x + \frac{1}{2}$
　　b　$y = x + 3\frac{1}{2}$

7 **a** Where will the line $y = x - 2$ cross the y axis?
   b Copy the axes on to squared paper.
   c Draw the line $y = x - 2$.
   Use this robot to help you.
   Copy and fill in:

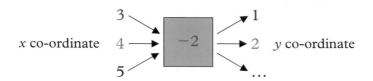

The points to plot are
$(3, 1)$ $(4, 2)$ $(5, ...)$
Join them with a straight line.
Label the line with its equation
$y = x - 2$
   d Was your answer to **a** correct?

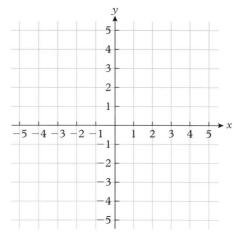

8 Where will these lines cross the y axis?
   a $y = x - 3$ **c** $y = x - 4$ **e** $y = x - 6$
   b $y = x - 7$ **d** $y = x + 6$ **f** $y = x$

9 Matthew knows that the line $y = x + 3$ crosses the y axis at 3.
   He wants to know if the rule still works for $y = 2x + 3$.
   He uses robot screens to help him draw the line.
   a Copy and fill in:

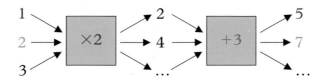

b Copy the axes on to squared paper.
Plot the points $(1, 5)$ $(2, 7)$ $(3, ...)$
Join them with a straight line.
Label the line with the equation
$y = 2x + 3$.

Does the rule still work?

10 Where will these lines cross the y axis?
   a $y = 2x - 4$ **c** $y = 3x - 5$
   b $y = 3x + 7$ **d** $y = 5x + 2$

11 Katy knows that the lines $y = x + 1$ and
$y = x + 2$ are parallel.
She wants to know if the lines $y = 2x + 1$
and $y = 2x + 2$ will be parallel.
   a Copy the axes on to squared paper.
   b Draw and label the line $y = 2x + 1$
      Use robot screens to help you.
   c Draw and label the line $y = 2x + 2$
      Use robot screens to help you.
   d Are the lines parallel?

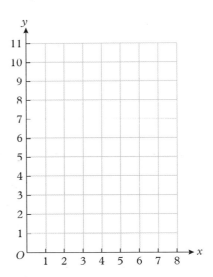

12 Look at each set of three lines.
Write down the two that are parallel.
   a $y = 3x + 5$ $y = 4x - 3$ $y = 3x - 1$
   b $y = 2x + 8$ $y = 3x - 5$ $y = 3x + 8$
   c $y = 5x - 4$ $y = 4x\ \ 5$ $y = 4x - 4$
   d $y = 7x + 5$ $y = 5x - 3$ $y = 7x - 1$

3 Finding the equation

This is the line $y = 2x + 3$
The **2** tells us how steep the line is.
The **3** tells us where the line will cross the y axis.

This is the line $y = 3x - 4$

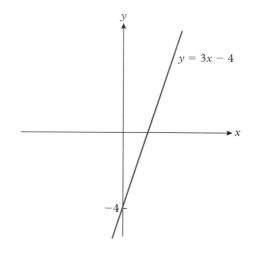

The **3** tells us how steep the line is.
The **−4** tells us where the line crosses the y axis.

This is the line $y = x + 7$
In algebra x means $1x$
So the equation is $y = 1x + 7$

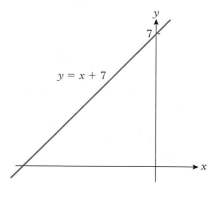

The **1** tells us how steep the line is.
The **+7** tells us where the line crosses the y axis.

["

3 $y = 3x + 4$

6 $y = 4x + 1$

4 $y = 2x + 1$

7 $y = 2x - 1$

5 $y = 3x - 5$

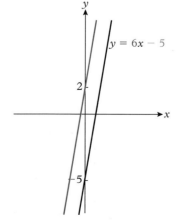

8 $y = 6x - 5$

9 Match the equation to the graph.

a

c

b

d
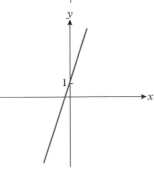

$$y = 3x + 1 \qquad y = x + 1 \qquad y = 2x - 3 \qquad y = x - 4$$

10 Match the equation to the graph.

a

c

b

d

$$y = 5x - 2 \qquad y = 2x + 2 \qquad y = x - 2 \qquad y = 2x - 1$$

Can't see the wood for the trees

The Forestry Commission has planted a new forest.
A tree is planted at each of the crossing points of a grid.

Look at the diagram showing part of the forest. It shows 25 trees on a 5 by 5 grid.
John is standing at the origin.
He can see the tree at (1, 1)
He can't see the trees at (2, 2), (3, 3), (4, 4) and (5, 5) because they are directly in line with (1, 1)

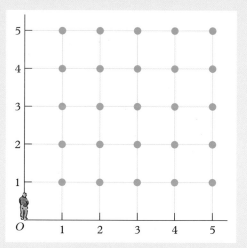

1   **a**   Which other trees can't he see?
    b   How many trees can't he see?

2   **a**   Draw a 6 by 6 grid.
    b   Mark on your grid the trees that John can't see.
    c   How many trees can't he see?

3   **a**   Try to predict how many trees John can't see on a 7 by 7 grid.
            Explain how you get this number.
    b   Draw the 7 by 7 grid to check.

4   Investigate other grids. Write a report about what you find out.

1 Write down the rules for these lines.

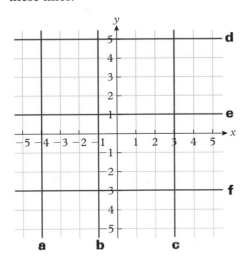

2 Write down the rules for these lines.

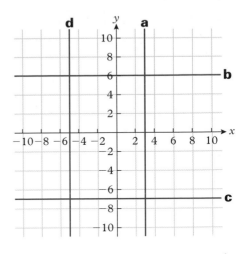

3 Write down the co-ordinates of the point of intersection of these lines.
   a $x = 5$ and $y = 7$
   b $x = 2$ and $y = 4$
   c $x = 4$ and $y = -5$
   d $x = -5$ and $y = -1$
   e $x = -2$ and $y = 0$
   f $y = 1$ and $x = 9$

4 Which vertical and horizontal lines have the point of intersection:
   a $(5, 8)$
   b $(0, 4)$
   c $(-5, 5)$
   d $(7, -1)$
   e $(6, 2)$
   f $(-3, 0)$

5 a Copy the axes in question **1** on to squared paper.
   b Draw a vertical line.
     Write down the rule of this line.
   c Draw a horizontal line.
     Write down the rule of this line.
   d Write down the co-ordinates of the point of intersection.

6 The vertices of a rectangle have co-ordinates
   $(-1, -2)$ $(-1, 6)$ $(3, 6)$ $(3, -2)$
   Write down the rules for the four sides of the rectangle.

7 The sides of a square have the rules
   $x = -2$ $y = -1$ $x = 5$ $y = 6$
   Write down the co-ordinates of the vertices of the square.

8 **a** Copy the axes on to squared paper.
  b Plot these points in order:
        $(1, 4)$ $(3, 6)$ $(6, 6)$ $(6, 5)$ $(4, 5)$ $(4, 4)$
        Join them with a ruler as you go.
  c Draw the line $y = 4$ on your axes.
  d Reflect the shape in the line $y = 4$
  e Write down the co-ordinates of the
        vertices of the new shape.

9 Which line is the steeper in each of these pairs?
  a $y = 3x$ or $y = 5x$
  b $y = 7x$ or $y = 4x$
  c $y = x$ or $y = 3x$
  d $y = 9x$ or $y = 10x$

10 Look at these three lines.
       $y = x + 3$ $y = x + 7$ $y = x + 2$

  a What can you say about the three lines?
  b Geoff plots the three lines.
        Which line is highest up the grid?
  c Which line is lowest on the grid?
  d Where does the line $y = x + 7$ cross the y axis?
  e Which pair of lines are closest together?
  f Which pair of lines are furthest apart?

11 Where will these lines cross the y axis?
  a $y = x + 3$ **c** $y = x + 1$ **e** $y = 2x + 5$
  b $y = x + 6$ **d** $y = x - 9$ **f** $y = 5x - 3$

12 Look at each set of three lines.
       Write down the two that are parallel.
  a $y = 2x + 1$ $y = x - 1$ $y = 2x - 1$
  b $y = 7x + 3$ $y = 4x + 3$ $y = 4x - 7$
  c $y = 8x + 9$ $y = 9x - 8$ $y = 8x + 8$
  d $y = 4x - 7$ $y = 7x - 4$ $y = 4x + 7$

13 Look at each set of three lines.
       Which line is the odd one out?
       Give the reason why.
  a $y = 3x - 1$ $y = 7x - 1$ $y = 6x + 1$
  b $y = 4x - 5$ $y = 5x + 4$ $y = 4x + 5$
  c $y = 7x - 1$ $y = x - 7$ $y = 7x + 7$

Write down the equation of each red line.

14

$y = 2x + 6$

−1

16

$y = 3x - 3$

1

15

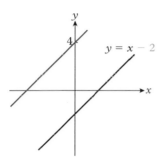

4

$y = x - 2$

17

$y = 4x - 3$

18 Match the equation to the graph.

a

4

c

b

−3

d

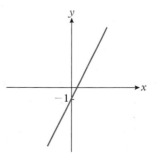

−1

$y = x$ $y = x - 3$ $y = 2x - 1$ $y = 2x + 4$

1 Three of the sides of a square have the rules
$$x = -1 \qquad y = 3 \qquad x = 6$$
There are two possible squares.
   a Write down the rule for the missing side of each square.
   b Write down the co-ordinates of the vertices of each square.

2 Draw a set of axes with x and y from -6 to $+6$.
Plot the lines $y = x + 1$ and $y = 2x - 1$
Use robot screens to help you.
Write down the co-ordinates of the point of intersection of
these two lines.

3 Three vertices of a rectangle have co-ordinates
$$(-5, 1) \qquad (4, 1) \qquad (4, -3)$$
Find the rules for the four sides of the rectangle.

4 We can use robots to see if a point lies on a line.
Does the point $(6, 20)$ lie on the line $y = 3x + 1$?

We put the x co-ordinate into the robot:

$$6 \longrightarrow \boxed{\times 3} \overset{18}{\longrightarrow} \boxed{+ 1} \longrightarrow 19$$

The robot tells us that the y co-ordinate is 19.
The point $(6, 19)$ lies on the line.
So the point $(6, 20)$ does not lie on the line.

Each of these questions has a point and a line.
Find out if the point lies on the line.
   a $(2, 3)$ $y = x - 1$ **d** $(4, 14)$ $y = 2x + 5$
   b $(5, 13)$ $y = 2x + 3$ **e** $(6, 24)$ $y = 5x - 4$
   c $(3, 7)$ $y = 4x - 5$ **f** $(8, 31)$ $y = 3x + 7$

5 Each of these questions has a line and some points.
The points lie on the line.
Find the missing co-ordinates.
   a $y = x - 2$ $(4, \ldots)$ $(10, \ldots)$ $(\ldots, 0)$
   b $y = 3x + 4$ $(5, \ldots)$ $(2, \ldots)$ $(10, \ldots)$
   c $y = 6x - 5$ $(3, \ldots)$ $(5, \ldots)$ $(4, \ldots)$
   d $y = 2x - 8$ $(4, \ldots)$ $(0, \ldots)$ $(5, \ldots)$

- All the points on this line have
  x co-ordinate $= 2$

  The rule for the line is
  $x = 2$

- **Point of intersection**
  The point where two lines cross is
  called a **point of intersection**.

  The point of intersection
  of these two lines is
  $(3, 1)$

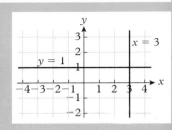

- **Equation**
  The rule of a line is called the **equation** of
  the line.

  The equation of this line is $y = x$

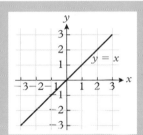

- Look at these lines.

  The red number tells us how steep the line is.
  The bigger the number the steeper the line.

  If two lines have the same number they are parallel.
  The lines $y = 2x + 3$ and $y = 2x + 5$ are parallel.

  Look at these lines.

  The blue number tells us where the line crosses
  the y axis.

  The line $y = x + 2$ crosses the y axis at 2
  The line $y = x + 5$ crosses the y axis at 5

1 Write down the rules for these lines.

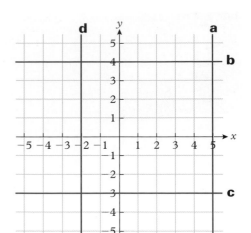

2 a Draw a set of axes as in question **1**.
  b Draw the line $x = 4$
  c Draw the line $y = 2$
  d The lines cross at a point.
    Write down the co-ordinates of
    the point of intersection.

3 Which vertical and horizontal lines cross at the point $(5, 3)$?

4 Look at these equations of lines.
  $y = 3x - 3$ $y = x + 7$ $y = 5x + 1$
  a Which line is the steepest?
  b Which line is the least steep?

5 Look at these three lines.
  $y = x + 4$ $y = x + 7$ $y = x$
  a What can you say about these lines?
  b Where does the line $y = x + 7$ cross the y axis?
  c Which line is highest up the grid?
  d Which line is lowest on the grid?
  e Which two lines would the line $y = x + 2$ be between?

6 Write down the equation of the red line.
  a

  b

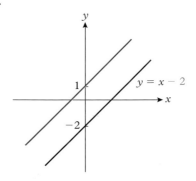

11 Ratio

Most maps of the UK are produced from the Ordnance Survey. The Board of Ordnance used to be in charge of defending Britain. (Ordnance means military supplies.) They wanted good maps for soldiers to use so they began the Ordnance Survey.

The Ordnance Survey put 'bench marks' in places like the stone of bridges or on the tops of hills. They use these points to measure from.

A bench mark

A large-scale Ordnance Survey map

The Ordnance Survey bring maps up to date from time to time. They mark new buildings and roads.

They produce large-scale maps and smaller-scale maps.

1 The metric system

· ·

Jane and Andy have broken a window.
Their father is measuring to find the size of glass that is needed to repair the window.
His tape measure has one side marked in feet and inches. The other side is marked in metric units.

Jane has a pencil and paper to write down the measurements.
Jane asks her father what units he is using.
He says he is using millimetres.

◄◄REPLAY►

Units of length

10 millimetres (mm) = 1 centimetre (cm)
100 centimetres = 1 metre (m)
1000 metres = 1 kilometre (km)

Example

| 0mm 10 | 20 | 30 | 40 | 50 | 60 | 70 | 80 |
| 0cm 1 | 2 | 3 | 4 | 5 | 6 | 7 | 8 |

This line measures 5.7 cm (or 57 mm).

Converting units within the metric system

Examples

1 Convert 6.75 m to cm

6.75 m = 6.75 × 100 cm
= 675 cm

2 Convert 6400 m to km

6400 m = 6400 ÷ 1000 km
= 6.4 km

Exercise 11:1

1 Convert the units in each of these.
  Think carefully whether you need to multiply or divide.
  a 50 mm to cm (10 mm = 1 cm)
  b 3000 m to km (1000 m = 1 km)
  c 9 m to cm (100 cm = 1 m)
  d 7 cm to mm (10 mm = 1 cm)
  e 4.5 cm to mm (10 mm = 1 cm)
  f 12 000 m to km (1000 m = 1 km)
  g 0.5 m to cm (100 cm = 1 m)
  h 56 mm to cm (10 mm = 1 cm)

2 Convert the units in each of these.
  Think carefully whether you need to multiply or divide by 10, 100 or 1000.
  a 4 km to m
  b 400 cm to m
  c 20 mm to cm
  d 6 cm to mm
  e 15 km to m
  f 2 m to cm
  g 30 mm to cm
  h 5000 m to km
  i 5 m to mm
  j 2000 mm to m

3 Convert the units in each of these.
  Think carefully whether you need to multiply or divide by 10, 100 or 1000.
  a 285 cm to m
  b 550 m to km
  c 8.7 cm to mm
  d 0.6 cm to mm
  e 7.4 km to m
  f 3.75 m to cm
  g 65 mm to cm
  h 0.9 km to m
  i 0.15 m to mm
  j 1250 mm to m

4 Write down the unit that completes each sentence.
  Choose from mm, cm, m, km.
  a A paperclip is about 30 ... long.
  b A door is about 2 ... high.
  c A teaspoon is about 13 ... long.
  d The distance from London to Cardiff is about 240 ...
  e A filing cabinet is about 45 ... wide.
  f A football pitch is about 70 ... wide.
  g A fingernail is about 10 ... wide.
  h The English Channel is about 33 ... across.

Converting Imperial units of length to metric units

1 in = 2.5 cm   1 yd = 0.9 m   1 mile = 1.6 km

Examples

1 Convert 3 in to cm
1 in = 2.5 cm
3 in = 3 × 2.5 cm
    = 7.5 cm

2 Convert 3.5 yd to m
1 yd = 0.9 m
3.5 yd = 3.5 × 0.9 m
     = 3.15 m

3 Convert 4 miles to km
1 mile = 1.6 km
4 miles = 4 × 1.6 km
     = 6.4 km

Exercise 11:2

1 Convert the units in each of these.
  a 2 in to cm   **c** 7 miles to km   **e** 20 miles to km
  b 6 yd to m   **d** 10 yd to m   **f** 12 inches (1 foot) to cm

2 Convert the red lengths into metric units.
  a Julie's book is 8 in by 6.5 in.
  b Deepal's bedroom door is 30 in wide.
  c A cricket pitch is 22 yd long.
  d Allison has a 1 foot ruler.
     She also has a smaller ruler 6 in long.
  e Paul runs the London marathon,
     which is 26.2 miles.
  f Stanthorne High's tennis court is
     26 yd by 12 yd.

1 inch is about $2\frac{1}{2}$ cm.
1 yard is a bit less than 1 metre.
1 mile is a bit more than $1\frac{1}{2}$ km.

Example

Estimate these lengths in metric units.

a 4 inches   **b** 18 yd   **c** 12 miles

a 1 inch is about $2\frac{1}{2}$ cm

$2 \times 4 = 8$

$\frac{1}{2}$ of 4 is 2

4 inches is about $8 + 2 = 10$ cm

b 1 yard is a bit less than 1 metre

18 yd is a bit less than 18 m

18 yd is about 16 or 17 m

c 1 mile is a bit more than $1\frac{1}{2}$ km

$\frac{1}{2}$ of 12 is 6

$12 + 6 = 18$

12 miles is a bit more than 18 km

12 miles is about 19 or 20 km

---

3 Estimate these in metric units.

a	6 inches	**e**	2 yd	**i**	2 miles	**m**	15 inches
b	8 inches	**f**	12 yd	**j**	30 miles	**n**	27 inches
c	10 inches	**g**	25 yd	**k**	1000 miles	**o**	17 miles
d	20 inches	**h**	100 yd	**l**	16 miles	**p**	55 miles

4 a 1 in = 2.5 cm, 1 yd = 0.9 m, 1 mile = 1.6 km

Use these and multiplication to convert the lengths in question **3** into metric units.

b Use your answers to **a** to check your estimates in question **3**.

Units of mass

Units of mass have similar names to units of length.

1000 milligrams (mg) = 1 gram (g)

1000 grams = 1 kilogram (kg)

1000 kg = 1 tonne (t)

A quarter teaspoon of sugar weighs about 1 gram.

An ordinary bag of sugar weighs 1 kilogram.

Converting units within the metric system

Examples

1 Convert 2.5 kg to g

$$2.5\,kg = 2.5 \times 1000\,g$$
$$= 2500\,g$$

2 Convert 5000 g to kg

$$5000\,g = 5000 \div 1000\,kg$$
$$= 5\,kg$$

Exercise 11:3

1 Convert the units in each of these.
Think carefully whether you need to multiply or divide.

a 4 kg to g (1000 g = 1 kg)
b 7000 mg to g (1000 mg = 1 g)
c 2000 g to kg (1000 g = 1 kg)
d 8000 kg to t (1000 kg = 1 t)
e 6 kg to g
f 55 kg to g

g 85 mg to g
h 0.6 kg to g
i 125 mg to g
j 0.3 g to mg
k 650 g to kg
l 1.5 t to kg

Converting Imperial units of mass to metric units

1 ounce is about 30 grams.
1 pound is a bit less than half a kilogram.
1 ton is a bit more than 1 tonne.

(16 ounces = 1 pound)
(14 pounds = 1 stone)

2 Estimate the red amounts in metric units.
a A newborn baby boy weighs about 8 pounds.
b An egg weighs about 2 ounces.
c A woman weighs about 140 pounds.
d A small car weighs about 2 tons.
e An orange weighs about 6 ounces.
f A large roast turkey weighs about 20 pounds.

Sometimes we need to be more accurate.

1 ounce (oz) = 28 g   1 pound (lb) = 450 g = 0.45 kg

Examples

1 Convert 3 ounces to g

1 oz = 28 g
3 ounces = 3 × 28 g
= 84 g

2 Convert 5 pounds to kg

1 pound = 0.45 kg
5 pounds = 5 × 0.45 kg
= 2.25 kg

3 Convert the units in each of these.

a 4 ounces to g
b 0.5 ounces to g
c 3 pounds to kg

d 6.5 pounds to kg
e 8 ounces to g
f 14 pounds to kg

g 100 pounds to kg
h 12 ounces to g
i 7 pounds to kg

4 One Imperial ton equals 2240 pounds.

a Convert one ton to kilograms using 1 pound = 0.4536 kg
Give your answer correct to the nearest whole number.
b How many kilograms larger is an Imperial ton than a metric tonne?
c Find the percentage extra in an Imperial ton.

Units of capacity

Units of capacity have similar names to units of length.

1000 millilitres (m*l*) = 1 litre (*l*)
100 centilitres (c*l*) = 1 litre

5 m*l*   75 c*l*   1 litre

The plastic medicine spoon holds 5 m*l*.
The bottle holds 75 c*l*.
The carton of fruit juice holds 1 litre.

We can convert units of capacity in the same way as
units of length or mass.

Exercise 11:4

1 Convert the units in each of these.
a 3000 ml to l (1000 ml = 1 l)   d 4.5 l to ml   g 800 ml to l
b 75 cl to l (100 cl = 1 l)   e 0.5 l to ml   h 5600 ml to l
c 7 l to ml   f 9000 ml to l   i 0.25 l to ml

Converting Imperial units of capacity to metric units

One pint is a bit more than half a litre.
One gallon is about $4\frac{1}{2}$ litres.

2 Estimate the red quantities in metric units.
a A washing-up bowl holds about 12 pints of water.
b A household bucket holds about 2 gallons of water.
c A dustbin would hold about 20 gallons of water.
d A classroom waste bin would hold about 7 gallons of water.

Sometimes we need to be more accurate.
1 pint = 0.57 l   1 gallon = 4.5 l   (8 pints = 1 gallon)

Examples

1 Convert 4 pints to litres.
1 pint = 0.57 l
4 pints = 4 × 0.57 l
= 2.28 l

2 Convert 3 gallons to litres.
1 gallon = 4.5 l
3 gallons = 3 × 4.5 l
= 13.5 l

3 Convert each of these quantities to litres.
a 7 pints   c 0.5 pints   e 5 pints   g 3.5 pints
b 15 gallons   d 5.6 gallons   f 9 gallons   h 1.4 gallons

4 An Imperial gallon is 4.546 litres.
An American gallon is smaller. It is 3.785 litres.
a Convert both kinds of gallon to millilitres.
b Find the difference between an Imperial and an American gallon in millilitres.

2 Introduction to ratio

4 cm

8 cm

⟵ 3 cm ⟶

⟵ 6 cm ⟶

Year 8 have had their photographs taken.
Sonya has bought the large size for her mother.
The small size is for her school record.

The width of the small photograph is half the width of the
large photograph.
Also, the length of the small photograph is half the length of the
large one.

We can write this fraction another way: **1 : 2** (said as 'one *to* two').

Ratio	**Ratio** is a measure of the relative size of two things.
Example	The ratio of the width of the small photograph to the width of the large photograph is 3 cm : 6 cm (said as 3 cm *to* 6 cm).

We can write ratios without units. $\quad$ 3 cm : 6 cm = 3 : 6

We can simplify ratios like fractions. $\quad \frac{3}{6} = \frac{1}{2}$ so 3 : 6 = 1 : 2

Exercise 11:5

1 a Measure this square.
Copy it into your book.
b Draw a new square with sides half as long.
c Copy and fill in:
(1) The ratio of the sides of the *small* square
to the sides of the *large* square is
? cm : 4 cm = ? : 4 = ? : 2
(2) The ratio of the sides of the *large* square to
the sides of the *small* square is
4 cm : ? cm = 4 : ? = 2 : ?

2 a Measure this rectangle.
Copy it into your book.
b Draw a new rectangle with sides three times as long.
c Copy and fill in:
(1) The ratio of the width of the *small* rectangle
to the width of the *large* rectangle is
2 cm : ? cm = 2 : ? = 1 : ?
(2) The ratio of the length of the *large* rectangle
to the length of the *small* rectangle is
? cm : 3 cm = ? : 3 = ? : 1

● 3 a Measure the length and width of each rectangle.
Copy them into your book.
Label each side with its length.

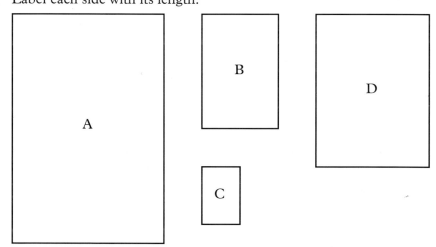

b Write down the ratio of width to length for rectangle A.
c Do the same for each of the other rectangles.
d Which rectangle does not have its width and length in the
same ratio as the others?

Example

A car-hire company has 8 cars and 4 vans for hire.
Find:

a the ratio of cars to vans
b the ratio of vans to cars
Give your answers in their simplest form.

a cars : vans $= 8 : 4$
$= 2 : 1$

b vans : cars $= 4 : 8$ (simplify like the fraction $\frac{4}{8} = \frac{1}{2}$)
$= 1 : 2$

Exercise 11:6

1 Polly is 7 years old. Her friend Abigail is 5 years old.
a What is the ratio of Polly's age to Abigail's age?
b What is the ratio of Abigail's age to Polly's age?

2 Gurjeet has £5 pocket money. His friend Dale has £3.
a What is the ratio of Gurjeet's pocket money to Dale's pocket money?
b What is the ratio of Dale's pocket money to Gurjeet's pocket money?

3 Laura works 4 hours a week. Nancy works 3 hours.
a What is the ratio of Nancy's work time to Laura's work time?
b What is the ratio of Laura's work time to Nancy's work time?

4 Alan is 12 years old. His little sister Claire is 6 years old.
a What is the ratio of Alan's age to Claire's age?
b What is the ratio of Claire's age to Alan's age?
Give your answers in their simplest form.

5 There are 30 pupils in 8L. 10 of them are girls.
a How many boys are there in 8L?
b What is the ratio of girls to boys?
c What is the ratio of boys to girls?
Give your answers to **b** and **c** in their simplest form.

6 Here are some counters.

   a What is the ratio of green counters to yellow counters?
   b What is the ratio of yellow counters to green counters?
   c What fraction of all the counters are green?
   d What fraction of all the counters are yellow?

7 Give your answers in their simplest form in this question.
   a What is the ratio of
      girls to boys?
   b What is the ratio of
      boys to girls?
   c What fraction of the
      children are girls?
   d What fraction of the
      children are boys?

8 Here are some patterns made with red and blue cubes.
For each pattern write down the ratio of red cubes to blue cubes.
Give your answers in their simplest forms.

   a

   b

   c

   d Make up some patterns of your own.
      Write down the ratio of red cubes to blue cubes for your patterns.

3   Proportion

• •

Robert is cooking some fruit buns.
The recipe is for 20 buns but
Robert only wants to make 10.
He needs to change the amounts
in the recipe.

Exercise 11:7

1   Here are the ingredients to make 20 fruit buns.

14 oz self-raising flour	7 oz margarine
4 oz sultanas	1 teaspoon mixed spice
2 oz raisins	2 small eggs
6 oz sugar	

   a   Write down the ingredients that you need to make 10 buns.

   b   What is the ratio of the amounts of ingredients for 10 buns to the amounts for 20 buns? Give the ratio in its simplest form.

   c   Write down the ingredients that you need to make 30 buns.

   d   What is the ratio of the amounts of ingredients for 30 buns to the amounts for 20 buns? Give the ratio in its simplest form.

2   The instructions on a bottle of orange squash say
'One part squash to five parts water.'
Louise is making a jug of the orange drink.

   a   Write down, in figures, the ratio of squash to water in the diluted drink.

   b   Louise dilutes 200 ml of the squash.
How much water does she use?

   c   How much of the orange drink does Louise have in her jug?

3   The instructions on a bottle of carpet shampoo say
'One part shampoo to 30 parts water.'

   a   Write down, in figures, the ratio of shampoo to water.

   b   The bottle of shampoo contains 500 ml.
How much water do you add if you use the whole bottle?

   c   How much diluted shampoo will you have altogether?

4 Mr Bean uses three parts sand to one part cement to make mortar.
   a Write down the ratio of sand to cement in figures.
   b (1) How much sand does Mr Bean mix with 6 kg cement?
      (2) How much mortar does this make altogether?
   c (1) How much cement does Mr Bean mix with 30 kg of sand?
      (2) How much mortar does this make altogether?

5 The instructions on a medicine bottle are
'Dilute with two parts water.'
   a Write down the ratio of medicine to water.
   b (1) How much water is needed to dilute 5 ml of medicine?
      (2) How much diluted medicine is there altogether?
   c A nurse measures 30 ml of water to mix with some of the medicine.
How much of the medicine is she using?

6 A rectangle is 5 cm long and 2 cm wide. It is enlarged to give a new
rectangle 20 cm long and 8 cm wide.
The ratio of lengths on the old rectangle to lengths on the new one
is $1 : n$
Write down the value of n.

7 A photograph is 7 cm long and
4.5 cm wide.
It is enlarged to give a photograph
21 cm long.
   a Sketch the two photographs.
Label the sides with their
lengths.
   b Write down the ratio of the
lengths on the small photograph
to the lengths on the large one.
   c Work out the width of the large
photograph.

7 cm
4.5 cm

21 cm
?

....

More simplifying of ratios

Example   Simplify these ratios.   **a** $8 : 12$ **b** $24 : 6$

      a 4 goes into 8 and 12 $8 : 12 = \dfrac{8}{4} : \dfrac{12}{4} = 2 : 3$

      b 6 goes into 24 and 6 $24 : 6 = \dfrac{24}{6} : \dfrac{6}{6} = 4 : 1$

Exercise 11:8

1   Simplify these ratios.

   a 5 : 15   **d** 18 : 30   **g** 100 : 20   **j** 9 : 27
   b 14 : 21   **e** 25 : 10   **h** 88 : 55   **k** 36 : 24
   c 16 : 20   **f** 30 : 20   **i** 12 : 18   **l** 30 : 25

• •

Sharing in ratios

Example

Carl and his sister Sian win a prize of £20. They decide to share the prize in the ratio of their ages.
Carl is 15 and Sian is 10.
How much do they each receive?

The ratio of Carl's age to Sian's age is $15 : 10 = 3 : 2$
Carl gets 3 shares and Sian gets 2 shares.
$3 + 2 = 5$ shares are needed.
One share is $£20 \div 5 = £4$
Carl gets $£4 \times 3 = £12$
Sian gets $£4 \times 2 = £8$
Check: $£12 + £8 = £20$

2   Share these amounts of money in the ratios given.
   You may need to simplify the ratio first.
   Check your answer each time.

   a £12   2 : 1   **e** £18   5 : 4   **i** £50   12 : 8
   b £15   1 : 4   **f** £30   7 : 3   **j** £100   15 : 35
   c £24   3 : 5   **g** £21   10 : 4   **k** £30   10 : 14
   d £28   3 : 4   **h** £75   18 : 12   **l** £27   20 : 4

3   Charmaine makes some lemon drink.
   She uses five parts water to one part lemon squash.
   How much water and how much squash are there in 3 litres of the drink?

4   A ready-mix concrete has one part cement, two parts sand and three parts gravel.
   How much of each is there in 60 kg of the mix?

4　Maps and scales

Tony wants to draw a plan of his room.
Denis helps Tony measure the room.
Tony has to choose a scale before he can draw his plan.

◄◄REPLAY►

Scale	The **scale** of a drawing gives the relative size of the actual length to the drawn length.

Exercise 11:9

1　Tony makes a scale drawing of his room. He uses a scale of 1 cm to 1 metre.

　a　(1) Measure the length of the drawing in centimetres.

　　　(2) Write down the actual length of the room in metres.

　b　(1) Measure the width of the drawing in centimetres.

　　　(2) Write down the actual width of the room in metres.

Scale: 1 cm to 1 m

2　Tony decides his drawing is too small.
He draws a new rectangle with sides twice as long.

　a　(1) Write down the length of the new rectangle in centimetres.

　　　(2) Write down the width of the new rectangle in centimetres.

　b　Write down the actual length and width of the room in metres.
Use your answers to question **1** to help you.

　c　How many centimetres represent 1 metre on the new scale?

We can find the length of a curved line.
We use a piece of string.
Place the string on top of the curved line.
Mark the length of the line on the string.
Measure the marked length of the string
with a ruler.

We can use this method for finding
distances on maps.

Tracey and Drew are planning a
walk. They are going from Cark
and Cartmel station south along
the road to West Plain Farm.
They will then turn west to
Cowpren Point along the
footpath.
From there they will walk back to
the station through Canon
Winder, Sand Gate and
Flookburgh.
Tracey and Drew can find out
how far they will walk using
the scale.

Scale: 2 cm to 1 km

3 **a** Copy this table. Fill it in.

Distance on map	1 cm	2 cm	3 cm	4 cm	5 cm
Actual distance		1 km	1.5 km		

b Give your answers to these in kilometres.
  (1) The length of the wide runway at Cark Airfield.
  (2) The distance going south from Cark and Cartmel station to
       West Plain Farm.
  (3) The distance a seagull flies from Cowpren Point to
       Flookburgh crossroads.
c (1) Estimate the length on the map of Tracey and Drew's walk.
       Use your string to help you.
  (2) Give the length of their walk in kilometres.

We can write map scales as a ratio of numbers.

Example   Express the scale 2 cm to 1 km as a ratio of numbers, 1 : ?

We need to convert 1 km to cm.   1 km = 1000 m
                                   1000 m = 1000 × 100 cm
                                          = 100 000 cm
The scale is 2 cm to 100 000 cm or 2 : 100 000 = 1 : 50 000
Answer: 2 cm to 1 km can be written as 1 : 50 000

Exercise 11:10

1 Copy and fill in:
1 km = … cm
A scale of 1 cm to 1 km = 1 : ?
A scale of 2 cm to 1 km = 2 : ? = 1 : ?
A scale of 4 cm to 1 km = 4 : ? = 1 : ?

● **2** Express the scale 1 cm to 2 km as a ratio in the form 1 : ?

Example   Sharon is drawing a plan of the school field.
She is using a scale of 1 : 500
   a What actual length does 4 cm on her plan represent?
   b The football pitch is 90 m long.
        How long will it be on Sharon's plan?

   a 4 cm represents 4 × 500 cm = 2000 cm
                          2000 cm = 2000 ÷ 100 m
                                  = 20 m

   b An actual length of 90 m is 90 × 100 cm = 9000 cm
                                     9000 cm ÷ 500 = 18 cm
        The pitch will be 18 cm long on Sharon's plan.

   Remember: Always check to see if your answers are sensible.

---

3 John has drawn a plan of his form room. He has used a scale of 1 : 100
   a The plan is 7 cm wide.
        How wide is John's form room?
   b John's form room is 9 m long.
        How long is the plan?

4 Mr Turner is making a play house for his daughter's fourth birthday.
It is a copy of Mr Turner's own house. The scale is 1 : 5

   a Mr Turner's house is 10 m high.
How high is the play house?

   b The play house is 3 m long.
How long is the actual house?

5 Nicholas is making a scale
model of an aeroplane.
The ratio of lengths on the
model plane to lengths on the
actual plane is 1 : 10
Copy the table.
Fill it in.

Part of plane	Model plane	Actual plane
length of wing	1 m	
door height	20 cm	
door width		90 cm
tail height	15 cm	
overall length		20 m
number of seats		60

6 This street map is of part of Runcorn
in Cheshire. It has a scale of 1 : 12 000

   a Measure the length of Park Road
on the map.

   b Work out the actual length of
Park Road.

   c Part of Heath Road is shown on
the map.
Heath Road has an actual length
of 2.4 km.
Work out the length of the whole
of Heath Road on this map.

7 Mr Singh has a road map with a
scale of 1 : 300 000

   a Two towns are 8 cm apart on the map.
What is their actual distance apart?

   b Two other towns are an actual distance of 60 km apart.
How many centimetres apart are they on Mr Singh's map?

1 Convert the units in each of these.
   a 380 cm to m   **e** 7250 g to kg   **i** 17.9 cm to mm
   b 1.7 kg to g   **f** 8.6 km to m   **j** 0.35 g to mg
   c 0.6 l to ml   **g** 50 000 ml to l   **k** 95 cm to m
   d 1900 mg to g   **h** 14.7 m to cm   **l** 0.25 m to mm

2 Give an estimate of these Imperial quantities.
   Use the metric unit given.
   a 12 inches or 1 foot (cm)   **d** 4 ounces (g)   **g** 4 pints (l)
   b 5 miles (km)   **e** 2 pounds (kg)   **h** 2 gallons (l)
   c 20 yd (m)   **f** 1 pound (g)

3 **a** Measure the sides of this rectangle.
   b Draw a larger rectangle so that the ratio
   of the sides of the small rectangle to the
   sides of the large rectangle is 1 : 4

4 Give each answer in its simplest form.
   a What is the ratio of dogs to cats?
   b What is the ratio of cats to dogs?
   c What fraction of the animals are cats?
   d What fraction of the animals are dogs?

5 A cake recipe uses one part sugar to four parts flour.
   a How much flour do you need when you use 150 g of sugar?
   b How much sugar do you need when you use 1 kg of flour?

6 Simplify these ratios.
   a 44 : 33   **b** 15 : 20   **c** 9 : 12   **d** 24 : 20

7 Share these amounts of money in the ratios given.
   Check your answer each time.
   a £50 3 : 7   **b** £15 15 : 10   **c** £240 16 : 8   **d** £90 7 : 2

8 Express these scales as ratios in the form 1 : ?
   a 1 cm to 1 m   **b** 1 cm to 2 m   **c** 2 cm to 1 m

9 Mr Brick the builder has a plan of a new housing estate.
   The scale is 1 : 1000
   a The actual road through the estate is 500 m long.
   How long is the road on the plan?
   b A bungalow is 1.2 cm wide on the plan.
   How wide is the actual bungalow?

1 Learn these to help you remember the size of some Imperial units.
- Two and a quarter pounds of jam
  weigh about a kilogram.
- A litre of water's a pint and three quarters.
- A metre measures three foot three,
  it's longer than a yard you see.

Can you think of any more helpful rhymes?

2 These are sayings, phrases and names of people.
The words that complete the sayings have been converted to metric units.
Write down the correct words.
  a 30 cm in the grave
  b 45 *l* hat
  c Sharon 6.4 kg
  d New Scotland 0.9 metres
  e 0.57 *l* sized
  f 0.45 kg of flesh
  g Give him 2.5 cm and he will take 1.6 km
  h A miss is as good as 1.6 km
  i It went down like 1016 kg of bricks
  j She hasn't got 28 g of common sense
  k Full 183 cm five thy father lies …
  l Pooh wandered into the 0.405 km² Wood
  m Spare the 5.03 m and spoil the child
  n A 20 m gang
  o Jack and 0.14 *l* went up the …

Can you make up some more of these yourself?

3 The instructions on a bottle of lemon squash say
'Dilute with six parts water.'
  a Write down the ratio of squash to water in the diluted drink.
  b (1) Gemma makes a jug of the drink. She measures 150 m*l* of squash.
    How much water does she need?
  (2) How much diluted squash does Gemma have altogether?
  c Gemma makes a second jug of the drink. She dilutes the squash in the
    same ratio as before to get 1.575 *l* of drink altogether.
    How much water does the diluted drink contain?

4 Find x and y **a** $5:8 = x:56$ **b** $2:9 = 11:y$

5 The angles of a triangle are in the ratio $3:4:5$
Work out the angles of the triangle.

6 A cake weighs 560 g.
There is twice as much flour as sugar and twice as much sugar as fat. There
are no other ingredients.
How much of each ingredient is there in the cake?

7 Look at these patterns of counters.

1   2   3

a Write down the ratio of white counters to black counters for each pattern.
Give your answers in the simplest form.

b Predict the answer for the fourth pattern.
Draw the fourth pattern to see if you are right.

c Copy this table.
Use the pattern to fill it in.

Number of pattern	1	2	3	4	5	6
Number of black counters	2	3	4			
Number of white counters	2	6				

d Write down the ratio of white counters to black counters for the nth pattern, where n is the number of the pattern.

e (1) How many black counters will there be in the 10th pattern?
    (2) How many white counters will there be in the 10th pattern?

f (1) How many white counters will there be in the 20th pattern?
    (2) Explain in words how you got this answer.

g Write a rule in algebra to find the number of *w*hite counters if you know the *n*umber of the pattern.

8 **a** (1) Draw a rectangle 3 cm by 4 cm.
    (2) Work out the perimeter of the rectangle.
    (3) Measure a diagonal of the rectangle.

  b (1) Draw a new rectangle with sides twice as long as the first one.
    (2) Work out the perimeter of the rectangle.
    (3) Measure a diagonal of the rectangle.

  c Write down and simplify these ratios.
    (1) perimeter of first rectangle : perimeter of second rectangle
    (2) diagonal of first rectangle : diagonal of second rectangle
    (3) Write down what you notice.

9 A map of Britain uses a scale of 1 : 1 500 000
  a How many kilometres does 1 cm represent?
  b On the map, Bournemouth and Swindon are 6.5 cm apart.
    Work out their actual distance apart.
  c The actual distance between Leicester and Norwich is 165 km.
    How many centimetres apart are they on the map?

- **Length** $10\,\text{mm} = 1\,\text{cm}$ $\quad 100\,\text{cm} = 1\,\text{m}$ $\qquad 1000\,\text{m} = 1\,\text{km}$
  1 inch is about $2\frac{1}{2}$ cm. $\qquad\qquad 1\,\text{in} = 2.5\,\text{cm}$
  1 yard is a bit less than 1 metre. $\quad 1\,\text{yd} = 0.9\,\text{m}$
  1 mile is a bit more than $1\frac{1}{2}$ km. $\quad 1\,\text{mile} = 1.6\,\text{km}$

- **Mass** $\quad 1000\,\text{mg} = 1\,\text{g}$ $\quad 1000\,\text{g} = 1\,\text{kg}$ $\quad 1000\,\text{kg} = 1\,\text{t}$
  1 ounce is about 30 grams. $\qquad\qquad$ 1 ounce (oz) $= 28$ g
  1 pound is a bit less than half a kilogram. $\quad$ 1 pound (lb) $= 450$ g $= 0.45$ kg
  1 ton is a bit more than 1 tonne $\qquad\qquad 1\,\text{kg} = 2.2$ pounds

- **Capacity** $\quad 1000\,\text{m}l = 1\,l$ $\quad 100\,\text{c}l = 1\,l$
  One pint is a bit more than half a litre. $\qquad$ 1 pint $= 0.57\,l$
  One gallon is about $4\frac{1}{2}$ litres. $\qquad\qquad$ 1 gallon $= 4.5\,l$

- **Ratio** **Ratio** is a measure of the relative size of two things.

  Example Simplify the ratio $8 : 12$

  4 goes into 8 and 12 $\qquad 8 : 12 = \dfrac{8}{4} : \dfrac{12}{4} = 2 : 3$

- *Example* Carl and his sister Sian win a prize of £20. They decide to share the prize in the ratio of their ages.
  Carl is 15 and Sian is 10.
  How much do they each receive?

  The ratio of Carl's age to Sian's age is $15 : 10 = 3 : 2$
  Carl gets 3 shares and Sian gets 2 shares.
  $3 + 2 = 5$ shares are needed.
  One share is £20 $\div 5 = $ £4
  Carl gets £4 $\times 3 = $ £12
  Sian gets £4 $\times 2 = $ £8 $\quad$ *Check:* £12 + £8 = £20

  Example Express the scale 2 cm to 1 km as a ratio of numbers, $1 : ?$

  We need to convert 1 km to cm. $\qquad 1\,\text{km} = 1000\,\text{m}$
  $1000\,\text{m} = 1000 \times 100\,\text{cm} = 100\,000\,\text{cm}$
  The scale is 2 cm to 100 000 cm or $2 : 100\,000 = 1 : 50\,000$

- *Example* Sharon is drawing a plan of the school field.
  She is using a scale of $1 : 500$
  What actual length does 4 cm on her plan represent?

  4 cm represents $4 \times 500\,\text{cm} = 2000\,\text{cm}$
  $\qquad\qquad 2000\,\text{cm} = 2000 \div 100\,\text{m} = 20\,\text{m}$

1   Convert the units in each of these.
    a   300 cm to m   **c**   8.6 m to cm   **e**   7.2 kg to g   **g**   3000 m*l* to *l*
    b   7 km to m   **d**   4500 g to kg   **f**   0.4 t to kg   **h**   4.8 *l* to m*l*

2   Estimate the red quantities in the metric unit given in brackets.
    a   Your middle finger is about 3 inches long. (cm)
    b   The Tyne bridge in Newcastle is 177 yd long. (m)
    c   The speed limit in towns is 30 miles an hour. (km)
    d   A medium sized apple weighs about 4 ounces. (g)
    e   A man weighs about 165 pounds. (kg)
    f   A large watering can holds about 3 gallons. (*l*)
    g   Two mugs of coffee make about a pint. (*l*)

3   **a**   Use multiplication to convert the red quantities accurately to
        metric units in question **2**.
    b   Use the answers to check your estimates in question **2**.

4   Melanie is 6 years old. Her brother Keith is 18 years old.
    a   What is the ratio of Melanie's age to Keith's age?
        Give your answer in its simplest form.
    b   Share a prize of £60 between Melanie and Keith in the ratio
        of their ages.

5   The instructions on a tin of concentrated orange juice say
    'add three parts water to one part orange juice'.
    a   A tin holds 250 m*l* of juice.
        How much water do you add?
    b   How much orange drink does this make altogether?

6   **a**   Simplify these ratios.
        (1)   12 : 20   (2)   15 : 10   (3)   50 : 45   (4)   10 : 1000
    b   Copy and fill in:
        A scale of 5 cm to 1 km = 5 : ? = 1 : ?

7   A map has a scale of 4 cm to 1 km.
    a   A road on the map is 24 cm long.
        How long is the actual road?
    b   A lake is 2.5 km wide.
        How wide is the lake on the map?

8   Helen makes a model aircraft carrier to a scale of 1 : 500
    a   The aircraft carrier is 300 m long.
        How long is the model?
    b   The model is 15 cm wide.
        How wide is the carrier?

12 Area

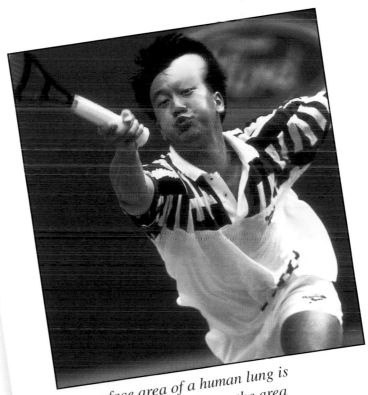

The surface area of a human lung is approximately the same as the area of a tennis court.

1 Perimeter and area

This is a picture of York.
It shows the old perimeter wall.
This goes all the way round
the outside of the old part of
the city.

Perimeter

The total distance around the
outside of a shape is called its
perimeter.

The red line is the perimeter of
this shape.
The perimeter is
$2 + 2 + 1 + 1 + 1 + 3 = 10$ cm

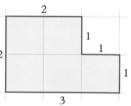

Each square has
an area of 1 cm^2

Area

The amount of space inside the shape is called its **area**.

The area of this shape is shaded green.
We use squares to measure area.

The area of this shape is 5 cm^2.

Exercise 12:1

Copy these shapes on to 1 cm squared paper.
Fill in the gaps.

1

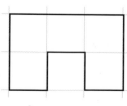

perimeter = ... cm
area = ... cm^2

2

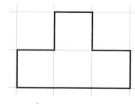

perimeter = ... cm
area = ... cm^2

3

perimeter = ... cm
area = ... cm²

4

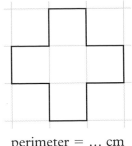

perimeter = ... cm
area = ... cm²

Area of a rectangle	**Area of a rectangle** $-$ *length* $\times$ *width* $= lw$

Example

Calculate the area of this rectangle.

Area = length $\times$ width
$= 4 \times 3$
$= 12\ \text{cm}^2$

3 cm

4 cm

Exercise 12:2

1 Find the perimeters and areas of these rectangles.

a

5 cm

6 cm

b

1 cm

8 cm

2 A dining room measures 4 m by 3 m. What is the area of the room?

3 A picture measures 30 cm by 25 cm. What is the perimeter of the picture?

4 The front of a Bran Flakes packet measures 19 cm by 27 cm. Find its area.

5 Peter wants to cover his back garden with grass.
  a What is the area of his back garden?
  b Grass seed costs 25 p for every m².
    How much will the grass seed cost?

10 m

15 m

6 Sinita is making new curtains for her bedroom.
The material is 2 metres wide.
She buys a length of 6 metres.
  a What area of material does she buy?
  b The material costs £5 per m².
    How much does Sinita's material cost?

7 The *area* of a rectangle is 65 cm².
The length is 13 cm.
What is the width?

8 The area of a wall is 48 m².
The height of the wall is 1.5 m.
What is the width?

- -

Example   Estimate the area of this leaf.

Count whole squares first.
There are 17 whole squares.

Now count squares which lie more than half inside the outline.
There are 12 of these.

An estimate of the area of the leaf is 29 squares.

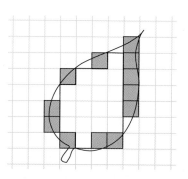

9 Estimate the areas of these leaves.

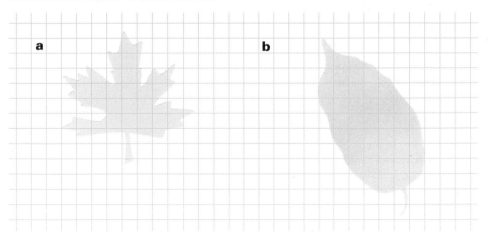

a

b

<table>
<tr><td>

Area of a triangle

</td><td>

Area of a triangle $= \dfrac{base \times height}{2}$

$= \dfrac{bh}{2}$

</td></tr>
</table>

Example Find the area of this triangle.

Area of triangle $= \dfrac{base \times height}{2}$

$= \dfrac{10 \times 8}{2}$

$= 40 \text{ cm}^2$

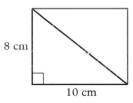

8 cm

10 cm

Exercise 12:3

Find the areas of these triangles.

1

5 cm

6 cm

2

8 cm

12 cm

3

10 cm

7 cm

4
9 cm
8 cm

5
10 cm
14 cm

6
17 cm
20 cm

Area of a parallelogram	**Area of a parallelogram** $= base \times height$ $= bh$ $= 8 \times 5$ $= 40 \text{ cm}^2$	

5 cm
8 cm

Find the areas of these parallelograms.

7
4 cm
9 cm

9
5 cm
6 cm

8
7 cm
10 cm

10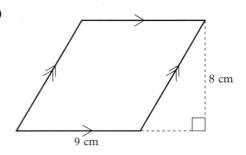
8 cm
9 cm

2   More areas

The O'Reilly family have moved into their new house.
They are going to grass the back garden which is a trapezium shape.
They need to work out the area of lawn to know how much turf to buy.

Exercise 12:4

You will need 1 cm squared paper.

1 Here is Mr O'Reilly's scale drawing of his back lawn.
 a Copy the drawing on to 1 cm squared paper.

You are going to find the area of Mr O'Reilly's lawn.
 b Mark the mid point of each of the sloping edges.
 Draw the red rectangle.
 c Write down the length of the rectangle.
 Write down its width.
 Find the area of the rectangle.
 d Explain why the rectangle has the same area as the trapezium.

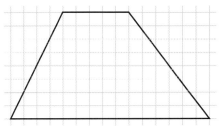

Scale: 1 square represents 1 m^2

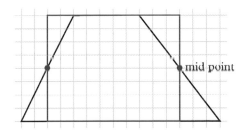

mid point

We do not always have a scale drawing.
We need a formula for finding the area of a trapezium.

Length of rectangle = mean (average) of side a and side b

$$= \frac{a + b}{2}$$

Area of a trapezium

Area of a trapezium = Area of rectangle

$$= \frac{a + b}{2} \times h$$

Example Calculate the area of this trapezium.

$a = 4\,\text{cm}$ $b = 12\,\text{cm}$ $h = 6\,\text{cm}$

$$\text{Area of trapezium} = \frac{a + b}{2} \times h$$

$$= \frac{4 + 12}{2} \times 6$$

$$= 48\,\text{cm}^2$$

4 cm

6 cm

12 cm

2 Calculate the area of this trapezium.
Copy and fill in:

$a = \ldots\,\text{cm}$ $b = \ldots\,\text{cm}$ $h = \ldots\,\text{cm}$

$$\text{Area of trapezium} = \frac{a + b}{2} \times h$$

$$= \frac{\ldots + \ldots}{2} \times \ldots$$

$$= \ldots\,\text{cm}^2$$

3 cm

4 cm

5 cm

Use the formula to find the areas of these trapeziums.

3

6 cm

5 cm

10 cm

6

15 cm

6 cm

20 cm

4

8 cm

6 cm

12 cm

7

30 mm

20 mm

50 mm

5

5 cm

5 cm

7 cm

8

15 m

15 m

25 m

These trapeziums are drawn accurately.
Find their areas.

9

10

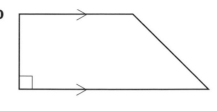

Exercise 12:5

1 The end of this drinking trough is
a trapezium.
Find its area.

2 The end wall of this shed is a
trapezium.
Find the area of the wall.

3 The side wall of this swimming
pool is a trapezium.
Find its area.

4 This buttress holds up a
church wall.
Find its area

To find the area of a complicated shape, divide it into simple shapes.

(1) Decide how to divide the shape.
(2) Find any missing lengths.
(3) Calculate the area of each part of the shape.
(4) Add the areas of the parts together.

Take extra care to show your working clearly.

Exercise 12:6

1 Find the area of this shape.
  a Copy the diagram.
  Divide the shape into a
  trapezium and a rectangle.
  b Find the width of the
  rectangle.
  Copy and fill in:
  $8\,m - 2\,m = \ldots m$
  c Copy and fill in:
  Area of rectangle $= lw$
  $= \ldots \times \ldots$
  $= \ldots m^2$
  d Copy and fill in:

  $$\text{Area of trapezium} = \frac{a+b}{2} \times h$$

  $$= \frac{\ldots + \ldots}{2} \times \ldots$$

  $$= \ldots m^2$$

  e Copy and fill in:
  Total area of shape $= \ldots m^2 + \ldots m^2$
  $= \ldots m^2$

Find the areas of these shapes in the same way.

2

3

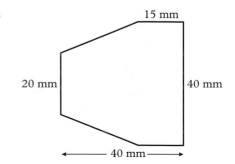

4 The picture shows the end wall of a barn.
Find the area of the wall.

6 This kitchen worktop can be divided into two trapeziums.
Find its area.

5 A badge is in the form of a yacht.
Find the area of the badge.

7 This castle turret is a piece of stage scenery.
Find its area.

8 The picture shows the side of a wooden shed with a rectangular window.
a Work out the total area of the side of the shed.
b Work out the area of the window.
c Find the area of wood in the side of the shed.

Exercise 12:7 The largest triangle

All the triangles in this exercise have a perimeter of 24 cm.
You will investigate which one has the largest area.

You will need a pair of compasses.
A set square is helpful for drawing the heights of triangles.

1 a Construct this triangle using your compasses.

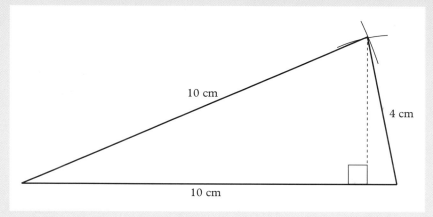

10 cm

4 cm

10 cm

b Draw and measure the height of the triangle.
c Calculate the area of the triangle.
d Calculate the perimeter of the triangle.

2 Another triangle has a base
10 cm long. One other side is 6 cm long.
The perimeter of the triangle is 24 cm.
a How long is the third side?
b Construct this triangle
using your compasses.
c Draw and measure the
height of the triangle.
d Calculate the area of the triangle.

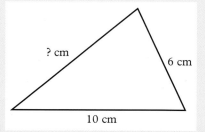

? cm

6 cm

10 cm

3 Investigate the areas of other triangles with base 10 cm and perimeter 24 cm.
Which triangle has the *largest* area?

4 Investigate the areas of triangles with bases of different lengths.
All your triangles should have a perimeter of 24 cm.

3 Enlargement and area

Alec needs to find the approximate area of this forest for his Geography homework.

Exercise 12:8

You will need 1 cm squared paper.

1 Copy this shape on to squared paper.
Label it A.
Work out the area of A.

2 Enlarge shape A by a scale factor of 2.
Label it B.
Work out the area of B.

3 Enlarge shape A by a scale factor of 3.
Label it C.
Work out the area of C.

4 Copy and fill in this table.
Only draw diagrams of D and E if you need to.

Shape	Area of A	Scale factor	New area
A	4	1	4
B	4	2	16
C	4	3	36
D	4	4	
E	4	5	

5 What is the rule for finding the new area?
Hint: It has something to do with the scale factor.

6 What will be the new area for a scale factor of 8?

7 What scale factor gives a new area of 400 cm²?

· ·

When a shape is enlarged, the area is multiplied by the square of the scale factor.

Example

The area of a rectangle is 8 cm².
The rectangle is enlarged by a scale factor of 3.
What is the new area?

Square of the scale factor is $3^2 = 9$
New area = original area × square of the scale factor
$$= 8 \times 9$$
$$= 72 \text{ cm}^2$$

Exercise 12:9

In questions **1–6** you are given the area of a shape.
The shape is enlarged by the scale factor given.
Find the new area.

1 4 cm²   scale factor 2   **4** 9 cm²   scale factor 10

2 7 cm²   scale factor 8   **5** 12 cm²   scale factor 6

3 6 cm²   scale factor 5   **6** 11 cm²   scale factor 4

7 The area of a patio is 9 m².
It is enlarged by a scale factor of 2.
What is the new area of the patio?

8 A car park has an area of 75 m².
It is to be enlarged by a scale factor of 1.5
What will the new area be?

9 The area of a vineyard is 950 m².
It is enlarged by a scale factor of 4.
What is the new area?

10 Jaswant has drawn a triangle of area 4.5 cm².
He enlarges his triangle by a scale factor of 6.
What is the new area?

· ·

Example

A lawn has been enlarged by a scale factor of 2.
The new area is 36 m².
What was the original area?

Square of the scale factor is $2^2 = 4$
New area = original area × square of the scale factor
$$36 = ? \times 4$$
Original area $= 36 \div 4$
$$= 9$$

The original area was 9 m².

Exercise 12:10

In questions **1–6** you are given the area of a shape.
The shape has been enlarged by the scale factor given.
Find the original area.

1   32 cm²   scale factor 2   **4**   64 cm²   scale factor 4

2   45 cm²   scale factor 3   **5**   700 cm²   scale factor 10

3   75 cm²   scale factor 5   **6**   640 cm²   scale factor 8

7   Louise has enlarged a rectangle by a scale factor of 2.
The new area is 36 cm².
What was the area of the rectangle before she enlarged it?

8   A farmer has enlarged his field by a scale factor of 2.
The area is now 12 hectares.
What was the original area of the field?

9   A Trading Estate has been enlarged by a scale factor of 3.
The new area is 1305 hectares.
What was the original area?

10   A rectangle has length 8 cm.
It is enlarged by a scale factor of 3.
The new area is 288 cm².
What was the width of the original rectangle?

1 Find the perimeters and areas of these rectangles.

a 7 cm
12 cm

b 5.5 cm
11 cm

c 3.7 cm
4.4 cm

2 Find the areas of these triangles.

a 6 cm
11 cm

b 14 cm
9 cm

c 10 cm
9 cm

3 Find the areas of these parallelograms.

a 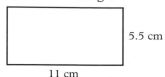 5 cm
11 cm

b 4 cm
7.5 cm

c 6 cm
8 cm

4 The end of the gutter on a house is a trapezium.
Find its area.

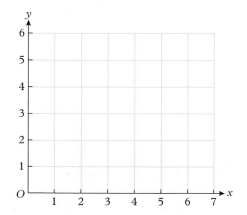

14 cm

8 cm

10 cm

5 Copy these axes on to squared paper.
  a Plot these points:
  A (1, 1) B (3, 1) C (6, 5)
  D (0, 5)
  Join the points to get trapezium ABCD.
  b Find the area of ABCD.

6 The sides of this metal waste
paper bin are trapeziums.
The base is square.
   a Work out the area of one side.
   b Work out the area of the base.
   c Find the total area of metal
       used to make the bin.

In questions 7–**10** you are given the area of a shape.
The shape is enlarged by the scale factor given.
Find the new area.

7 5 cm²   scale factor 4   **9**   3 cm²   scale factor 5

8 6 cm²   scale factor 2   **10** 7 cm²   scale factor 12

In questions **11–14** you are given the area of a shape.
The shape has been enlarged by the scale factor given.
Find the original area.

11 81 cm²   scale factor 3   **13**   147 cm²   scale factor 7

12 48 cm²   scale factor 2   **14**   175 cm²   scale factor 5

15 A shape has an area of 15 cm².
It is enlarged by a scale factor of 5.
What is the new area?

16 A play area has an area of 60 m².
It is enlarged to 540 m².
What scale factor is used?

17 Pauline has enlarged her drawing by a scale factor of 3.
The new area is 396 cm².
What was the area of her original drawing?

1 Find the lengths marked with letters.

a

6 cm

a

Area = 42 cm²

b

b

← 12 m →

Area = 60 m²

c

8 cm

c

← 20 cm →

Area = 126 cm²

2 Copy these axes on to squared paper.

  a Plot the points (1, 1) (1, 8) (7, 8)
  These are three vertices of a rectangle.
  Write down the co-ordinates of the fourth vertex.
  Draw the rectangle.

  b Plot and label these points:
  A (1, 4) B (4, 8) C (7, 6) D (5, 4)
  E (5, 1)
  Join them with straight lines in order.

  c Find the area of the shape ABCDE.
  Hint: Find the area of the rectangle and then subtract areas until you are left with the shape ABCDE.

3

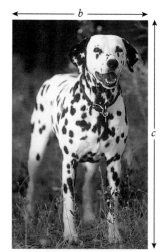

b

c

7 cm

a

Area = 84 cm²   Area = 3024 cm²

Find the values of a, b and c.

- **Perimeter**   The total distance around the outside of a shape is called its **perimeter**.

  Area   The amount of space inside the shape is called its **area**.

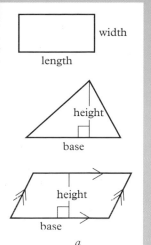

Area of a rectangle $= l\text{ength} \times w\text{idth}$
$$= lw$$

Area of a triangle $= \dfrac{base \times height}{2}$
$$= \dfrac{bh}{2}$$

Area of a parallelogram $= base \times height$
$$= bh$$

Area of a trapezium $= \dfrac{a + b}{2} \times h$

- *Example*   Calculate the area of this trapezium.
  $a = 4\,\text{cm} \quad b = 12\,\text{cm} \quad h = 6\,\text{cm}$

  Area of trapezium $= \dfrac{a + b}{2} \times h$
  $$= \dfrac{4 + 12}{2} \times 6$$
  $$= 48\,\text{cm}^2$$

- When a shape is enlarged, the area is multiplied by the square of the scale factor.

  Example   The area of a rectangle is $8\,\text{cm}^2$.
  The rectangle is enlarged by a scale factor of 3.
  What is the new area?

  Square of the scale factor is $3^2 = 9$
  New area = original area $\times$ square of the scale factor
  $$= 8 \times 9$$
  $$= 72\,\text{cm}^2$$

1 Find the areas of these shapes.

a

8 m

6.5 m

d

15 mm

18 mm

35 mm

b

12 cm

10 cm

e

7 cm

5 cm

c

20 mm

14 mm

f

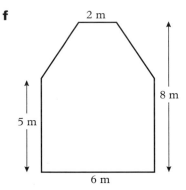

2 m

5 m

8 m

6 m

2 Find the perimeter of shape **a** in question **1**.

3 A shape has an area of 15 cm^2.
It is enlarged by a scale factor of 10.
What is the new area?

4 Alan has enlarged a triangle using a scale factor of 2.
The new area is 48 cm^2.
What was the area of the triangle before the enlargement?

13 Statistics: getting it together

Crazy Cricket Calculations

Frank and Paul play for the same cricket team.

In the first half of the season, Frank averaged more runs per innings than Paul. He hoped he might win the trophy for the best batting average of the season.

Frank's average for the second half of the season was also better than Paul's.

Think how upset Frank was when he found out that Paul's average for the **whole** season was the best, so Paul won the trophy!

How could this happen?

1 Averages and range

◀◀REPLAY▶

Year 8 pupils are in eight forms at Stanthorne High.
The forms do not all have the same number of pupils.
One form has 25 pupils, three have 27, two have 28 and two have 29.

Mean	To find the **mean** of a set of data:

(1) Find the total of all the data values.
(2) Divide by the number of data values.

Example

Find the mean number of pupils in a Year 8 form at Stanthorne High.

The total is:
$$25 + 27 + 27 + 27 + 28 + 28 + 29 + 29 = 220$$
The mean is $220 \div 8 = 27.5$

You cannot really have 27.5 people in a form! You must not round the mean to a whole number even if you think the answer is silly.

Exercise 13:1

1 Stanthorne High has a school nurse. She counted the number of pupils with bad asthma every day for two weeks.
Here are her results:

3   15   0   3   1   0   4   3   1   4

Work out the mean number of pupils with asthma.

2 Tony timed his journeys to and from school for a week.
Here are his times in minutes:

25   21   24   26   21   24   26   27   21   27

Find the mean time for Tony's journeys.

3 Some children were weighed and measured as part of a medical examination.

Height (cm)	148	136	130	127	137	143	139	141	144	129
Weight (kg)	65	55	46	41	51	61	58	61	59	49

a Find the mean height.
b Find the mean weight.

4 These are the monthly rainfall figures in millimetres for South Wales for one year.

Jan	115.8	Apr	63.5	Jul	85.4	Oct	114.3
Feb	76.2	May	76.2	Aug	99.1	Nov	116.8
Mar	58.4	Jun	55.8	Sep	91.4	Dec	109.1

a Work out the mean rainfall per month.
b Write down the months that had a rainfall lower than the mean.
c Write down the months that had a rainfall higher than the mean.

- -

Mode	The **mode** is the most common or the most popular data value. This is sometimes called the **modal value**.

Example

Find the modal number of pupils in a Year 8 form at Stanthorne High.

The numbers in the forms are:
25   27   27   27   28   28   29   29
The most common number is 27.

The modal value is 27 pupils.

5 Here are the school nurse's results on bad asthma.
She wrote down the number of cases every day for two weeks.
3   15   0   3   1   0   4   3   1   4
Write down the modal number of asthma cases.

6 Here are Tony's times in minutes for his journeys to and from school.
25   21   24   26   21   24   26   27   21   27
Write down the modal time for Tony's journeys.

7 Mrs Brown gets cross if 8B forget their maths exercise books.
She counts the number of forgotten books for eight lessons.
Here are her results:
0   1   3   1   2   0   1   1
Write down the mode.

8 The mode does not have to be a number.
Here is a pie-chart of the ways 8M and their teacher come to school.

a What is the mode?

b Explain how you can find the mode from the pie-chart.

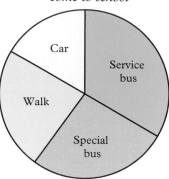

Pie-chart of the ways 8M come to school

| **Median** | There is a third type of average called the **median**. |

There is a third type of average called the **median**.
The median is the middle value of the data.
You must make sure that your data is in order from smallest to largest.

Examples

1 These are the amounts that Manisha spent on her school lunches in one week.

   75 p   92 p   95 p   88 p   98 p

Find the median amount Manisha spent.

Write the numbers in order:

   75 p   88 p   **92 p**   95 p   98 p

The middle value is 92 p so this is the median.

2 Find the median number of pupils in a Year 8 form at Stanthorne High.

The numbers in the forms are:

   25   27   27   27   28   28   29   29

There are two middle values.

The median is $\dfrac{27 + 28}{2} = 27.5$

Like the mean, the median does not have to be one of the data values.

---

9 Find the the median of each of these sets of numbers.

a 7   5   6   7   4   8   3

b 14   16   17   12   13

10 Here are the school nurse's results on bad asthma.
She wrote down the number of cases every day for two weeks.

    3   15   0   3   1   0   4   3   1   4

Work out the median.

11 Here are Tony's times in minutes for his journeys to and from school.

    25   21   24   26   21   24   26   27   21   27

Work out the median time for Tony's journeys.

- -

Range

For any set of data, the **range** is the biggest value take away the smallest value.

Example

Find the range of the number of pupils in Year 8 forms at Stanthorne High.

The numbers in the forms are:

    25   27   27   27   28   28   29   29

The biggest value is 29. The smallest value is 25.
The range is $29 - 25 = 4$

Exercise 13:2

1 Here are the school nurse's results on bad asthma.
She wrote down the number of cases every day for two weeks.

    3   15   0   3   1   0   4   3   1   4

Find the range.

2 Here are Tony's times in minutes for his journeys to and from school.

    25   21   24   26   21   24   26   27   21   27

Find the range of his times.

3 Some children were weighed and measured as part of a medical examination.

Height (cm)	148	136	130	127	137	143	139	141	144	129
Weight (kg)	65	55	46	41	51	61	58	61	59	49

a Find the range of the heights.
b Find the range of the weights.

- -

Choosing a sensible average

Example Here are the numbers of pupils at chess club for ten weeks.

   12   12   12   13   15   16   17   17   18   46

The three averages are: **mean 17.8, mode 12, median 15.5**
Which average is the most sensible to choose?

The mode is too small.
The mean is too large because of the 46 (the Christmas party).
The median is the most sensible.

Using the range

The range tells us how the data is spread out around the mean.

Example Here are the runs scored by two cricketers in their last six innings.

Jack	44	73	39	60	68	40
Ian	120	7	84	26	9	90

50 runs are needed to win.
Who is the best choice as batsman?

Jack has **mean 54** runs and **range 34** runs for his innings.
Ian has **mean 56** runs and **range 113** runs for his innings.
The mean scores are nearly the same but Ian's range is much larger
than Jack's. Jack's scores are usually reliable, but Ian's vary more.
Jack is a better choice if 50 runs are needed to win.

Exercise 13:3

1 Look at this data. You have already found the three averages and
the range.
  a The school nurse's daily numbers of pupils with bad asthma:
     3   15   0   3   1   0   4   3   1   4
  b Tony's times in minutes for his journeys to and from school:
     25   21   24   26   21   24   26   27   21   27
  For each set:
  Write down the mean, mode and median.
  Say which average or averages it is sensible to use.

2 a Write down the mean and range of Tony's times from question **1**.

b Here are Tony's journey times for a different two weeks:

26   22   20   28   24   18   27   19   28   30

Work out the mean and range for this second two weeks.

c Tony travels by bus. During the second two weeks the council tried using different traffic lanes for buses.

Use your answers to **a** and **b** to decide which system is better for getting the buses to run on time.

Explain how you chose your answer.

Tally-table	When there is a lot of data we make a **tally-table**. We use tally marks.
Tally marks	**Tally marks** are done in groups of five. The fifth tally mark goes across the other four: 卌

Exercise 13:4

1 These are the numbers of pupils in each form for Years 7 to 11 at Stanthorne High.

Year 7	30	27	26	28	29	30	28	29
Year 8	25	27	28	27	29	27	28	29
Year 9	28	27	29	27	26	29	25	27
Year 10	28	24	27	28	26	27	28	27
Year 11	25	26	27	29	27	28	26	28

a Find the range of the numbers of pupils in a form.

b Copy this tally-table. Continue the first column to 30. Fill the table in.

Number of pupils in a form	Tally	Total
24		
25		

c Use the table to find the mode.

2 The headteacher wants to know the mean number of pupils per form at Stanthorne High.

a Use the data from question **1**.

Copy the table. Fill it in.

You can add an extra column to the table for question **1** if you prefer.

Add the numbers in the third column to find the total number of pupils.

Number of pupils in a form	Number of forms	Total number of pupils
24	1	$24 \times 1 =$
25	3	$25 \times 3 =$

b Copy and fill in:

Mean number of pupils

$= $ total number of pupils $\div$ total number of forms

$= \ldots \div 40$

$= \ldots$

3 Some pupils at Stanthorne High come to school by car.

One morning 8J did a survey of how many pupils arrived in each car.

Here are their results:

Number of pupils in a car	1	2	3	4
Number of cars	38	27	12	3

a Write down the mode.

b Copy this table for the survey.

Fill it in to find the total number of pupils.

Number of pupils in a car	Number of cars	Total number of pupils
1	38	$1 \times 38 =$

c Copy and fill in:

Mean number of pupils $=$ total number of pupils $\div$ 80

$= \ldots \div 80$

$= \ldots$

d Find the range of the number of pupils in a car.

2 Grouping data

Children's books are often given a reading age.
This measures how difficult a book is to read.

There are a few ways of measuring reading age.
One way is to count the length of the words. Books for older children may have longer words.
Another way is to count the number of words in each sentence.

Word length and sentence length are examples of discrete data.

Discrete data	When data can only be certain individual values it is called **discrete**.
Example	Shoe size is an example of discrete data. The values can only be 1, $1\frac{1}{2}$, 2, $2\frac{1}{2}$, etc. There are no shoe sizes in between these.

Exercise 13:5

 1 a Look at the two pages from children's books. Copy this tally-table for Book A. Fill it in.

b Now make a tally-table for Book B.

Word length (letters)	Tally	Total
1		
2		
3		
4		
5		
6		
7		
8		
9		
10		

To compare the two books it is best to draw some diagrams.

2 **a** Copy the axes on to graph paper.

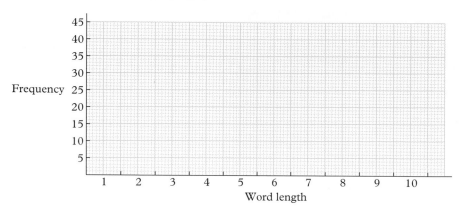

b Use your tally-table for Book A to draw a bar-chart.
c Copy the axes again.
d Use your tally-table for Book B to draw another bar-chart.

3 Use your two bar-charts to answer these questions.
   a Which book has the most 2-letter words?
   b Which book has the most 6-letter words?
   c Which book do you think is easier to read?
      Explain your answer.

4 **a** Which is the most common length of word in Book A?
   b Copy and fill in:
        The modal word length for Book A is ... letters.
   c Which is the most common length of word in Book B?
   d Copy and fill in:
        The modal word length for Book B is ... letters.

5 **a** Add a fourth column to your tally-tables.

Word length (letters)	Tally	Total	Total number of letters (= word length × total)

   b Fill in the fourth column.
      Add up the numbers in the column.
      This is the total number of letters.
   c Divide your answer to **b** by the total number of words.
      This is the mean word length.
   d Which book has the smallest mean word length?
   e Does this match your answer to question **3c**? Explain.

There is another way of measuring how difficult books are to read.
You can count the number of words in a sentence.
This is called the sentence length.

Exercise 13:6

W 1   **a**   Go back to your page from Book A.
Count the number of words in each sentence.
Write down each sentence length in your book.

b   Count the length of the sentences in the page from Book B.
Write down each sentence length in your book.

Sentences can be lots of different lengths.
It is sensible to put these in groups before you make a tally-table.

Length of sentence (in words)	Tally	Total
1–5		
6–10		
11–15		
16–20		
21–25		
26–30		
31–35		

Sentences with 1, 2, 3, 4 or 5 words go into the 1–5 group.
Sentences with 6, 7, 8, 9 or 10 words go into the 6–10 group
and so on.

Then you can draw a bar-chart from the grouped data.

2   **a**   Copy the tally-table.
b   Tally the sentence lengths from Book A.
Use the numbers you wrote down in question **1**.
c   Copy the tally-table again.
Tally the sentence lengths from Book B.

3 a Copy the axes on to squared paper.

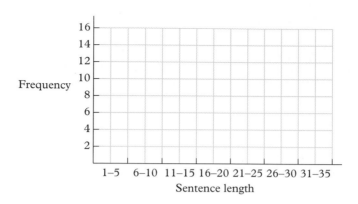

b Use your tally-table for Book A to draw a bar-chart.
Don't leave gaps between the bars.
c Copy the axes again.
d Use your tally-table for Book B to draw another bar-chart.

4 a Which group has the most sentences in it for Book A?
b Copy and fill in:
The modal sentence length for Book A is … words.
c Which group has the most sentences in it for Book B?
d Copy and fill in:
The modal sentence length for Book B is … words.
e Think about your answers to **b** and **d**.
Which book do you think is easier to read?
Explain your answer.

5 You can work out the mean sentence length.
a Write down the total number of words on the page from Book A.
b Write down the total number of sentences on the page from Book A.
c Copy and fill in:
mean sentence length
= total number of words ÷ total number of sentences
= … ÷ …
= …
d Write down the total number of words on the page from Book B.
e Write down the total number of sentences on the page from Book B.
f Work out the mean sentence length for Book B.

Continuous data	Data is **continuous** when it can take *any* value in a certain range.

Example The lengths of earthworms, the heights of pupils in Year 8, the weights of hamsters are all examples of continuous data.

When you are grouping continuous data you need to think very carefully about the beginning and end of each group.

Exercise 13:7

1 In a Science survey Howard measured the lengths of some earthworms in centimetres.
Here are his results to the nearest millimetre.

6.2	5.4	8.9	12.1	6.5
9.3	7.2	12.7	10.2	5.4
7.7	9.5	11.1	8.6	7.0
13.5	12.7	5.6	15.4	12.3
13.4	9.5	6.7	8.6	9.1
11.5	14.2	13.5	8.8	9.7

Howard put the data into groups like this:

Length in cm	Tally	Total
5 but less than 7		
7 but less than 9		
9 but less than 11		
11 but less than 13		
13 but less than 15		
15 but less than 17		

a Which group does 13.5 go into?
b Which group does 7.0 go into?
c Copy the tally-table.
    Tally all the results in your table.
d Draw a bar-chart of this grouped data.
    Don't leave gaps between the bars.

2 Mariza used different groups.
  a Copy this table.

Length in cm	Tally	Total
5 but less than 9 9 but less than 13 13 but less than 17		

  b Tally all the results from question **1** in your new table.
  c Draw a bar-chart of your new table.
    Don't leave gaps between the bars.
  d Which bar-chart do you think is best for showing the data?
    Explain your answer.

3 These are the weights of 30 adults in kilograms.

47	65	52	43	58	69	71	49	56	60
82	54	91	54	70	56	95	47	82	86
75	79	96	99	100	57	98	63	80	92

  a Copy this table.

Weight in kg	Tally	Total
40 but less than 50 50 but less than 60 60 but less than 70 70 but less than 80 80 but less than 90 90 but less than 100 100 but less than 110		

  b Which group does a weight of 100 kg go into?
  c Which group does a weight of 80 kg go into?
  d Tally all the results in your table.
  e Draw a bar-chart of this grouped data.
    Don't leave gaps between the bars.

4 Sian did a survey of how long her friends took to get to school.
  Here are her results in minutes to the nearest minute.

8	13	21	5	16	24	9	14	16	17
7	5	25	31	14	17	19	23	5	12
8	12	16	19	21	24	5	2	33	4

  a Choose sensible groups for this data.
  b Make a tally-table for these groups.
  c Fill in your tally-table.
  d Draw a bar-chart of your table.

3   Frequency polygons

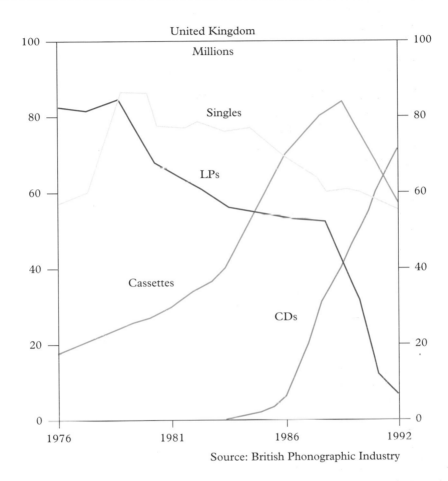

United Kingdom

Millions

Singles

LPs

Cassettes

CDs

1976   1981   1986   1992

Source: British Phonographic Industry

These frequency polygons show the sales of LPs, cassettes, CDs and singles since 1976.

Frequency polygon	**Frequency polygons** are often used to compare two sets of data.
Trend	The points are joined together to show the **trend**. The trend shows how the data is changing. You do not read information from the lines in between the points.

Exercise 13:8

1 Look at this table.
It shows the total number of goals scored in 40 football matches played one Saturday.

Number of goals	0	1	2	3	4	5	6
Number of matches	5	9	12	5	7	1	1

a Look at the figures in red.
How many matches had 2 goals in them?
b Look at the figures in green.
How many matches had 6 goals in them?
c Write down all the possible final scores that have 6 goals in them.
Start with 6–0, 5–1, 4–2, …

Here is a frequency polygon showing this information.

Frequency polygon to show the number
of goals scored in 40 football matches

Number of matches

Number of goals

d How many matches had 5 goals in them?
Is this the same as in the table?
e How many matches had 2 goals in them?

2 Look at this frequency polygon.
It shows the number of pupils in each year at a boys' secondary school.

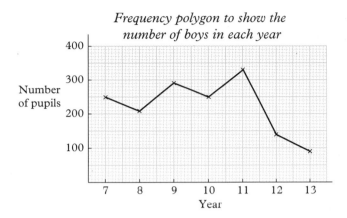

Frequency polygon to show the number of boys in each year

Copy this table.

Year	7	8	9	10	11	12	13
Number of pupils							

Fill in the table. Get the information from the frequency polygon.

3 This frequency polygon shows the number of pupils at the nearby girls' school.

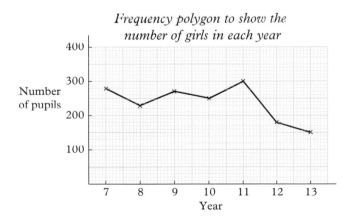

Frequency polygon to show the number of girls in each year

Copy the table from question **2** again.
Fill it in. Get the information from the frequency polygon.

The frequency polygons from question **2** and question **3** can be drawn on the same diagram.
This makes them easier to compare.

4 a Copy the frequency polygon from question **2** on to graph paper.
  b Copy the frequency polygon from question **3** on to the same
    set of axes.
  c Which school has the most Year 7 pupils?
  d Which school has more pupils in Year 9?
  e In which year do both schools have the same number of pupils?
  f How many more boys are there in Year 9 than girls?
  g How many more girls are there in Year 8 than boys?

5 Look at these frequency polygons.
  They show the number of pupils at two schools.

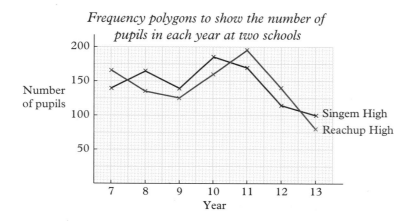

Frequency polygons to show the number of pupils in each year at two schools

  a Which school has the most Year 7 pupils?
  b Which school has the most Year 9 pupils?
    How many more Year 9 pupils has it got?
  c Make a list of the number of pupils in each year at Singem High.
    How many pupils does it have altogether?
  d How many pupils are there at Reachup High?

6 8P have been comparing two reading books. The books are for pupils
  in junior school.
  8P have counted the numbers of letters in the first 50 words of each
  book.
  Here are two tables showing their results.

Number of letters in a word	1	2	3	4	5	6	7
Number of words in *Read for fun*	3	5	14	17	6	4	1

Number of letters in a word	1	2	3	4	5	6	7
Number of words in *Reading made easy*	4	5	9	13	10	7	2

a Copy the axes on to squared paper.

Frequency polygons of the numbers of letters in a word for two books

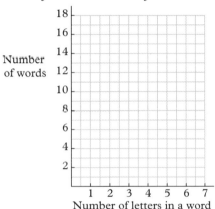

b Draw a frequency polygon for *Read for fun*.
c Draw a frequency polygon for *Reading made easy* on the same diagram.
Use a different colour.
d Which book do you think is easier to read?
Explain your answer.

7 Results are collected each year about casualties in traffic accidents. These are the numbers of school-age casualties in Derbyshire in one year.

Age	5	6	7	8	9	10	11	12	13	14	15	16	17	18	19
Number	37	35	42	52	56	56	52	62	63	87	58	113	167	188	167

a Draw a frequency polygon to show this data.
b Describe how the number of casualties changes as people get older.
c Do you think this trend will continue?
Explain your answer.

If the data is grouped then the points of the frequency polygon are plotted in the middle of each group.
This is like joining up the middle of the top of each bar on a bar-chart.

Here is a table of the casualty data from Exercise **13:8**.
The data has been grouped.

Age	5–7	8–10	11–13	14–16	17–19
Number	114	164	177	258	522

Exercise 13:9

1 **a** Draw a bar-chart of this grouped data. Use a pencil and draw it as lightly as possible.
   b Put a small cross in the middle of the top of each bar.
   c Join your crosses with straight lines.
   You now have a frequency polygon.

2 Here is the casualty data for older age groups.

Age	20–22	23–25	26–28	29–31	32–34
Number	485	406	359	292	246

   a Draw a bar-chart for this data. Use a pencil and draw it lightly.
   b Draw a frequency polygon over the top of your bar-chart.
   c Describe the trend of the casualties as the people get older.
   d Suggest why the trend is like this.

3 Here is a third set of casualty data for Derbyshire.

Age	41–43	44–46	47–49	50–52	53–55
Number	158	166	156	130	98

   a Plot all three sets of casualty data on one frequency polygon.
   Do NOT join up 33 to 42.
   Use this scale on the bottom axis.

5–7 8–10 11–13 14–16 17–19 20–22 22–25 26–28 29–31 32–34 35–37 38–40 41–43 44–46 47–49 50–52 53–55

   b By looking at the trend of the graph, suggest values for the groups that are missing: 35–37 and 38–40.

1   Stanthorne High under-15 football team has played three matches.
    The mean number of goals they have scored is two.
    a What is the total number of goals scored?
    b They play another match and score four goals.
       What is the new mean?

2   8L collect 40 leaves from a tree.
    They measure them in centimetres correct to the nearest millimetre.
    Here are their results:

6.0	5.2	6.1	5.3	8.2	6.4	5.7	7.1	6.5	6.4
7.2	8.7	4.8	5.6	7.3	4.9	6.5	8.3	6.8	7.8
7.4	7.9	5.5	7.0	7.5	5.8	5.1	7.6	6.8	5.4
8.1	6.3	6.4	5.9	4.7	8.4	6.1	6.7	8.8	7.7

    a Copy the table. Fill it in.

Length of leaf in cm	Tally	Total
4 but less than 5		
5 but less than 6		
6 but less than 7		
7 but less than 8		
8 but less than 9		

    b Draw a bar-chart of your table.
    c Write down the modal group.

3   Here is a table showing the numbers of pupils in two schools.

Number of pupils	Year 7	Year 8	Year 9	Year 10	Year 11
The Burton School	170	160	180	200	150
The Bravo School	150	160	140	120	150

    a Copy the axes on to squared paper.
    b Plot the points for The Burton School. Join them with straight lines.
    c Plot the points for The Bravo School. Join them with straight lines. Use a different colour.

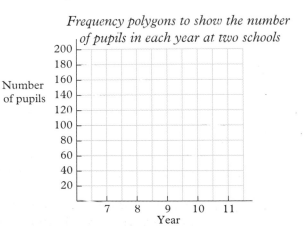

Frequency polygons to show the number of pupils in each year at two schools

295

1   Elmtown Council is trying to get people to share cars when they go to work. This helps to reduce the traffic.

The council do regular surveys to see if more people are sharing. Here is a set of their results for 50 cars.

Number of people in a car	Number of cars
1	15
2	18
3	11
4	4
5	2

   a   Work out the mean number of people in a car.

   b   Write down the mode.

   c   The median of the results is found to be 2. Choose one of the three averages to estimate the number of people in 500 cars.

   d   What is the probability that a car contains more than one person?

2   40 pupils took their pulse rates after exercising.

Here are their results in beats per minute.

124	120	137	122	124	122	129	124	128	126
132	122	120	120	126	124	122	128	136	110
134	120	126	115	122	126	132	124	118	112
128	122	128	119	125	124	122	118	112	130

   a   Choose sensible groups for this data.

   b   Make a tally-table for these groups.

   c   Fill in your tally-table.

   d   Draw a bar-chart of your results.

3   Gemma and Kath have done a survey of two brands of carrots. Both brands cost the same and the carrots are about the same size. They have opened eight tins of each brand and counted the number of carrots in each tin.

Here are their results:

Brand A	32	41	28	31	34	37	39	30
Brand B	32	34	36	30	32	35	33	32

   a   Work out the mean number of carrots per tin for each brand. Which brand looks better value?

   b   Work out the range for each brand of carrots. Explain what the range shows. Which brand of carrots would you buy next time?

- **Mean** To find the **mean** of a set of data:
  (1) Find the total of all the data values.
  (2) Divide by the number of data values.

  Mode The **mode** is the most common or the most popular data value.

  Median The **median** is the middle value when the data is in order from smallest to largest.

- **Range** The **range** is the biggest value take away the smallest value.

- **Discrete data** **Discrete data** can only be certain individual values.

  Continuous data Data is **continuous** when it can take *any* value in a certain range.

- **Grouping data** It is sensible to put data in groups before you make a tally-table.

  Example

Length of sentence (words)	Tally	Total
1–5		
6–10		
11–15		

  Sentences with 1, 2, 3, 4 or 5 words go into the 1–5 group.
  Sentences with 6, 7, 8, 9 or 10 words go into the 6–10 group and so on.
  Then you can draw a bar-chart from the grouped data.

- **Frequency polygons**
  Frequency polygons are often used to compare two sets of data.

  Trend
  The points are joined together to show the **trend**.
  The trend shows how the data is changing.
  You do not read information from the lines in between the points.

Frequency polygon to show the number of goals scored in 40 football matches

1 Look at these numbers:

      7   6   9   0   3   4   7   6   4   7

a Work out the mean.   **c** Find the median.

b Write down the mode.   **d** Work out the range.

2 8J recorded the number of people in 50 cars passing the school. Here are their results:

Number of people	Number of cars	Total number of people
1	23	$1 \times 23 =$
2	17	$2 \times 17 =$
3	7	$3 \times 7 =$
4	3	$4 \times 3 =$
Total		

a Write down the mode.

b Copy the table. Fill it in.

c Work out the mean number of people per car.

d Draw a frequency polygon to show the data.

3 8F measured the heights of 40 seedlings four weeks after the seeds were planted.

Here are their results, given in centimetres correct to the nearest millimetre.

2.8	10.3	3.6	6.3	8.1	7.2	4.7	7.1	4.3	8.2
5.9	8.0	2.5	7.4	5.3	9.1	1.9	6.8	4.8	5.1
9.4	7.3	3.8	7.9	9.0	8.7	5.5	8.4	3.6	8.5
7.9	7.8	9.7	7.7	1.8	6.2	7.3	6.9	10.5	6.5

a Copy the table.

Tally all the results in the table.

Length in cm	Tally	Total
0 but less than 2		
2 but less than 4		
4 but less than 6		
6 but less than 8		
8 but less than 10		
10 but less than 12		

b Write down the modal group.

c Draw a bar-chart of this grouped data.

d Draw a frequency polygon on your bar-chart.

14 Volume: filling the space

The average adult human female has 4.5 litres of blood in her body.

A male has slightly more.

If you give blood to the National Blood Service they take less than half a litre.

Altogether they collect 1.5 million litres each year.

This is the same as about 300 000 full bodies worth!

1 Pack it in!

The world record for the number of people in a phone box is 23.
This is a lot of people in a very small space!

Volume	The amount of space that an object takes up is called its **volume**.

Exercise 14:1

1 Look at these objects.

List the objects in order of volume. Start with the *biggest*.

2 Look at these objects.

List the objects in order of volume. Start with the *smallest*.

| Capacity | The **capacity** of a hollow object is the volume of space inside it. |

3 Look at these containers.

List the objects in order of capacity.
Start with the *biggest*.

Units of volume

Volume is measured in cubic units.
These can be mm³, cm³ or m³

| **1 cm³** | **1 cm³** is the space taken up by a cube with all its edges 1 cm long. |

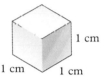

Units of capacity

| **1 ml** | This cube is filled with water. The volume of water inside is **1 millilitre**. This is written **1 ml** **1 ml** is the same as **1 cm³** |

4 Look at these containers.
  a List the containers in order of volume. Start with the *smallest*.
  ● b Peter makes an ice cream float from the Coke and ice cream.
       His glass has a capacity of 350 ml.
       He puts all the ice cream into the glass first.
       Will all of the Coke now fit in the glass?

We measure large volumes in **litres**.
   1 litre = 1000 ml

This lemonade bottle holds 2 litres.
This petrol can holds 5 litres.
A petrol tanker holds 34 000 litres.

Exercise 14:2

1 Estimate the volume of these containers.
   Write your answers in litres.

a   **c**   **e**

b   **d**

2 Estimate the volume of these containers.
   Write your answers in millilitres.

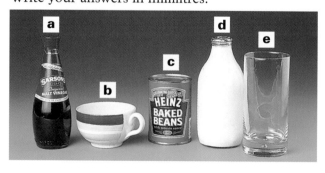

3 Estimate the volume of these containers.
   You need to choose millilitres or litres.

a   **b**   **c**

2 Stacking

Supermarkets stack their shelves so that you can see what they are selling.
They want to fit in as much as they can.
The shelf stackers need to work out how much they can fit in.

Example

Rachel is stacking cornflakes boxes.
First she sees how many boxes fit along the shelf.
5 boxes fit on this shelf.

Then she sees how many rows of boxes she can fit in.
She can fit 4 rows on this shelf.

She multiplies the number of boxes in each row by the number of rows.
This tells her how many boxes will fit in.

$5 \times 4 = 20$ boxes
20 boxes will fit on the shelf.

Exercise 14:3

For each question:
a Write down the number of boxes in one row.
b Write down the number of rows that will fit on the shelf.
c Work out how many boxes will fit altogether.

1

2

3

Example

Rachel also has to stack boxes of pizzas in the freezer.
She works out how many will fit in one layer.

Then she works out how many layers she can fit in.
She multiplies the number in one layer by the number of layers.
This tells her the total number of pizzas she can fit in.

In this freezer she can fit 12 boxes in each layer and 5 layers.
She can fit $12 \times 5 = 60$ pizzas in altogether.

Exercise 14:4

For each question work out:
a The number of boxes in one layer.
b The number of layers.
c The total number of boxes in the stack.

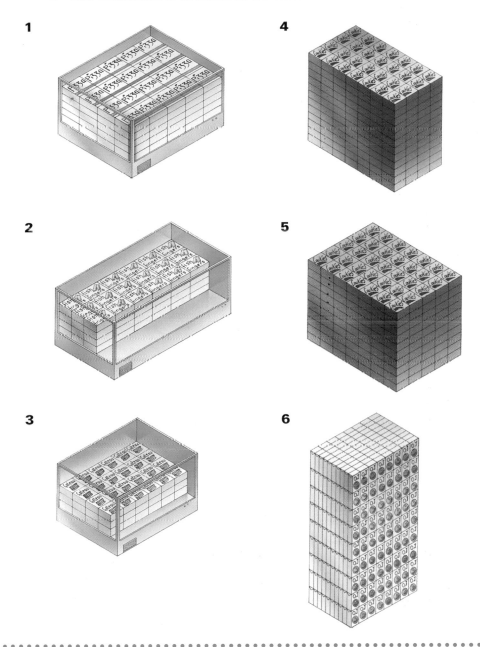

1

4

2

5

3

6

James is playing with wooden cubes.
He has learned to build them into towers.

Exercise 14:5

For each question work out:
a How many cubes James has in each layer.
b How many layers of cubes James has.
c How many cubes James has altogether.

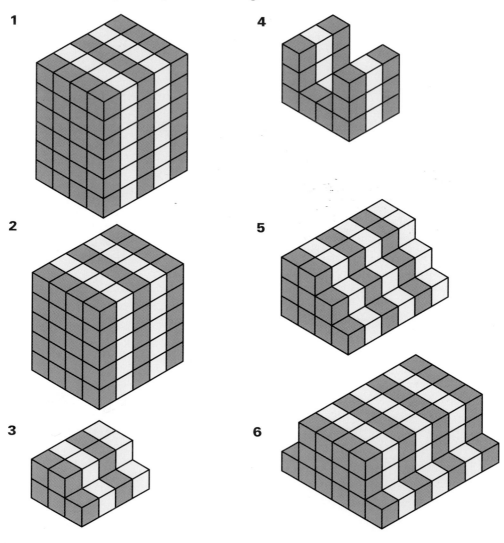

1

2

3

4

5

6

| 1 cm³ | A cube that has sides of 1 cm is called a 1 cm cube.
We say that it has a volume of 1 cm cubed.
We write this as **1 cm³** |

Example   This rectangle of 1 cm cubes has
a volume of 12 cm³

Exercise 14:6

Work out the volume of these rectangles of 1 cm cubes.
Write your answers in cm³

1

3

2

4

Work out the volume of these blocks of 1 cm cubes.
Write your answers in cm³

5

7

6

8

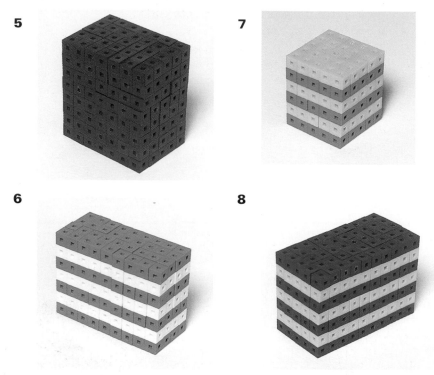

Exercise 14:7

Work out the volume of these shapes made from 1 cm cubes.
To do this:
a Work out the number of cubes in one layer.
b Multiply by the number of layers.

1

2

3

6

4

7

5

8

MCT

3   Prisms

This is a picture of a triangular prism.

It is used to split white light into the colours of the rainbow.

Prism

A **prism** is a solid which is exactly the same shape all the way through.
Wherever you cut a slice through the shape it is the same size and shape.

Cross section

The shape of this slice is called the **cross section** of the solid.

These shapes are prisms.

These shapes are not prisms.

Exercise 14:8

Look at these solids.
Write down the letters
of the prisms.

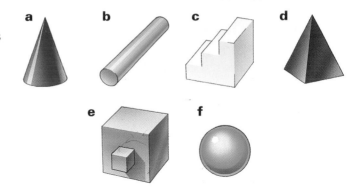

a   **b**   **c**   **d**

e   **f**

· ·

To find the volume of a prism:

(1) Find the number of cubes in one layer.

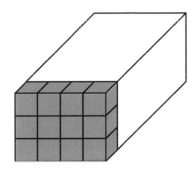

This is the same as the area of
the cross section.

3 cm   4 cm

(2) Find the number of layers in the prism.

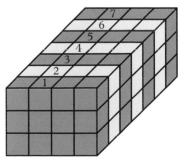

This is the same as the length of the prism.

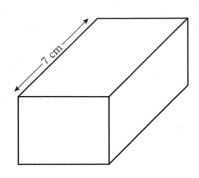

(3) Multiply the number of cubes in one layer by the number of layers. This is the same as multiplying the area of the cross section by the length.

| **Volume of a prism** | The volume of a prism is **area of cross section × length** |

If the prism is a cuboid this is the same as
length × width × height

Example

Find the volume of this prism.

Area of cross section
$$= 6 \times 8$$
$$= 48 \text{ cm}^2$$

Volume $= 48 \times 15$
$$= 720 \text{ cm}^3$$

or   length × width × height $= 6 \times 8 \times 15 = 720 \text{ cm}^3$

Exercise 14:9

Work out the volume of these prisms.

1

2

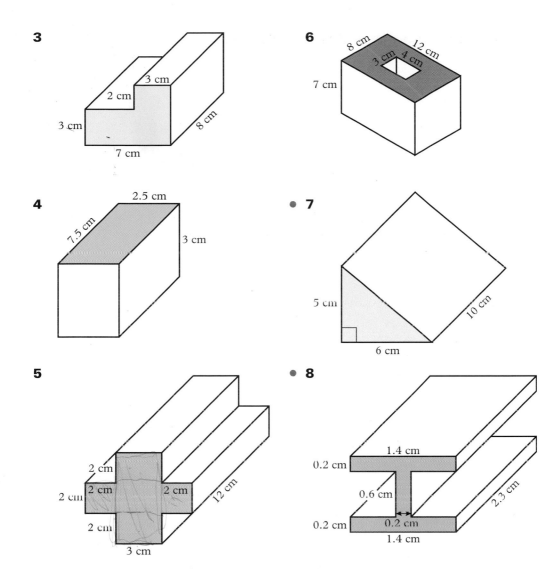

3

2 cm
3 cm
3 cm
7 cm
8 cm

6

8 cm
12 cm
3 cm
4 cm
7 cm

4

2.5 cm
7.5 cm
3 cm

7

5 cm
6 cm
10 cm

5

2 cm
2 cm
2 cm
2 cm
2 cm
3 cm
12 cm

8

1.4 cm
0.2 cm
0.6 cm
0.2 cm
0.2 cm
1.4 cm
2.3 cm

Exercise 14:10

For each question:
a Sketch the shape.
Mark on the measurements.
b Colour the area of the cross section.
c Find the area of the cross section.
d Multiply the area of the cross section by the length to find the volume.

1 A cuboid with sides of length 5 cm, 8 cm and 3 cm.

2 A cube with sides 6 cm long.

3 A 750 g size cereal box has sides of length 7 cm, 19 cm and 29 cm.

4 A 1 litre carton of fruit juice is in the shape of a cuboid.
It measures 5.9 cm by 9 cm by 19.5 cm.

5 A new type of tea is sold in a T-shaped box.
The measurements are shown in the diagram.

Exercise 14:11

1 A 1 litre carton of milk is in the shape of a cuboid.
It measures 7 cm by 7 cm by 21 cm.
  a Find the volume of the carton.
  b 1 cm³ takes up the same space as 1 m*l*.
  The carton contains 1 *l* of milk.
  How much space is left inside the carton?

2 A Toblerone box is in the shape of a triangular prism.
The triangle has base of length 6 cm and height 5 cm.
The length of the box is 30 cm.
  a Find the area of the cross section.
  b Find the volume of the box.

3 A trench is dug to lay some pipes.
The cross section of the trench is
in the shape of a trapezium.
It is 30 m long.

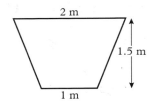

2 m

1.5 m

1 m

   a Find the area of the cross
   section of the trench.
   b Find the volume of earth dug
   out of the trench.

4 Saleem looks at two chocolate milkshake drinks.
One is in a bottle which has a capacity of 750 m*l*.
The other is in a carton which measures 8 cm by 6 cm by 15 cm.
Both containers are full.
Which one has the most milkshake in it?

5 A bottle of fabric softener holds 1.5 litres.
The manufacturer wants to produce a carton to refill the bottle.
The carton must also hold 1.5 litres.
The base of the carton is a square with sides 8 cm.
How high does the carton need to be?
Give your answer to the nearest millimetre.

6 A petrol tank in a car measures 60 cm by 50 cm by 30 cm.
   a Work out the volume of the tank in cm^3
   b Write your answer to part **a** in litres.
   c 1 gallon is about 4.5 litres.
   About how much petrol does the tank hold in gallons?

7 **a** Hotchoc is sold in circular tins.
   The area of the end of the tin
   is 100 cm^2
   The tin is 15 cm high.
   Find the volume of the tin.
   b The Hotchoc company wants to
   change to rectangular tins.
   The new tin must have the same
   volume as the tin in part **a**.
   Suggest possible measurements
   for the new tin.

Exercise 14:12 Building a box

Get a piece of squared paper exactly 18 cm by 24 cm.

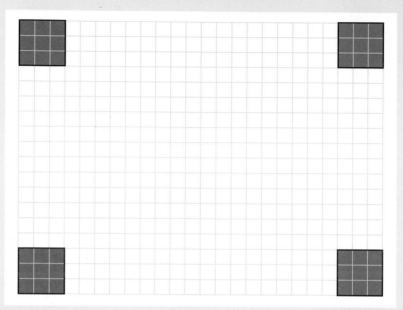

Cut squares out of each corner. This makes your paper into the net of a box.
Fold the paper to make the box.
Stick the corners with sticky tape.
The box will not have a lid.

Find the volume of the box.

Use more pieces of squared paper
18 cm by 24 cm to make more boxes.
Try changing the size of the squares
at the corners.

Find the volume of each box you make.
You will need to organise your results.

What is the biggest volume you can get?

Other things to try:
● The sides of the corner squares do not need to be a whole number
  of centimetres.
● You could make a box with a lid.
  How would this affect the volume?
● You could start with a piece of A4 paper.

Write a report on what you have found out.

1 Estimate the volume of these containers.
You need to choose millilitres or litres.

2 Find the volume of these prisms.

a

5 cm
3 cm
12 cm

c

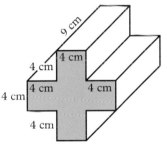

13 cm
12 cm
4 cm
4 cm
12 cm

b

3.5 cm
3.5 cm
13 cm

d

9 cm
4 cm
4 cm
4 cm
4 cm
4 cm

3 For each question:
(1) Sketch the shape.
Mark on the measurements.
(2) Colour the area of the cross section.
(3) Find the area of the cross section.
(4) Multiply the area of the cross section by the length to find the volume.

a A cuboid with sides of length 3.5 cm, 5 cm and 7.5 cm.
b A cube with sides 8.5 cm long.
c A box of computer discs which has sides of length 10 cm, 10 cm and 4.5 cm.

10 cm

10 cm
4.5 cm

d A CD case with sides of length 14.2 cm, 12.4 cm and 1.1 cm.

4 Find the volume of this piece of guttering in cm^3. (Its total length is 5 m.)

20 cm
8 cm
12 cm

317

1 Here is the cross section of a swimming pool.

The pool is 15 m wide.
a Find the area of the cross section.
b Find the volume of the pool in m³
c Find the volume of the pool in litres. (1 m³ = 1000 *l*)

2 A set of child's bricks contains 24 cubes with sides of 4 cm.
a Find the volume of each brick.
b Find the total volume of the whole set of bricks.
c The cubes are packed into a box.
Suggest possible measurements for the box.
d These boxes are to be packed into crates containing 100 boxes.
Find the volume of each crate.

3 The cistern of Pauline's toilet is in the shape of a cuboid.
The cistern measures 18 cm by 44 cm by 30 cm.
The cistern fills with water so that it is three quarters full.
a Find the volume of water in the cistern in cm³
b Find the volume in litres.

4 This giant Toblerone box is in the
shape of a triangular prism.
The triangle has base of length
15 cm and height 12.5 cm.
The length of the box is 1 m.

a Find the area of the cross section.
b Find the volume of the box in cm³
This is a small Toblerone box.
c How many times bigger are
the lengths of the sides of the
big box?
d How many times more chocolate
do you get in the big box?

- **Volume** The amount of space that an object takes up is called its **volume**.

- **Capacity** The **capacity** of a hollow object is the volume of space inside it.

- **Units of volume** Volume is measured in cubic units. These can be mm³, cm³ or m³

  1 cm³ **1 cm³** is the space taken up by a cube with all its edges 1 cm long.

  Units of capacity This cube is filled with water. The volume of water inside is **1 millilitre**. This is written **1 ml**

  1 ml **1 ml is the same as 1 cm³**

  We measure large volumes in litres.
  1 litre = 1000 ml

- **Prism** A **prism** is a solid which is exactly the same shape all the way through.
  Wherever you cut a slice through the shape it is the same size and shape.

  Cross section The shape of this slice is called the **cross section** of the solid.

- **Volume of a prism** The volume of a prism is **area of cross section × length**

  If the prism is a cuboid this is the same as
  length × width × height

Example Find the volume of this prism.

Area of cross section = 6 × 8
$$= 48 \text{ cm}^2$$

Volume = 48 × 15
$$= 720 \text{ cm}^3$$

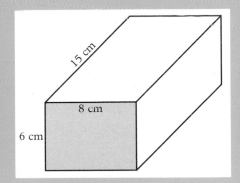

or length × width × height = 6 × 8 × 15 = 720 cm³

1 Look at these objects.
List the objects in order of volume.
Start with the *biggest*.

2 Estimate the volume of these containers.
You need to choose millilitres or litres.

3 Find the volume of these
blocks of 1 cm cubes.
Write your answers in cm³

4 Find the volume of these prisms.

a

13 cm
5 cm
5 cm
5 cm
5 cm
5 cm

b

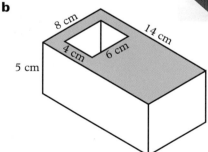

8 cm
14 cm
4 cm
6 cm
5 cm

5 Find the volume of this kitchen
cupboard in cm³

78 cm
40 cm
25 cm

15 More or less?

A supertanker holds 300 000 tonnes of crude oil. This makes about 267 million litres of petrol.

A Mini covers about 13 km on 1 litre of petrol. The distance of the Sun from the Earth is about 150 million km.

So Bill could drive his car to the Sun and back more than 11 times!

1 Trial and improvement

◄◄REPLAY►

Josie is practising her passing and shooting in hockey.
She sets up a target and tries to hit it.
If her ball goes to the right of the target she aims to the left next time.
If the ball goes to the left of the target she aims to the right next time.
She is getting closer to the target.

This happens in Maths.
You can solve equations by guessing different values. You then try to get closer to the right answer.

This method is called **trial and improvement**.

Example

To solve $3x + 3 = 45$ by trial and improvement:
(1) try different values of x
(2) write your results in a table like this.

Value of x	Value of $3x + 3$	
10	33	too small
15	48	too big
14	45	correct

Answer: $x = 14$

Exercise 15:1

Solve these equations by trial and improvement.
For each question:
    copy the table
    fill it in
    add more rows until you find the answer.

1　$5x - 4 = 36$

Value of x	Value of $5x - 4$	
5		
10		

2　$13x - 24 = 262$

Value of x	Value of $13x - 24$	
10		

3　$53x + 214 = 1751$

Value of x	Value of $53x + 214$	
10		

4　$113x - 214 = 3854$

Value of x	Value of $113x - 214$	
30		

Example　　　　Solve $12x - 35 = 163$

Value of x	Value of $12x - 35$	
10	85	too small
20	205	too big
16	157	too small
17	169	too big
16.5	163	correct

Answer: $x = 16.5$

5 $4x - 23 = 27$

Value of x	Value of $4x - 23$	
10		
12		
13		

6 $8p + 25 = 221$

Value of p	Value of $8p + 25$	
20		
30		
24		
25		

7 $25y - 124 = 356$

Value of y	Value of $25y - 124$	
10		
20		
19		
19.5		

Example Solve $x^2 = 1444$

Value of x	Value of x^2	
30	900	too small
40	1600	too big
38	1444	correct

Answer: $x = 38$

Exercise 15:2

Solve these equations by trial and improvement.

1 $x^2 = 2025$

Value of x	Value of x^2	
40		

2 $x^2 - 253 = 3111$

Value of x	Value of $x^2 - 253$	

● **3** $2x^2 = 2738$ *Remember: $2x^2$ means $2 \times x^2$*

Value of x	Value of $2x^2$	

Sometimes answers do not work out exactly.
When this happens you may have to give your answer correct to 1 dp.

Example

Solve $x^2 = 135$

Value of x	Value of x^2	
11	121	too small
12	144	too big
11.5	132.25	too small
11.6	134.56	too small
11.7	136.89	too big
11.65	135.7225	too big

x is between 11 and 12
x is between 11.5 and 12
x is between 11.6 and 12
x is between 11.6 and 11.7
x is between 11.6 and 11.65

11.6   11.65   11.7

x must be somewhere in the green part of the number line. Any number in the green part rounds down to 11.6 to 1 dp.

Answer: $x = 11.6$ to 1 dp.

Exercise 15:3

1 Solve $x^2 = 153$
Copy this table. Fill it in.
Add more rows until you have found x correct to 1 dp.

Value of x	Value of x^2	
12	144	too small
13	169	too big
12.5	156.25	too big

2 Solve these equations by trial and improvement.
Make a table to help you.
Give your answers to 1 dp.
a $x^2 = 189$
b $x^2 = 349$
c $x^2 = 456$

3 The area of this square is 559 cm^2.
Use trial and improvement to find the length of a side.
Give your answer to 1 dp.

● 4 The length of this garden is
three times its width.
The area is 45 m^2.
Find the width of the garden
using trial and improvement.
Give your answer to 1 dp.

● 5 The length of this picture frame is
4 cm more than its width.
The area of the frame is 65 cm^2.
a Use trial and improvement to
find the width of the frame to
1 dp.
b Write down the length correct
to 1 dp.

2 Inequalities

Mary wants to go on this ride.
She has to be at least 120 cm tall.
Her height must be greater than
or equal to 120 cm.
We write   height $\geqslant$ 120
This is called an **inequality**.

Number line   We can show positive and negative numbers on a
number line.

Negative direction
numbers are getting
smaller

Positive direction
numbers are getting
larger

Look at this number line. Part of it is coloured red.
What can we say about all the numbers that are on the
red part?

They are all equal to or greater than 1.
In algebra we write $x \geqslant 1$
Some possible values for x are 2, 2.5, 3.2, $5\frac{1}{2}$, 8, 39.03,
67, 500 000 and so on.

On this number line the numbers on the red part are all
less than or equal to 3.

In algebra we write $x \leqslant 3$

Exercise 15:4

Use algebra to describe the numbers on the red part of the number line.

Inequalities   The signs $<$ $\leqslant$ $>$ $\geqslant$ are all called inequality signs.

$x < 3$ $x \leqslant 5$ $x > 1$ $x \geqslant -2$ are called **inequalities**.

Draw a number line for each question.
Colour part of the number line to show the inequality.

7 $x \geqslant 2$ **9** $x \geqslant 0$ **11** $x \leqslant 1$

8 $x \geqslant -3$ **10** $x \leqslant 3$ **12** $x \leqslant -2$

Examples   **1** Write down the possible values of x if x is a whole number and $x \geqslant 2$

The possible values of x are 2, 3, 4, 5, 6, ...
(... means that the numbers carry on in this way)

2 Write down the first five possible values of x if x is a whole number and $x > 2$

The first five possible values are 3, 4, 5, 6, 7

Exercise 15:5

Write down the first five possible values of x if x is a whole number and:

1 $x \geqslant 4$ **4** $x < 2$ **7** $x \leqslant -2$

2 $x > -3$ **5** $x \geqslant 0$ **8** $x < -8$

3 $x \leqslant 5$ **6** $x < 0$ **9** $x \geqslant -7$

Sometimes you are asked to give just one of the possible values of x.
You can choose any one that you want.

Write down one possible value for x if x is a whole number and:

10 $x > 2$ **12** $x < -1$ **14** $x > -9$

11 $x \leqslant 3$ **13** $x \geqslant 8$ **15** $x \leqslant 1$

16 Write down one possible value for x if $x > 2$ and x is a square number.

17 Write down the highest value x can have if $x < 5$ and x is a whole number.

18 Write down the lowest value x can have if $x \geqslant 2$ and x is a whole number.

Nathan wants to show $x > 1$ on a number line.
He starts colouring the line. He doesn't know how to show that 1 is not a possible value.

He draws a line above the number line like this:

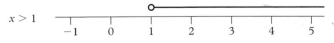

The circle above the 1 is not coloured in.
This shows that 1 is not a possible value of x.

Nathan shows $x \geq 1$ on a number line like this:

$x \geq 1$

The circle above the 1 is coloured in. This shows that 1 is a possible value of x.

$x \leq 3$ on a number line is

$x < 3$ on a number line is

Exercise 15:6

Show these inequalities on number lines.

1 $x \geq 2$ **4** $x \geq -1$ **7** $x < -3$

2 $x > 1$ **5** $x \leq 3$ **8** $x > -4$

3 $x < 4$ **6** $x \leq -2$ **9** $x \geq 0$

Write down the inequality shown on the number line.

10

11

12

13

14

15

Michael wants to go on a fairground ride. He can only go on this ride if his height is at least 120 cm but less than 160 cm.
We write $h \geqslant 120$ and $h < 160$
We can show these on a number line.

$h \geqslant 120$
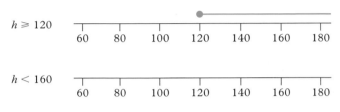

$h < 160$

Michael's height must fit both the inequalities. We look for the overlap of the lines.

In algebra we write $120 \leqslant h < 160$
We have made the two inequalities into one double inequality.

Exercise 15:7

Show these inequalities on number lines.

1 $2 \leqslant x < 4$ **3** $0 < x \leqslant 5$ **5** $-5 \leqslant x \leqslant -1$

2 $1 \leqslant x \leqslant 6$ **4** $-4 \leqslant x < 3$ **6** $-3 < x < 0$

Write down the inequality shown on the number line.

7

10

8

11

9

12

Example   Write down all the possible values of x if x is a
whole number and $1 \leqslant x \leqslant 5$

$1 \leqslant x \leqslant 5$ on a number line is

But x can only be a whole number.
The possible values of x are 1, 2, 3, 4, 5

Write down all the possible values of x if x is a whole number and:

13 $3 \leqslant x \leqslant 5$ **15** $7 \leqslant x \leqslant 10$ **17** $-7 \leqslant x \leqslant -3$

14 $0 \leqslant x \leqslant 4$ **16** $-2 \leqslant x \leqslant 1$ **18** $2 \leqslant x \leqslant 3$

Example   Write down all the possible values of x if x is a
whole number and $2 \leqslant x < 4$

$2 \leqslant x < 4$ on a number line is

But x can only be a whole number.
The possible values of x are 2, 3
(4 is not a possible value because $x < 4$ means that 4 is
not included.)

Exercise 15:8

Write down all the possible values of x if x is a whole number and:

1 $1 \leqslant x < 6$ **3** $3 < x \leqslant 7$ **5** $7 < x < 13$

2 $-2 \leqslant x < 3$ **4** $-6 < x \leqslant 0$ **6** $-9 \leqslant x < -2$

Write down one possible value for x if x is a whole number and:

7 $5 \leqslant x < 8$ **9** $3 < x < 5$ **11** $-7 < x < -5$

8 $-1 < x \leqslant 2$ **10** $0 \leqslant x < 5$ **12** $0 \leqslant x \leqslant 2$

3 Solving simple linear inequalities

The lift cable will break if there are too many people in the lift.
The cable is safe if the total weight of the lift and people is
less than or equal to 1400 kg.

weight of people + weight of lift ≤ 1400

The weight of the lift is 824 kg.

$$w + 824 \leqslant 1400$$

We need to solve the inequality to find the maximum safe weight of people.
We do this in the same way as we solved equations.
We use inverses.

$$w + 824 \leqslant 1400$$

The inverse of + 824 is −824

$$w + 824 - 824 \leqslant 1400 - 824$$
$$w \leqslant 576$$

We have solved the inequality.
The maximum safe weight of people is 576 kg.

Exercise 15:9

Solve these inequalities using inverses.

1 $x + 3 \geqslant 5$ **2** $x + 6 \leqslant 9$ **3** $x + 2 < 6$

Example

Solve the inequality $x - 3 < 7$
Show the answer on a number line.

$$x - 3 + 3 < 7 + 3$$
$$x < 10$$

Solve these inequalities.
Show the answers on number lines.

4 $x + 1 < 2$ **6** $x - 1 \leqslant 3$ **8** $x - 6 > 1$

5 $x - 2 \geqslant 7$ **7** $x + 4 \leqslant 6$ **9** $x - 5 \leqslant 4$

10 Bill's small van cannot carry more than 1000 kg.
This includes Bill's weight.

weight of boxes + Bill's weight $\leqslant 1000$

Bill weighs 85 kg.
What is the greatest weight of boxes that Bill can put in the van?

Write down the first five possible values for x if x is a whole number and:

11 $x + 1 \leqslant 5$ **13** $x - 5 \geqslant 3$ **15** $x - 1 \leqslant 1$

12 $x - 3 > 2$ **14** $x + 6 < 7$ **16** $x - 3 < 0$

Write down one possible value for x if x is a whole number and:

17 $x - 2 > 12$ **19** $x + 7 < 20$ **21** $x + 9 > 1$

18 $x + 6 \leqslant 5$ **20** $x - 8 \geqslant 2$ **22** $x + 5 \geqslant 0$

Example

Solve the inequality $3x \geqslant 12$

$3x$ means that x is multiplied by 3.
The inverse of $\times 3$ is $\div 3$

$$\frac{3x}{3} \geqslant \frac{12}{3}$$

Remember: $\dfrac{12}{3}$ means $12 \div 3$

$$x \geqslant 4$$

Exercise 15:10

Solve these inequalities.

1 $5x > 25$ **4** $3x < 21$

2 $2x \leqslant 8$ **5** $10x \geqslant 40$

3 $4x \geqslant 12$ **6** $6x \leqslant 18$

Example   Solve the inequality $\dfrac{x}{4} > 2$

$\dfrac{x}{4}$ means that x is divided by 4.

The inverse of $\div 4$ is $\times 4$

$$\dfrac{x}{4} \times 4 \geqslant 2 \times 4$$
$$x \geqslant 8$$

Solve these inequalities.

7 $\dfrac{x}{2} < 6$ **10** $\dfrac{x}{8} \geqslant 5$

8 $\dfrac{x}{5} \geqslant 3$ **11** $\dfrac{x}{3} > 7$

9 $\dfrac{x}{7} \leqslant 10$ **12** $\dfrac{x}{9} \leqslant 11$

13 A chef cuts a large cheesecake into 24 slices.
Each slice must weigh at least 150 g.

$$\dfrac{\text{weight of cheesecake}}{24} \geqslant 150$$

Solve this inequality to find the minimum weight of the cheesecake.

1 Solve these equations by trial and improvement.
For each question:
  copy the table
  fill it in
  add more rows until you find the answer to 1 dp.

a $x^2 + 25 = 210$

Value of x	Value of $x^2 + 25$	
10		
20		

b $x^2 + 140 = 615$

Value of x	Value of $x^2 + 140$	
20		
30		

2 Solve $3a^2 = 1083$ by trial and improvement.
Remember: $3a^2$ means $3 \times a^2$

3 Show these inequalities on number lines.

a $x < 5$ c $x \leqslant -3$ e $x \leqslant 1$

b $x \geqslant -4$ d $x > 0$ f $x > -6$

4 Write down the inequality shown on the number line.

a

b

c

d

5 Write down the first five possible values of x if x is a whole number and:

a $x \geqslant 5$ c $x \leqslant 3$ e $x > 7$

b $x \geqslant -3$ d $x \leqslant -6$ f $x < -1$

6 Write down one possible value for x if $x > 11$ and x is a square number.

7 Write down one possible value for x if $x \geq 8$ and x is a prime number.

8 Write down one possible value for x if $x \geq 12$ and x is a cube number.

9 Write down the highest value x can have if $x < 8$ and x is a whole number.

10 Write down the lowest value x can have if $x \geq 6$ and x is a whole number.

11 Write down one possible value for x if $x < 7$ and x is a square number.

12 Write down one possible value for x if $x \leq 9$ and x is an even number.

13 Show these inequalities on number lines.
   a $5 \leq x < 8$ **c** $-2 < x \leq 5$ **e** $-7 \leq x < -3$
   b $0 < x \leq 4$ **d** $-5 \leq x \leq 0$ **f** $-1 \leq x < 0$

14 Write down all the possible values of x if x is a whole number and:
   a $3 \leq x < 7$ **c** $0 \leq x \leq 4$ **e** $-7 < x \leq -3$
   b $-1 < x \leq 5$ **d** $-2 \leq x < 0$ **f** $-9 \leq x < -8$

15 Solve these inequalities.
   Show the answers on number lines.
   a $x + 9 \leq 15$ **c** $x - 5 > 0$ **e** $x + 5 < 2$
   b $a - 3 \geq 10$ **d** $s - 8 \geq -3$ **f** $x + 7 \geq 7$

16 Write down the first five possible values of x if x is a whole number and:
   a $x - 10 \geq 6$ **c** $\dfrac{x}{2} \geq 16$ **e** $\dfrac{x}{8} \leq 5$

   b $4x < 12$ **d** $6x > 24$ **f** $\dfrac{x}{9} > 3$

1 Solve $x^2 + x = 153$ by trial and improvement.
Copy this table to help you.
Give your answer correct to 1 dp.

Value of x	Value of $x^2 + x$	

2 Solve $2x^2 + x = 271$ by trial and improvement.
Copy this table to help you.
Give your answer correct to 1 dp.

Value of x	Value of $2x^2 + x$	

3 **a** Write down all the possible values of x if x is a whole number and
$2 \leqslant x \leqslant 5$
b These inequalities give the same possible values of x as part **a**.
Copy and fill in:
$\ldots < x \leqslant 5$ $\qquad \ldots < x < \ldots$ $\qquad \ldots \leqslant x < \ldots$

In questions 4–7 x is a whole number.

4 Write down the four inequalities that have 5, 6, 7, 8, 9 as the
possible values of x.

5 Write down the four inequalities that have -3, -2, -1, 0 as the
possible values of x.

6 What inequalities have 7 as the only possible value of x?

7 What inequalities have -4 as the only possible value of x?

- ## *Trial and improvement*

  Example   Solve $x^2 = 135$

Value of x	Value of x^2	
11	121	too small
12	144	too big
11.5	132.25	too small
11.6	134.56	too small
11.7	136.89	too big
11.65	135.7225	too big

  x is between 11 and 12
  x is between 11.5 and 12
  x is between 11.6 and 12
  x is between 11.6 and 11.7
  x is between 11.6 and 11.65

  x must be somewhere in the green part of the number line. Any number in the green part rounds down to 11.6 to 1 dp.

  11.6   11.65   11.7

  Answer: $x = 11.6$ to 1 dp.

- **Inequalities** The signs $< \leqslant > \geqslant$ are called inequality signs.

  $x < 3$ $x \leqslant 5$ $x > 1$ $x \geqslant -2$ are all called **inequalities**.

- *Example*   Write down the possible values of x if x is a whole number and $x \geqslant 2$

  The possible values are 2, 3, 4, 5, 6, ...

- *Example*   Write down all the possible values of x if x is a whole number and $2 \leqslant x < 4$

  $2 \leqslant x < 4$ on a number line is

  But x is a whole number.
  The possible values of x are 2, 3
  (4 is not a possible value because $x < 4$ means that 4 is not included.)

- *Example*   Solve the inequality $x - 3 < 7$
  Show the answer on a number line.

  $x - 3 + 3 < 7 + 3$
  $x < 10$

1 Solve $x^2 + 56 = 622$ by trial and improvement.
Copy this table. Fill it in.
Add more rows until you have found x correct to 1 dp.

Value of x	Value of $x^2 + 56$	
20		

2 Show these inequalities on number lines.
 a $x \geqslant -1$ **c** $x < 4$
 b $3 < x \leqslant 6$ **d** $-1 \leqslant x < 2$

3 Write down all the possible values of x if x is a whole number and $7 \leqslant x < 11$

4 Write down the highest value x can have if $x < 7$ and x is a whole number.

5 Write down the lowest value x can have if $x \geqslant 8$ and x is a whole number.

6 Solve these inequalities.
Show the answers on number lines.
 a $x + 3 < 7$ **b** $x - 4 \geqslant 1$

7 Solve these inequalities.
 a $3x \geqslant 18$ **b** $\dfrac{x}{4} \leqslant 2$

8 Write down the inequality shown on the number line.

16 The crossing point

Each symbol in the diagram has a value. The total values are placed alongside some rows and columns. What number should replace the question mark to give the value of the bottom row?

1 Intersecting lines

You can use robots to draw lines.

Example

The robot has to draw the line
$y = 2x + 1$
He uses the x values 1, 2, 3

He plots the points (1, 3) (2, 5)
(3, 7)
He joins them with a ruler.
He labels his line with its
equation $y = 2x + 1$

You only need two points to
draw a straight line. The third
point acts as a check.

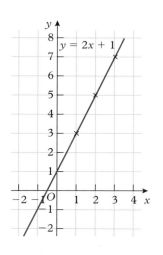

Exercise 16:1

Use robot screens to do this question.
Use the *x* values 1, 2, 3.

1 Copy the axes on to squared paper.
  a Draw the line $y = x + 2$
    Label your line.
  b On the same set of axes draw the line $y = 3x - 2$
    Label your line.
  c Write down the co-ordinates of the
    point where the two lines cross.
    Remember: this is called a
    point of intersection.

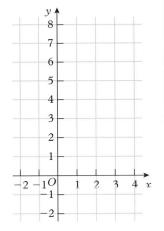

2 Copy the axes from question **1**.
  a Draw and label the line $y = 2x - 1$
  b Draw and label the line $y = 3$
  c Write down the co-ordinates of the point of intersection of the lines.

You can use tables to plot graphs instead of robots.

Example   Draw the line $y = 2x + 3$

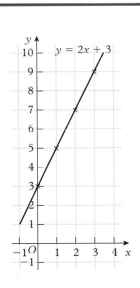

We can find the value of *y* when $x = 1$
$$y = 2 \times 1 + 3$$
$$= 2 + 3$$
$$= 5$$

Similarly: when $x = 2$ when $x = 3$
          $y = 2 \times 2 + 3$ $y = 2 \times 3 + 3$
             $= 4 + 3$ $= 6 + 3$
             $= 7$ $= 9$

This gives the points (1, 5) (2, 7) (3, 9)
We can put these points in a table.

x	1	2	3
y	5	7	9

We can now draw the line $y = 2x + 3$

3 Copy the axes from question **1** again.

  a (1) Make a table for $y = 3x - 1$

     (2) Draw and label the line $y = 3x - 1$

  b (1) Make a table for $y = x - 1$

     (2) Draw and label the line $y = x - 1$

  c Write down the co-ordinates of the point of intersection of the lines.

Make a table for each of these lines. Do not draw the lines.
Use the x values 1, 2, 3.

4 $y = 4x + 1$ **7** $y = 3x - 7$

5 $y = 5x - 3$ **8** $y = 4x - 8$

6 $y = 4 + 2x$ **9** $y = 6 - x$

10 Copy the axes on to squared paper.

  a (1) Make a table for $y = 3 - x$

     (2) Draw and label the line $y = 3 - x$

  b (1) Make a table for $y = 2x - 3$

     (2) Draw and label the line $y = 2x - 3$

  c Write down the co-ordinates of the point of intersection of the lines.

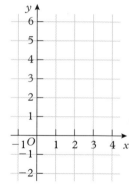

11 Copy the axes on to squared paper.

  a (1) Make a table for $y = 3x + 1$

     (2) Draw and label the line $y = 3x + 1$

  b (1) Make a table for $y = 3x - 3$

     (2) Draw and label the line $y = 3x - 3$

  c Explain why there is no point of intersection of the lines.

2 Lines that do not start with y

Sometimes equations of lines are written in a different way.

Example   Draw the line $x + y = 5$

We do not use $x = 1$, 2 and 3 for this type of equation.
It is easier to find points when $x = 0$ and when $y = 0$

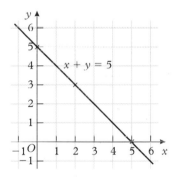

When $x = 0$ When $y = 0$
  $0 + y = 5$ $x + 0 = 5$
     $y = 5$ $x = 5$
This gives (0, 5)   This gives (5, 0)

It is useful to find a third point.
Try another value of x
$x = 2$ $2 + y = 5$
               $y = 3$
This gives (2, 3)

We could use (1, 4) (3, 2) or (4, 1)
They all follow the rule $x + y = 5$

We now have three points so we can draw the line.

Exercise 16:2

1 Copy the axes on to squared paper.
  a Find the co-ordinates of three points on the line $x + y = 6$
  b Plot the points.
    They should be in a straight line.
    Draw and label the line $x + y = 6$

Repeat question **1** for these lines.
Plot all the lines on the same diagram.
Label each line.

2 $x + y = 7$

3 $x + y = 4$

4 $x + y = 3$

5 $x + y = 2$

Example Draw the line $x + 2y = 4$

When $x = 0$ When $y = 0$
$0 + 2y = 4$ $x + 2 \times 0 = 4$
$2y = 4$ $x + 0 = 4$
$y = 2$ $x = 4$
This gives $(0, 2)$ This gives $(4, 0)$

Sometimes it is difficult to find a
third point.
We will use just two.

---

6 Copy the axes from question **1**.
  a Find the co-ordinates of two points on the line $x + 3y = 6$
  b Plot the points.
    Draw and label the line $x + 3y = 6$

Find two points on each of these lines. Do not draw the lines.

7 $3x + y = 9$

8 $2x + y = 8$

9 $5x + y = 10$

10 $x + 4y = 8$

11 $4x + y = 4$

12 $2x + 5y = 10$

13 $4x + 3y = 12$

● **14** $x - y = 2$

● **15** $2x + 3y = 18$

3   Solving problems with lines

You can use graphs of intersecting lines to solve problems.

Example   Charlotte and Brendan are buying presents.
Charlotte buys one *perfume* spray and one bottle of *aftershave* for £5.
Brendan buys three *perfume* sprays and two bottles of *aftershave* for £12.
Find the cost of a perfume spray and the cost of a bottle of aftershave.

Charlotte's equation is $p + a = 5$
Two points on this line are $(0, 5)$
and $(5, 0)$

Brendan's equation is $3p + 2a = 12$
Two points on this line are $(0, 6)$
and $(4, 0)$

The lines intersect at $(2, 3)$
This means that $p = 2$ and $a = 3$

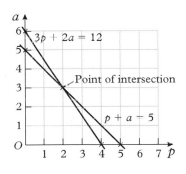

So a perfume spray costs £2 and a bottle of aftershave costs £3.

Check: We can check the answer.

Charlotte buys one perfume spray and one bottle of aftershave.
They cost £2 + £3, which is £5.

Brendan buys three perfume sprays and two bottles of aftershave.
They cost $3 \times £2 + 2 \times £3$, which is £12.

Simultaneous equations   Equations we solve at the same time like this are called **simultaneous equations**.

Exercise 16:3

Draw graphs to solve these problems.
Check your answers in the original problem each time.

1 A shop is having a sale of CDs and
games.
Sonya buys one **C**D and
one **g**ame for £10.
Jamie buys three **C**Ds and
two **g**ames for £24.
Find the cost of one CD and the
cost of one game.

2 The Smith family and the Patel
family go to the theatre together.
The Smiths buy one **a**dult ticket
and four **c**hildren's tickets at
a cost of £12.
The Patels buy two **a**dult tickets and
one **c**hild's ticket at a cost of £10.
Find the cost of an adult ticket and
the cost of a child's ticket.

3

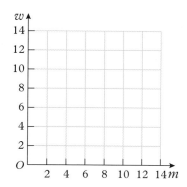

Denis is going fishing. He uses maggots and worms as bait for the fish.
Ten **m**aggots and four **w**orms cost 40 p.
One **m**aggot and one **w**orm cost 7 p.
Find the cost of one maggot and the cost of one worm.

4

Emma hires out boats.
Her charges are for one hour's hire of a rowing boat or canoe.
One Saturday morning she hires out one *r*owing boat and
two *c*anoes during the first hour.
She takes £10 for these.
During the second hour she hires out three *r*owing boats and
four *c*anoes and takes £24.
Find the cost of an hour's hire of a rowing boat and the cost of
an hour's hire of a canoe.

5 Stanthorne High is having
a school fair.
At the cake stall Henry
buys two *b*uns and five
pieces of *f*lapjack for 50 p.
His friend Wasim is less
greedy. Wasim only buys
one *b*un and one piece of
*f*lapjack for 13 p.
Find the cost of one bun
and the cost of one piece
of flapjack.

Kate has found a puzzle in a newspaper.

She has to find the value of each shape.

Example

Here is Kate's newspaper problem.
The shapes add up to the number shown.
Kate has to find the value of each shape.

▲	▲	●	●	10
▲	▲	●	■	12
■	■	■	■	16

She sees that four squares add up to 16.
One square must have value 4.

Two *t*riangles and two *c*ircles add up to 10. $2t + 2c = 10$

Two triangles, one circle and one square add up to 12.
Two *t*riangles and one *c*ircle must add up to 8. $2t + c = 8$

Two points on $2t + 2c = 10$ are $(0, 5)$ and $(5, 0)$
Two points on $2t + c = 8$ are $(0, 8)$ and $(4, 0)$

The lines intersect at $(3, 2)$
A triangle has value 3 and a circle has value 2.

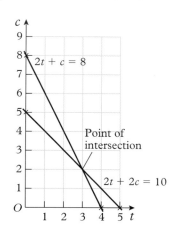

Exercise 16:4

Solve these picture puzzles.

1

♥	♣	♥	♥	9
♦	♦	♦	♦	20
♦	♦	♥	♣	15

2

B	A	A	C	16
B	B	A	A	14
C	C	C	C	32

You don't always need lines to solve puzzles.
Here are some puzzles to solve without lines.

Exercise 16:5

1 The numbers in ◯ and ◯ add up to the number in ☐ like this:

a Copy these.
Fill in the missing numbers.

(1)

(3)

(2) ...

b Write down the value of each letter:

(1)

(3)

(2)

(4)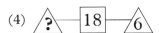

2 The numbers in △ and △ are multiplied to give the number in ☐ like this:

a Copy these.
Fill in the missing numbers.

(1)

(2) ...

b Write down the value of each letter.

(1)

(3)

(2)

1 **a** Copy the axes on to squared paper.
　b Use a robot screen to draw the
　　line $y = 3x + 1$
　　Use the x values 1, 2, 3.
　　Label your line.
　c On the same set of axes draw the
　　line $x = 2$
　　Label your line.
　d Write down the co-ordinates of the
　　point of intersection of the lines.

2 Copy the axes from question **1** again.
　a (1) Make a table for $y = x + 5$
　　 (2) Draw and label the line $y = x + 5$
　b (1) Make a table for $y = 4x - 4$
　　 (2) Draw and label the line $y = 4x - 4$
　c Write down the co-ordinates of the point of intersection of the lines.

3 Copy the axes on to squared paper.
　a Find the co-ordinates of three
　　points on the line $x + y = 7$
　b Plot the points.
　　They should be in a straight line.
　　Draw and label the line $x + y = 7$
　c Find the co-ordinates of three
　　points on the line $x + y = 3$
　d Plot the points.
　　They should be in a straight line.
　　Draw and label the line $x + y = 3$
　e What can you say about the
　　two lines?

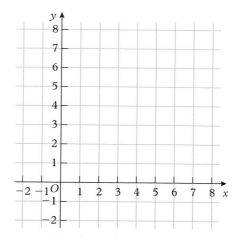

4 Find two points on each of these lines. Do not draw the lines.
　a $x + 9y = 18$　　　　**c** $3x + 5y = 15$
　b $3x + y = 30$　　　　**d** $2x + 7y = 14$

352

5 Copy the axes on to squared paper.
At the Stanthorne High school fair,
a school enterprise company is
selling scarves and ties.
The headteacher buys five *scarves*
and three *ties* for £30.
Paula buys one *scarf* and one *tie*
for £8.
Find the cost of a scarf and the
cost of a tie.

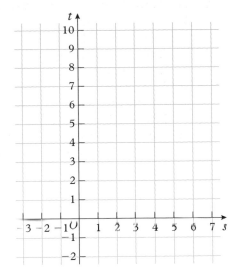

6 Copy the axes on to squared paper.
Two families go out ten-pin
bowling together.
The Morley family pay £24 for
two *adults* and one *child*.
The Pleavin family pay £27 for
one *adult* and three *children*.
Find the cost of a child's ticket and
the cost of an adult's ticket.

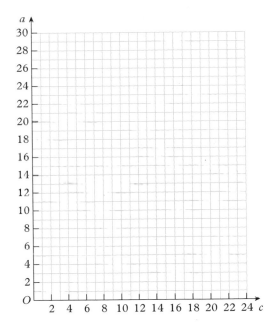

Solve these picture puzzles.

7

▲	▲	▲	▲	36
■	■	▲		19
▲	■		▲	25

8

♥	♥	♣	♦	15
♣	♣	♣	♣	28
♥	♣	♦	♦	17

1 a Three points on this line are
marked ×.
Write down their co-ordinates.
Look at the numbers in the
co-ordinates of each point.
What do you notice?

b These points lie on the line.
Use your answer to **a** to find the
missing co-ordinates.

(8, ...)   (..., 13)
$(5\frac{1}{2}, ...)$ $(..., 7\frac{1}{2})$

c The point (1, 6) is above the line.
Look at these points:

(7, 4)   (6, 9)   (5, 11)   (9, 10)

(1) Which one of these points is above the line?
Explain your answer.
(2) Which points are below the line?

d The point (..., 20) is above the line.
Write down a possible x co-ordinate for the point.

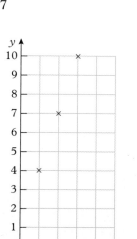

2 Solve this puzzle.

P	P	P	P	P	30
B	B	B	A	A	18
P	P	B	A	A	22

3 Look at these pairs of lines.
Which pair of lines will not intersect?
Explain your answer.

a $y = 2x + 3$ **b** $y = 4x - 1$ **c** $y = x + 8$
$y = 3x + 2$ $y = 4x + 1$ $x + y = 7$

4 Karen and Adam are playing a game
using a set of axes.
Karen chooses an equation of a
straight line without telling Adam.
She puts crosses on the grid in red
until Adam can guess the equation
of the line.
Look at the grid and write down the
co-ordinates of Karen's crosses.
Work out the equation of the line.

● *Example* Draw the graph of $y = 2x + 3$

When $x = 1$ When $x = 2$ When $x = 3$
$y = 2 \times 1 + 3$ $y = 2 \times 2 + 3$ $y = 2 \times 3 + 3$
$\quad = 2 + 3$ $\quad = 4 + 3$ $\quad = 6 + 3$
$\quad = 5$ $\quad = 7$ $\quad = 9$

This gives the points $(1, 5)$ $(2, 7)$ $(3, 9)$
You can put these points in a table.

x	1	2	3
y	5	7	9

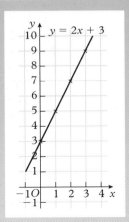

● *Example* Draw the line $x + 2y = 4$

When $x = 0$ When $y = 0$
$0 + 2y = 4$ $x + 2 \times 0 = 4$
$\quad 2y = 4$ $\quad x + 0 = 4$
$\quad\quad y = 2$ $\quad\quad x = 4$
This gives $(0, 2)$ This gives $(4, 0)$

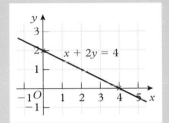

Sometimes it is difficult to find a third point. You can draw a graph with two.

● *Example*

Charlotte and Brendan are buying presents.
Charlotte buys one *perfume* spray and
one bottle of *aftershave* for £5.
Brendan buys three *perfume* sprays and
two bottles of *aftershave* for £12.
Find the cost of a perfume spray and the
cost of a bottle of aftershave.

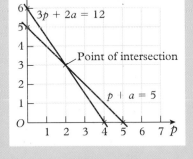

Charlotte's equation is $p + a = 5$
Two points on this line are $(0, 5)$ and $(5, 0)$

Brendan's equation is $3p + 2a = 12$
Two points on this line are $(0, 6)$ and $(4, 0)$

The lines intersect at $(2, 3)$
This means that $p = 2$ and $a = 3$

So a perfume spray costs £2 and a bottle of aftershave costs £3.

Simultaneous equations Equations we solve at the same time like this are called **simultaneous equations**.

1 Copy the axes on to squared paper.
  a (1) Make a table for $y = x + 1$
       Use the x values 1, 2, 3.
     (2) Draw and label the line $y = x + 1$
  b (1) Make a table for $y = 2x - 3$
     (2) Draw and label the line $y = 2x - 3$
  c Write down the co-ordinates of the
     point of intersection of the lines.

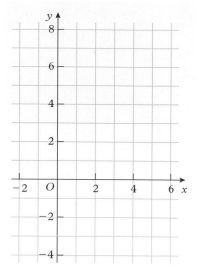

2 Find two points on each of these lines. Do not draw the lines.
  a $x + y = 7$ **c** $x + 3y = 6$
  b $2x + y = 4$ **d** $3x + 2y = 12$

3 Steven buys two **c**hicken and chips and three **s**ausage and chips for £12.
  Keeley buys four **c**hicken and chips and two **s**ausage and chips for £16.

  a Copy the axes on to squared paper.
  b Write the things that Keeley and Steven
     buy as two equations.
  c Solve the two equations by plotting lines.
     Write down the cost of one chicken and
     chips and one sausage and chips.
  d Check your answers in the original
     problem.

Help yourself

1 Adding

You should set out additions in columns.

Example

$14 + 8$

```
  1 4
+   8
  2 2
  ₁
```

Here are some more examples.

$36 + 28$

```
  3 6
+ 2 8
  6 4
  ₁
```

$237 + 46$

```
  2 3 7
+   4 6
  2 8 3
    ₁
```

$685 + 78$

```
  6 8 5
+   7 8
  7 6 3
  ₁ ₁
```

Exercise 1

Copy these into your book.
Work out the answers.

1.
```
  2 5
+   9
```

2.
```
  2 8
+ 1 6
```

3.
```
  3 7
+ 2 5
```

4.
```
  1 4 7
+   2 8
```

5.
```
  2 7 5
+   2 4
```

6.
```
  5 6 8
+   9 3
```

7.
```
  2 4 8
+ 1 8 5
```

8.
```
  5 2 6
+ 4 1 9
```

9. $38 + 57$

10. $95 + 46$

11. $114 + 97$

12. $57 + 253$

13. $85 + 438$

14. $757 + 864$

Other words

All these words can also mean **add**.

plus   **sum**   **total**

Examples
Work out 25 **plus** 14
Find the **sum** of 25 and 14
Find the **total** of 25 and 14

all mean
```
    2 5
+   1 4
    3 9
```

2 Subtracting

Subtractions should also be set out in columns.

Example

$54 - 28$

The 5 is worth
5 lots of 10.
We can 'borrow' →
one of these 10s.
We change it into
ten ones.

```
  5 4
- 2 8
```
← The 8 is
bigger
than
the 4.

Our working now looks like this:

$$\begin{array}{r} \overset{4}{\cancel{5}}\overset{1}{4} \\ -\ 2\ 8 \\ \hline 2\ 6 \end{array}$$ ← We can now take the 8 away from the 14.

Here is another example:

$75 - 39$

$$\begin{array}{r} 7\ 5 \\ -\ 3\ 9 \\ \hline \end{array} \rightarrow \begin{array}{r} \overset{6}{\cancel{7}}\overset{1}{5} \\ -\ 3\ 9 \\ \hline \end{array} \rightarrow \begin{array}{r} \overset{6}{\cancel{7}}\overset{1}{5} \\ -\ 3\ 9 \\ \hline 3\ 6 \end{array}$$

Here are some more difficult examples:

$92 - 45 \qquad 278 - 159 \qquad 734 - 457$

$$\begin{array}{r} \overset{8}{\cancel{9}}\overset{1}{2} \\ -\ 4\ 5 \\ \hline 4\ 7 \end{array} \qquad \begin{array}{r} 2\ \overset{6}{\cancel{7}}\overset{1}{8} \\ -\ 1\ 5\ 9 \\ \hline 1\ 1\ 9 \end{array} \qquad \begin{array}{r} \overset{6}{\cancel{7}}\overset{12}{\cancel{3}}\overset{1}{4} \\ -\ 4\ 5\ 7 \\ \hline 2\ 7\ 7 \end{array}$$

Exercise 2

Copy these into your book.
Work out the answers.

1 $\quad\begin{array}{r} 3\ 7 \\ -\ 1\ 8 \\ \hline \end{array}$ **4** $\quad\begin{array}{r} 2\ 5\ 3 \\ -\ 3\ 5 \\ \hline \end{array}$

2 $\quad\begin{array}{r} 8\ 6 \\ -\ 4\ 9 \\ \hline \end{array}$ **5** $\quad\begin{array}{r} 4\ 2\ 3 \\ -\ 3\ 1\ 9 \\ \hline \end{array}$

3 $\quad\begin{array}{r} 5\ 4 \\ -\ 2\ 7 \\ \hline \end{array}$ **6** $\quad\begin{array}{r} 6\ 3\ 4 \\ -\ 1\ 6\ 6 \\ \hline \end{array}$

7 $193 - 58$ **10** $621 - 438$

8 $275 - 167$ **11** $417 - 309$

9 $513 - 374$ **12** $526 - 438$

You cannot borrow from the next column if there is a zero in it.
You may need to borrow across more than one column.

Example

$$\begin{array}{r} 5\ 0\ 0 \\ -\ 1\ 8\ 6 \\ \hline \end{array} \rightarrow \begin{array}{r} \overset{4}{\cancel{5}}\overset{1}{0}\ 0 \\ -\ 1\ 8\ 6 \\ \hline \end{array} \rightarrow \begin{array}{r} \overset{4}{\cancel{5}}\overset{9}{\cancel{0}}\overset{1}{0} \\ -\ 1\ 8\ 6 \\ \hline 3\ 1\ 4 \end{array}$$

Exercise 3

Copy these into your book.
Work out the answers.

1 $\quad\begin{array}{r} 4\ 0\ 0 \\ -\ 1\ 7\ 3 \\ \hline \end{array}$ **3** $\quad\begin{array}{r} 8\ 0\ 0\ 0 \\ -\ 3\ 6\ 4 \\ \hline \end{array}$

2 $\quad\begin{array}{r} 8\ 0\ 0 \\ -\ 2\ 3\ 6 \\ \hline \end{array}$ **4** $\quad\begin{array}{r} 7\ 0\ 0\ 0 \\ -\ 4\ 3\ 2\ 8 \\ \hline \end{array}$

Other words

All these words can also mean **subtract**.

| take away | take |
| minus | difference |

Examples
Find 54 **take away** 26
Work out 54 **take** 26
Find 54 **minus** 26
Find the **difference** between 54 and 26

all mean $\quad\begin{array}{r} \overset{4}{\cancel{5}}\overset{1}{4} \\ -\ 2\ 6 \\ \hline 2\ 8 \end{array}$

Checking

You can always check a subtraction by adding.

Example

$256 - 183$

$$\begin{array}{r} \overset{1\ 1}{2}56 \\ -\ 183 \\ \hline 73 \end{array} \qquad \text{check} \qquad \begin{array}{r} 183 \\ +\ 73 \\ \hline 256 \end{array}$$

Go back to your answers for Exercise **5**. Check each of them by adding.

3 Multiplying

When we are adding lots of the same number it is quicker to multiply.

Example

$$\begin{array}{r} 31 \\ 31 \\ 31 \\ 31 \\ +\ 31 \\ \hline 155 \end{array} \quad \text{is the same as} \quad \begin{array}{r} 31 \\ \times\ \ 5 \\ \hline 155 \end{array}$$

To do $\begin{array}{r} 31 \\ \times\ \ 5 \\ \hline \end{array}$ first do 5×1 $\begin{array}{r} 31 \\ \times\ \ 5 \\ \hline 5 \end{array}$

then do 5×3 $\begin{array}{r} 31 \\ \times\ \ 5 \\ \hline 155 \end{array}$

Remember to keep your numbers in columns.

Here are some more examples:

$$\begin{array}{r} 62 \\ \times\ \ 4 \\ \hline 248 \end{array} \qquad \begin{array}{r} 51 \\ \times\ \ 9 \\ \hline 459 \end{array}$$

Exercise 4

1 $\begin{array}{r} 23 \\ \times\ \ 2 \\ \hline \end{array}$ **2** $\begin{array}{r} 213 \\ \times\ \ \ \ 3 \\ \hline \end{array}$

3 52×4 **4** 331×3

Sometimes we need to carry.

Example

$$\begin{array}{r} 26 \\ \times\ \ 3 \\ \hline 8 \\ \scriptstyle 1 \end{array} \quad \longrightarrow \quad \begin{array}{r} 26 \\ \times\ \ 3 \\ \hline 78 \\ \scriptstyle 1 \end{array}$$

$3 \times 2 = 6$
Then add the 1 to give 7

Exercise 5

1 $\begin{array}{r} 37 \\ \times\ \ 2 \\ \hline \end{array}$ **2** $\begin{array}{r} 45 \\ \times\ \ 2 \\ \hline \end{array}$

3 46×4 **7** 146×9

4 124×3 **8** 178×9

5 259×2 **9** 357×5

6 637×5 **10** 803×4

Other words

These words can also mean **multiply**.

times   **product**   **of**

Examples

Find 24 **times** 16
Find the **product** of 24 and 16
Find one half **of** 24

4 Multiplying by 10

When we multiply by 10, all the digits move across **one** column to the **left**. This makes the number 10 times bigger.
We can use the headings **Th H T U** to help.
They mean **Th**ousands, **H**undreds, **T**ens and **U**nits. Units is another way of saying 'ones'.

Example 1

23 × 10 = 230

H   T   U

         2   3
      2   3   0

Example 2

Th H   T   U

         4   6   46 × 10 = 460
      4   6   0

      2   5   3   253 × 10 = 2530
   2   5   3   0

Exercise 6

Multiply each of these numbers by 10.

1	39	4	756	7	5000
2	45	5	684	8	8007
3	128	6	1562		

5   Multiplying by 100, 1000, ...

When we multiply by 100, all the digits move across **two** columns to the **left**.

This makes the number 100 times bigger.
This is because 100 = 10 × 10. So multiplying by 100 is like multiplying by 10 twice.

Example

74 × 100 = 7400

Th   H   T   U

7   4   0   0

When we multiply by 1000 all the numbers move across three columns to the left.

This is because 1000 = 10 × 10 × 10. This means that multiplying by 1000 is like multiplying by 10 three times.

Example

74 × 1000 = 74 000

TTh Th H   T   U

7   4   0   0   0

Exercise 7

Write down the answers to these.

1	75 × 100	7	5243 × 100
2	82 × 100	8	800 × 1000
3	36 × 1000	9	5004 × 1000
4	178 × 100	10	815 × 10 000
5	3190 × 100	11	302 × 10 000
6	420 × 1000	12	835 × 100 000

6 Multiplying by 20, 30, ...

When we multiply by 20 it is like multiplying by 2 then by 10. This is because $20 = 2 \times 10$.

Example

To do 18×20
first do

$$\begin{array}{r} 18 \\ \times\ \ 2 \\ \hline 36 \\ \hline {\scriptstyle 1} \end{array}$$

Then do $\quad 36 \times 10 = 360$

So $\quad 18 \times 20 = 360$

In the same way multiplying by 30 is the same as multiplying by 3 and then multiplying by 10.

Example

To do 26×30:
first do

$$\begin{array}{r} 26 \\ \times\ \ 3 \\ \hline 78 \\ \hline {\scriptstyle 1} \end{array}$$

Then do $\quad 78 \times 10 = 780$

So $\quad 26 \times 30 = 780$

Exercise 8

Work these out.

1	28×20	**7**	83×40
2	36×20	**8**	45×50
3	27×30	**9**	62×50
4	34×30	**10**	213×20
5	58×30	**11**	371×30
6	26×40	**12**	425×70

362

7 Multiplying decimals by 10

We can multiply decimals by 10 in the same way.

Example

56.87×10

$$56.87 \times 10 = 568.7$$

Exercise 9

Multiply these decimals by 10.

1	9.5	**3**	17.83	**5**	10.7
2	28.2	**4**	86.31	**6**	0.9

8 Multiplying decimals by 100

When we multiply by 100, all the digits move across **two** columns to the **left**.

Example

27.65×100

$$27.65 \times 100 = 2765$$

Exercise 10

Multiply these decimals by 100.

1	42.91	**3**	71.6	**5**	60.59
2	57.04	**4**	137.4	**6**	7.08

9 Long multiplication

When we want to multiply two quite large numbers we have to do it in stages.
Here are two methods. You only have to know one of them.

Method 1

Example
146 × 24

First do 146 × 4

```
    1 4 6
  ×     4
    5 8 4
    1 2
```

Then do 146 × 20

```
    1 4 6
  ×     2
    2 9 2
      1
```

292 × 10 = 2920

Now add the two answers together.

```
    5 8 4
  + 2 9 2 0
    3 5 0 4
```

Usually the working out looks like this:

```
    1 4 6
  ×   2 4
    5 8 4
  2 9 2 0
  3 5 0 4
```

Here is another example.

```
    2 2 3
  ×   3 6
  1 3 3 8  ← (223 × 6)
  6 6 9 0  ← (223 × 30)
  8 0 2 8
  1 1
```

Method 2

Example
125 × 23

First set out the numbers with boxes,
like this:

Now draw in the diagonals like this:

Fill in like a table square then add
along the diagonals like this:

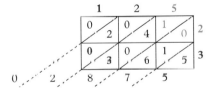

$1 \times 3 = 3$

Notice the 0 in the top box when the answer is a single digit.

So 125 × 23 = **2875**

Here is another example.
When the diagonal adds up to more
than 10, we carry into the next one.

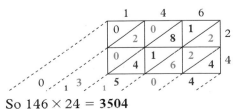

So 146 × 24 = **3504**

Exercise 11

Use the method you prefer to work these out.

1	34×25	**7**	391×43
2	63×34	**8**	172×84
3	123×42	**9**	545×33
4	314×26	**10**	612×65
5	271×35	**11**	754×61
6	257×53	**12**	989×98

Exercise 12

Work these out.

1	$12 \div 3$	**7**	$45 \div 9$
2	$45 \div 5$	**8**	$80 \div 10$
3	$30 \div 6$	**9**	$14 \div 2$
4	$20 \div 4$	**10**	$42 \div 6$
5	$32 \div 4$	**11**	$40 \div 8$
6	$21 \div 7$	**12**	$54 \div 9$

10 Dividing

Multiplying is like doing lots of additions. In the same way dividing is like doing lots of subtractions.

To find out how many 4s make 12 we can see how many times we can take 4 away from 12.

$12 - 4 = 8$ (once)
$8 - 4 = 4$ (twice)
$4 - 4 = 0$ (three times)

So there are 3 lots of 4 in 12.

We can say 12 divided by 4 is 3

or $12 \div 4 = 3$

Example

$15 \div 3 = ?$
$15 - 3 = 12$ (once)
$12 - 3 = 9$ (twice)
$9 - 3 = 6$ (three times)
$6 - 3 = 3$ (four times)
$3 - 3 = 0$ (five times)

So $15 \div 3 = 5$

When the numbers get bigger, this method takes too long. We need a new way to work it out.

Example

$68 \div 2$

$$2\overline{)68}$$

First work out $6 \div 2 = 3$. Put the 3 above the 6:

$$2\overline{)6\,8}^{\,3}$$

Now work out $8 \div 2 = 4$. Put the 4 above the 8:

$$2\overline{)6\,8}^{\,34}$$

So $68 \div 2 = 34$

Here is another example: $84 \div 4$

$$4\overline{)8\,4}^{\,21}$$

So $84 \div 4 = 21$

Exercise 13

Work these out.

1 2)84

2 3)93

3 5)55

4 96 ÷ 3

5 64 ÷ 2

6 884 ÷ 4

3 72 ÷ 4

4 64 ÷ 4

5 84 ÷ 7

6 76 ÷ 4

7 96 ÷ 6

8 128 ÷ 8

9 424 ÷ 4

10 276 ÷ 2

11 621 ÷ 3

12 364 ÷ 7

Sometimes we need to 'carry'. This happens when a number does not divide exactly.

Example

72 ÷ 4

4)72

First do 7 ÷ 4. This is 1 with 3 left over.
Put the 1 above the 7 and carry the 3 like this.

$$\overset{1}{4)7^32}$$

Now do 32 ÷ 4. This is 8. Put the 8 above the ^{3}2 like this

$$\overset{1\,8}{4)7^32}$$

So 72 ÷ 4 = 18

Here is another example: 85 ÷ 5

$$\overset{1\,7}{5)8^35}$$

So 85 ÷ 5 = 17

Exercise 14

Work these out.

1 2)58

2 3)54

11 Dividing by 10

When we divide by 10, all the digits move across **one** column to the **right**. This makes the number smaller.

Example

230 ÷ 10 = 23

H   T   U

2   3   0

2   3

Here are some more examples.

580 ÷ 10 = 58

2460 ÷ 10 = 246

Exercise 15

Divide these numbers by 10.

1 740

2 80

3 5960

4 830

5 9040

6 7200

7 5000

8 700 000

12 Dividing by 100, 1000, ...

When we divide by 100, all the digits move across **two** columns to the **right**. This is because $100 = 10 \times 10$. So dividing by 100 is like dividing by 10 twice.

Example

$7400 \div 100 = 74$

Th	H	T	U
7	4	0	0

$$\begin{array}{cccc} 7 & 4 & 0 & 0 \\ & \div 100 & \div 100 & \\ & & 7 & 4 \end{array}$$

When we divide by 1000, all the numbers move across **three** columns to the **right**.

Example

$74\,000 \div 1000 = 74$

TTh	Th	H	T	U
7	4	0	0	0

$$\begin{array}{ccccc} 7 & 4 & 0 & 0 & 0 \\ & \div 1000 & \div 1000 & & \\ & & & 7 & 4 \end{array}$$

Exercise 16

Work these out.

1	$7800 \div 100$	**5**	$78\,000 \div 100$
2	$5300 \div 100$	**6**	$78\,000 \div 1000$
3	$6400 \div 100$	**7**	$200\,000 \div 1000$
4	$42\,000 \div 1000$	**8**	$200\,000 \div 10\,000$

13 Dividing by 20, 30, ...

When we divide by 20, it is like dividing by 2 then by 10. This is because $20 = 2 \times 10$.

Example

To do $360 \div 20$

first do
$$\begin{array}{r} 1\,8\,0 \\ 2\overline{)3\,^1 6\,0} \end{array}$$

Then do $\quad 180 \div 10 = 18$

So $\qquad 360 \div 20 = 18$

In the same way dividing by 30 is the same as dividing by 3 then by 10.

Example

To do $780 \div 30$

first do
$$\begin{array}{r} 2\,6\,0 \\ 3\overline{)7\,^1 8\,0} \end{array}$$

Then do $\quad 260 \div 10 = 26$

So $\qquad 780 \div 30 = 26$

Exercise 17

Work these out.

1	$640 \div 20$	**5**	$7540 \div 20$
2	$240 \div 30$	**6**	$2820 \div 30$
3	$5680 \div 40$	**7**	$1890 \div 90$
4	$2350 \div 50$	**8**	$24\,240 \div 80$

14 Dividing decimals by 10

We can divide decimals by 10 in the same way.

Example 1

$47.1 \div 10$

T	U	.	$\frac{1}{10}$	$\frac{1}{100}$
4	7	.	1	

$47.1 \div 10 = 4.71$

$$\begin{array}{ccccc} 4 & 7 & . & 1 & \\ & \div 10 & \div 10 & \div 10 & \\ & 4 & . & 7 & 1 \end{array}$$

Example 2

$2.9 \div 10$

U	.	$\frac{1}{10}$	$\frac{1}{100}$

2 . 9

$2.9 \div 10 = 0.29$

0 . 2   9

Exercise 18

Divide each of these decimals by 10.

1 51.7   **3** 4.3   **5** 4.02

2 86.2   **4** 5.69   **6** 10.5

15 Dividing decimals by 100

When we divide by 100, all the digits move across **two** columns to the **right**.

Example 1

$257.1 \div 100$

H	T	U	.	$\frac{1}{10}$	$\frac{1}{100}$	$\frac{1}{1000}$

2   5   7 . 1 $257.1 \div 100$
                          $= 2.571$
         2 . 5   7   1

Example 2

$52.3 \div 100$

T	U	.	$\frac{1}{10}$	$\frac{1}{100}$	$\frac{1}{1000}$

5   2 . 3 $52.3 \div 100$
                        $= 0.523$
    0 . 5   2   3

Exercise 19

Divide each of these decimals by 100.

1 193.4   **3** 38.5   **5** 10.6

2 362.8   **4** 16.9   **6** 27.04

Other words

These words can also mean **divide**.

share   **quotient**

Examples

Share 240 by 12
Find the **quotient**   } both mean
of 240 and 12   } $240 \div 12$

16 Multiplying by 0.1, 0.01, …

The decimal 0.1 is one tenth.
This means that if you multiply by 0.1 you are multiplying by one tenth.
Finding a tenth of something is the same as dividing by 10.
So multiplying by 0.1 is the same as dividing by 10.

Example

34×0.1
This is the same as $34 \div 10 = 3.4$

So $34 \times 0.1 = 3.4$

In the same way, multiplying by 0.01 is the same as dividing by 100

multiplying by 0.001 is the same as dividing by 1000

and so on.

Exercise 20

Work these out.

1 25×0.1 **7** 23.4×0.01

2 57×0.1 **8** 3.6×0.01

3 722×0.01 **9** 72×0.001

4 244×0.01 **10** 349×0.001

5 3.7×0.1 **11** 1.67×0.01

6 9.3×0.1 **12** 3.9×0.001

17 Dividing by 0.1, 0.01, ...

The decimal 0.1 is one tenth.
This means that if you divide by 0.1 you are dividing by one tenth.
Dividing into tenths gives you ten times as many parts, which is what you get by multiplying by 10.
So dividing by 0.1 is the same as multiplying by 10.

Example

$48 \div 0.1$

This is the same as $48 \times 10 = 480$

So $48 \div 0.1 = 480$

In the same way, dividing by 0.01 is the same as multiplying by 100

dividing by 0.001 is the same as multiplying by 1000

and so on.

Exercise 21

Work these out.

1 $25 \div 0.1$ **7** $18.4 \div 0.01$

2 $31 \div 0.1$ **8** $74.6 \div 0.01$

3 $673 \div 0.01$ **9** $2 \div 0.001$

4 $245 \div 0.01$ **10** $3.9 \div 0.001$

5 $1.9 \div 0.1$ **11** $9.17 \div 0.01$

6 $7.8 \div 0.1$ **12** $6.3 \div 0.001$

18 Adding fractions

To add fractions, the bottom numbers (denominators) **must** be the same.

Examples

$\frac{1}{3} + \frac{1}{3} = \frac{2}{3}$

one third + one third = two thirds

$\frac{2}{7} + \frac{3}{7} = \frac{5}{7}$

two sevenths + three sevenths = five sevenths

$\frac{3}{5} + \frac{3}{5} = \frac{6}{5} = 1\frac{1}{5}$

three fifths + three fifths = six fifths = One and one fifth

Exercise 22

Work these out.

1 $\frac{3}{5} + \frac{1}{5}$ **7** $\frac{2}{9} + \frac{5}{9}$

2 $\frac{1}{6} + \frac{3}{6}$ **8** $\frac{5}{12} + \frac{4}{12}$

3 $\frac{7}{9} + \frac{1}{9}$ **9** $\frac{8}{12} + \frac{5}{12}$

4 $\frac{4}{11} + \frac{3}{11}$ **10** $\frac{4}{5} + \frac{3}{5}$

5 $\frac{5}{13} + \frac{7}{13}$ **11** $\frac{6}{8} + \frac{5}{8}$

6 $\frac{3}{8} + \frac{2}{8}$ **12** $\frac{9}{11} + \frac{5}{11}$

Sometimes the two bottom numbers are different. Before we can add the fractions we **must** make them the same.

Example

$\frac{2}{3} + \frac{1}{6}$

We need to find a number that 3 and 6 both divide into exactly.

Numbers that 3 goes into:
3 ⑥ 9 12 ...
Numbers that 6 goes into:
⑥ 12 18 ...

The first number that is in both lists is 6. The 6 is called the common denominator.

Now write the fractions with 6 as the bottom number:

$\frac{2}{3} = \frac{?}{6}$ so $\frac{2}{3} \xrightarrow{\times 2} \frac{4}{6}$ so $\frac{2}{3} = \frac{4}{6}$

We can see this in a diagram.

The $\frac{1}{6}$ does not need changing.

So $\frac{2}{3} + \frac{1}{6} = \frac{4}{6} + \frac{1}{6} = \frac{5}{6}$

Here is another example

$\frac{2}{3} + \frac{1}{4}$

Numbers that 3 goes into:
3 6 9 (12) 15 …

Numbers that 4 goes into:
4 8 (12) 16 …

We need to change both fractions to twelfths. 12 is the common denominator.

$\frac{2}{3} = \frac{?}{12}$ $\frac{2}{3} \xrightarrow{\times 4} \frac{8}{12}$

$\frac{1}{4} = \frac{?}{12}$ $\frac{1}{4} \xrightarrow{\times 3} \frac{3}{12}$

So $\frac{2}{3} + \frac{1}{4} = \frac{8}{12} + \frac{3}{12} = \frac{11}{12}$

Exercise 23

Work these out.

1 $\frac{1}{4} + \frac{1}{2}$ 7 $\frac{1}{3} + \frac{1}{5}$

2 $\frac{1}{5} + \frac{1}{10}$ 8 $\frac{2}{7} + \frac{1}{2}$

3 $\frac{2}{5} + \frac{3}{10}$ 9 $\frac{2}{5} + \frac{1}{3}$

4 $\frac{5}{8} + \frac{1}{4}$ 10 $\frac{1}{7} + \frac{4}{5}$

5 $\frac{5}{12} + \frac{1}{6}$ 11 $\frac{1}{8} + \frac{3}{7}$

6 $\frac{5}{9} + \frac{1}{3}$ 12 $\frac{1}{2} + \frac{1}{3} + \frac{1}{4}$

19 Subtracting fractions

This works just like adding fractions.

Example

$\frac{3}{5} - \frac{2}{5} = \frac{1}{5}$

The two bottom numbers must still be the same. *Example*

$\frac{3}{8} - \frac{1}{4}$

Numbers that 8 goes into:
(8) 16 24 …
Numbers that 4 goes into:
4 (8) 12 16 …

$\frac{1}{4} = \frac{?}{8}$ $\frac{1}{4} \xrightarrow{\times 2} \frac{2}{8}$

The $\frac{3}{8}$ does not need changing.

So $\frac{3}{8} - \frac{1}{4} = \frac{3}{8} - \frac{2}{8} = \frac{1}{8}$

Exercise 24

Work these out.

1 $\frac{7}{8} - \frac{2}{8}$ 7 $\frac{1}{4} - \frac{1}{5}$

2 $\frac{2}{5} - \frac{1}{5}$ 8 $\frac{3}{6} - \frac{1}{3}$

3 $\frac{7}{11} - \frac{3}{11}$ 9 $\frac{6}{7} - \frac{2}{3}$

4 $\frac{3}{5} - \frac{1}{10}$ 10 $\frac{3}{4} - \frac{2}{3}$

5 $\frac{5}{8} - \frac{1}{4}$ 11 $\frac{5}{8} - \frac{2}{5}$

6 $\frac{11}{12} - \frac{2}{3}$ 12 $\frac{10}{11} - \frac{5}{8}$

20 Simplifying fractions

This is also known as **cancelling**.

We look for a number that divides exactly into both the top and bottom numbers.

Example 1

Simplify $\frac{6}{15}$

3 goes into both 6 and 15 exactly

We can divide by more than one number.

Example 2

Simplify $\frac{18}{24}$

Exercise 25

Simplify these.

1 $\frac{3}{6}$ **5** $\frac{8}{12}$ **9** $\frac{24}{36}$

2 $\frac{4}{6}$ **6** $\frac{20}{50}$ **10** $\frac{18}{30}$

3 $\frac{10}{15}$ **7** $\frac{12}{18}$ **11** $\frac{15}{45}$

4 $\frac{14}{21}$ **8** $\frac{16}{24}$ **12** $\frac{28}{70}$

CHAPTER 1

1 **a** DM10 = £5   **b** DM12 = £6   **c** DM6 = £3

2 **a**

Number of hours	1	2	3	4	5
Wages £	5	10	15	20	25

b

Graph to show Alison's wages

3 **a** (1) 06 45   (2) 20 20   (3) 12 00
  b (1) 6.25 pm   (2) 7.45 am   (3) 10.10 pm

4 **a** Stopped from 7.50 to 8.00 which is 10 minutes.   **b** 35 km
  c (1) Mohammed travelled faster in the first part.
     (2) The graph is steeper from 7.30 to 7.50.

CHAPTER 2

1 **a** 289   **b** 12.96   **c** 0.0064

2 **a** 25   **b** 2.8   **c** 111.1   **d** 6.7

3 **a** 53.29 cm²   **b** 15.8 cm

4 **a** 16 807   **b** 28 561   **c** 592.704   **d** 0.000 064

5 **a** 93   **c** 132   **e** 640   **g** 12
  b 83   **d** 19   **f** 48   **h** 4

6 **a** 6   **b** 70   **c** 600   **d** 1700

7 **a** 3   **b** 90   **c** 500   **d** 2000

8 **a** (1) estimate 300 + 600 = 900   (3) estimate 6 × 3 = 18
     (2) estimate 1300 − 900 = 400   (4) estimate 500 ÷ 20 = 25
  b (1) 916   (2) 327   (3) 17.92   (4) 28
  The estimates are all quite close to the correct answers. Part (3) is very close.

9 **a** $\sqrt{25}$ = 5, $\sqrt{36}$ = 6, $\sqrt{30}$ is about 5.5
  b $\sqrt{49}$ = 7, $\sqrt{64}$ = 8, $\sqrt{61}$ is about 7.8
  c $\sqrt{64}$ = 8, $\sqrt{81}$ = 9, $\sqrt{80}$ is about 8.9
  d $\sqrt{16}$ = 4, $\sqrt{25}$ = 5, $\sqrt{17}$ is about 4.1

  As all these are estimates, allow yourself any answer which is close to them.

CHAPTER 3

1 **a**

Time taken (min)	Tally	Total
1–5	⑴⑴ I	6
6–10	⑴⑴ ⑴⑴	10
11–15	III	3
16–20	IIII	4
21–25	⑴⑴	5
26–30	II	2

b *Time taken by 8J to get to school*

2 **a** $\frac{100}{200} = \frac{1}{2}$ said Radio 1, $\frac{25}{200} = \frac{1}{8}$ said Radio 2,

$\frac{25}{200} = \frac{1}{8}$ said Atlantic 252, $\frac{50}{200} = \frac{1}{4}$ said Radio 5 Live

b *Year 8's favourite radio station*

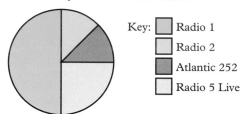

Key:
Radio 1
Radio 2
Atlantic 252
Radio 5 Live

3 **a** $360° \div 30 = 12°$

b

	Number of pupils	Working	Angle
Radio 1	10	10×12	120°
Radio 2	4	4×12	48°
Radio 5 Live	9	9×12	108°
Atlantic 252	7	7×12	84°
Total	30		360°

c *8J's favourite radio station*

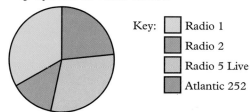

Key:
Radio 1
Radio 2
Radio 5 Live
Atlantic 252

CHAPTER 4

1 a

b

Number of blue tiles	1	2	3	4	5
Number of white tiles	5	8	11	14	17

$+3$ $+3$ $+3$ $+3$

c 3 white tiles

d number of white tiles = 3 × number of blue tiles

e add 2

f number of *white* tiles = 3 × number of *blue* tiles + 2

g $3 \times 17 + 2 = 51 + 2 = 53$ white tiles

h $\longrightarrow$ [× 3] $\longrightarrow$ [+ 2] $\longrightarrow$

i $\longleftarrow$ [÷ 3] $\longleftarrow$ [− 2] $\longleftarrow$

j $20 \longleftarrow$ [÷ 3] $\xleftarrow{60}$ [− 2] $\longleftarrow 62$

2 term 1: $4 \times 1 + 3 = 7$
term 2: $4 \times 2 + 3 = 11$
term 3: $4 \times 3 + 3 = 15$

3
a $2 \times 2 + 10 = 14$
b $2 \times 5 + 7 = 17$
c $7 \times 7 = 49$
d $5 \times 5 \times 5 = 125$
e $2 \times 5 \times 5 = 50$
f $(2 \times 5)^2 = 10 \times 10 = 100$

CHAPTER 5

1 a   **b**

2 **a**   **b**   **c**

3 **a**   **b**

4

5 **a**

b

CHAPTER 6

1 $-5\,°C, -3\,°C, -1\,°C, 0\,°C, 1\,°C, 2\,°C, 6\,°C$

2 **a** $5\,°C > 3\,°C$ **b** $-6\,°C > -8\,°C$ **c** $-4\,°C < 0\,°C$

3 $9 + 43 = 52\,°C$

4 **a** 6 **b** -6 **c** -9 **d** 1

5 **a** 10 **c** -4 **e** -15 **g** -60
   b -7 **d** -8 **f** 8 **h** 5

6 **a** -1736 **c** -17 **e** 20
   b -7 **d** 23 **f** 1035

7 **a** $r = 68 - 25$ **b** $r = 12 - 25$ **c** $r = -35 - 25$
     $= 43$ $= -13$ $= -60$

8 **a** $v = 5 \times 6 - 12$ **b** $v = 5 \times 2 - 12$ **c** $v = 5 \times 4 - 12$
     $= 18$ $= -2$ $= -32$

9 **a** $-2 \times -2 = 4$ **b** $5 \times -2 \times -2 = 20$ **c** $8 \times -2 \times -2 = 32$

10 **a** $E = 5 \times 3 \times 3$ **b** $E = 5 \times 1 \times 1$ **c** $E = 5 \times -5 \times -5$
     $= 45$ $= 5$ $= 125$

CHAPTER 7

1 **a** $a = 180° - 71° - 41° = 68°$
   b $b = 360° - 107° - 90° = 163°$
   c $c = 180° - 32° = 148°$,
     $d = 32°$ (opposite angles),
     $e = 148°$ (opposite angles)
   d isosceles triangle: $f - 34°$,
     $g = 180° - (2 \times 34°) = 112°$

2 **a** $i = 48°$ $g = 48°$ $h = 132°$ **b** $m = 72°$ $n - 108°$
     $j = 132°$ $k = 48°$ $p = 108°$ $q = 72°$
     $l = 132°$ $r = 108°$ $s = 72°$

3 **a** $s = 112°$ (corresponding)
   b $t = 57°$ (alternate)
   c $u = 99°$ (interior)

4 **a** Octagon can be divided into 6 triangles.
     So interior angle sum $= 6 \times 180° = 1080°$
   b One interior angle $= 1080° \div 8 = 135°$

5 **a** $240° - 180° = 60°$
Bearing of A from B $= 060°$
b $115° + 180° = 295°$
Bearing of A from B $= 295°$
c $77° + 180° = 255°$
Bearing of A from B $= 255°$

CHAPTER 8

1 There are 14 sweets in the bag.
a $\frac{4}{14} = \frac{2}{7}$ **b** $\frac{10}{14} = \frac{5}{7}$

2 There are 15 pencils in the case.
a (1) $3 \times 2 = 6$ (2) $5 \times 2 = 10$ (3) $7 \times 2 = 14$
b (1) $3 \times 6 = 18$ (2) $5 \times 6 = 30$ (3) $7 \times 6 = 42$

3 $1 - \frac{2}{5} = \frac{3}{5}$

4 $\frac{1}{6} + \frac{3}{6} = \frac{4}{6}$

Probability it will last for more than 20 minutes $= 1 - \frac{4}{6}$
$= \frac{2}{6}$
$= \frac{1}{3}$

5 **a** $P(A) = \frac{3}{6}$ (3 odd numbers out of 6) **b** $P(\text{not A}) = 1 - P(A)$
$= \frac{1}{2}$
$= 1 - \frac{1}{2}$
$= \frac{1}{2}$

6 **a** 8
b

		Dice			
		1	2	3	4
Coin	H	H, 1	H, 2	H, 3	H, 4
	T	T, 1	(T, 2)	T, 3	(T, 4)

c $\frac{2}{8} = \frac{1}{4}$

CHAPTER 9

1 12 out of 50 is the same as 24 out of 100, which is 24%

2 **a** 10% of £9.50 = 95p
b 10% of £12.50 = £1.25
c 10% of £14.80 = £1.48

3   **a**   10% of £400 = £40

      b   40% of £400 = 4 × £40 = £160

      c   50% of £340 = £170, so 25% is £170 ÷ 2 = £85

4   **a**   48% of 6700 = 0.48 × 6700 = 3216 people

      b   38% of 1200 = 0.38 × 1200 = 456 m

      c   7% of 1327 = 0.07 × 1327 = £92.89

      d $67\frac{1}{2}$% of 750 = 0.675 × 750 = 506.25 g

5   **a** $17\frac{1}{2}$% of 30 = 0.175 × 30 = £5.25

      b $17\frac{1}{2}$% of 40 = 0.175 × 40 = £7

6 $\frac{26}{40}$ = 26 ÷ 40 = 0.65 = 65%

7   **a**   2400 + 3600 = 6000 cars

      b $\frac{2400}{6000}$ = $\frac{24}{60}$ = 24 ÷ 60 = 0.4 = 40%

8   **a** $\frac{1}{7}$ of 28 = 28 ÷ 7 = 4, so $\frac{2}{7}$ of 28 is 4 × 2 = 8 teeth

      b $1 - \frac{2}{7} = \frac{5}{7}$ are not filled

9   **a**   Total cakes sold = 24 + 28 + 28 + 36 + 44 = 160

        Fraction sold on Friday is $\frac{44}{160} = \frac{11}{40}$

      b   Percentage sold on Monday is 15%. $\frac{24}{160}$ = 24 ÷ 160 = 0.15 = 15%

CHAPTER 10

1   **a** $x = 5$ **b** $y = 4$ **c** $y = -3$ **d** $x = -2$

2   **d**   The lines cross at (4, 2)

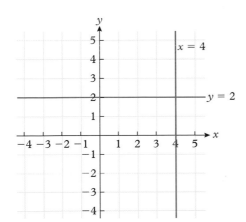

3 $x = 5$, $y = 3$

4　**a**　$y = 5x + 1$ is the steepest　　**b**　$y = x + 7$ is the least steep

5　**a**　the lines are parallel
　　b　$y = x + 7$ crosses the y axis at 7
　　c　$y = x + 7$ is highest up the grid
　　d　$y = x$ is lowest on the grid
　　e　$y = x + 2$ would be between $y = x$ and $y = x + 4$

6　**a**　$y = 2x + 4$　　**b**　$y = x + 1$

CHAPTER 11

1　**a**　$300\,cm = 300 \div 100\,m = 3\,m$　　　**f**　$7.2\,kg = 7.2 \times 1000\,g = 7200\,g$
　　b　$25\,mm = 25 \div 10\,cm = 2.5\,cm$　　**g**　$0.4\,t = 0.4 \times 1000\,kg = 400\,kg$
　　c　$7\,km = 7 \times 1000\,m = 7000\,m$　　**h**　$3000\,ml = 3000 \div 1000\,l = 3\,l$
　　d　$8.6\,m = 8.6 \times 100\,cm = 860\,cm$　　**i**　$4.8\,l = 4.8 \times 1000\,ml = 4800\,ml$
　　e　$4500\,g = 4500 \div 1000\,kg = 4.5\,kg$

2　**a**　$2 \times 3 = 6$
　　　　$\frac{1}{2}$ of $3 = 1\frac{1}{2}$
　　　　3 inches is $6 + 1\frac{1}{2} = 7\frac{1}{2}$ cm
　　b　177 yd is a bit less than 177 m, about $160 - 170$ m
　　c　$\frac{1}{2}$ of 30 is 15, $30 + 15 = 45$
　　　　30 miles per hour is a bit more than 45 km per hour, 48 km per hour
　　d　4 ounces is about $4 \times 30\,g = 120\,g$
　　e　165 pounds is a bit less than half of 165, 82.5 kg. It is about 75 kg.
　　f　3 gallons is a bit less than 3×5 or $15\,l$.
　　g　1 pint is a bit more than $\frac{1}{2}\,l$

3　**a**　$3\,in = 3 \times 2.5\,cm = 7.5\,cm$
　　b　$177\,yd = 177 \times 0.9\,m = 159.3\,m$
　　c　30 miles an hour $= 30 \times 1.6$ km an hour $= 48$ km an hour
　　d　4 ounces $= 4 \times 28\,g = 112\,g$
　　e　165 pounds $= 165 \times 0.45\,kg = 74.25\,kg$
　　f　3 gallons $= 3 \times 4.5\,l = 13.5\,l$
　　g　1 pint $= 0.57\,l$

4　**a**　6 years : 18 years $= 6 : 18 = 1 : 3$
　　b　$1 + 3 = 4$ shares are needed.
　　　　One share is $60 \div 4 = £15$
　　　　So Melanie gets £15, Keith gets $3 \times 15 = £45$.

5　**a**　You add　$3 \times 250\,ml = 750\,ml$ of water
　　b　$750 + 250 = 1000\,ml = 1\,l$ of orange drink is made

6   **a**   (1) $3:5$ (2) $3:2$ (3) $10:9$ (4) $1:100$

     b   A scale of $5\,cm$ to $1\,km = 5:100\,000 = 1:20\,000$

7   **a** $24 \div 4 = 6\,km$ **b** $2.5 \times 4 = 10\,cm$

8   **a** $300\,m = 300 \times 100\,cm = 30\,000\,cm$

        On the model $30\,000\,cm$ is $30\,000 \div 500 = 60\,cm$

     b $15 \times 500 = 7500\,cm = 75\,m$

CHAPTER 12

1   **a**   Area = length $\times$ width $= 6.5 \times 8 = 52\,m^2$

     b   Area $= \dfrac{\text{base} \times \text{height}}{2} = \dfrac{10 \times 12}{2} = 60\,cm^2$

     c   Area = base $\times$ height $= 14 \times 20 = 280\,mm^2$

     d   Area $= \dfrac{a+b}{2} \times h = \dfrac{15+35}{2} \times 18 = \dfrac{50}{2} \times 18 = 450\,mm^2$

     e   Area $= \dfrac{\text{base} \times \text{height}}{2} = \dfrac{5 \times 7}{2} = 17.5\,cm^2$

     f

Area of A $= \dfrac{a+b}{2} \times h = \dfrac{6+2}{2} \times 3$

$\qquad\qquad\quad = 4 \times 3$

$\qquad\qquad\quad = 12\,m^2$

Area of B $= 6 \times 5 = 30\,m^2$

Total area $= 12 + 30 = 42\,m^2$

2   Perimeter $= 8 + 6.5 + 8 + 6.5 = 29\,m$

3   Square of the scale factor is $10^2 = 100$

     New area $= 15 \times 100 = 1500\,cm^2$

4   New area   = original area $\times 2^2$

     Original area = new area $\div 2^2$

$\qquad\qquad\qquad = 48 \div 4 = 12\,cm^2$

CHAPTER 13

1   **a**   Mean $= \dfrac{7+6+9+0+3+4+7+6+4+7}{10}$

$\qquad\qquad = 53 \div 10 = 5.3$

     b   Mode is the most common number $= 7$

     c   Writing the numbers in order: 0   3   4   4 $\boxed{6 \quad 6}$ 7   7   7   9

        Median is the mean of the two middle numbers $= 6$

     d   Range = biggest number $-$ smallest number

$\qquad\qquad = 9 - 0 = 9$

2 a Mode is the most common number of people in cars = 1

b

Number of people	Number of cars	Total number of people
1	23	$1 \times 23 = 23$
2	17	$2 \times 17 = 34$
3	7	$3 \times 7 = 21$
4	3	$4 \times 3 = 12$
Total	50	90

Mean number of people per car = $90 \div 50 = 1.8$

c

Frequency polygon to show the number of cars passing the school

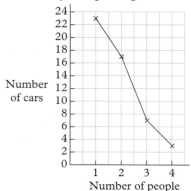

3 a

Length in cm	Tally	Total
0 but less than 3	IIII	4
3 but less than 6	IIII IIII	10
6 but less than 9	IIII IIII IIII IIII	20
9 but less than 12	IIII I	6

b Modal group is 6 but less than 9 because it has the most seedlings in it.

c, d

Heights of 40 seedlings

380

CHAPTER 14

1 (3) Ariel, (1) Corn flakes, (2) Dairy Milk, (4) Butter

2   **a** 1 litre   **b** 60 ml

As both these are estimates allow yourself any answer that is close to them.

3   **a** $9 \times 3 \times 3 = 81 \, \text{cm}^3$ **b** $7 \times 3 \times 3 = 63 \, \text{cm}^3$

4   **a** The cross section has five squares. Each square is 5 cm × 5 cm.

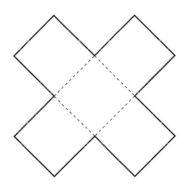

Area of cross section
$$= 5 \times 5 \times 5$$
$$= 125 \, \text{cm}^2$$

Volume of prism
$$= 125 \times 13$$
$$= 1625 \, \text{cm}^3$$

  b Area of top face $= (8 \times 14) - (4 \times 6)$
$$= 88 \, \text{cm}^2$$
Volume of prism $= 88 \times 5$
$$= 440 \, \text{cm}^3$$

5 Volume $= 78 \times 40 \times 25$
$$= 78\,000 \, \text{cm}^3$$

CHAPTER 15

1

Value of x	Value of $x^2 + 56$	
20	456	too small
30	956	too big
25	681	too big
24	632	too big
23	585	too small
23.8	622.44	too big
23.7	617.69	too small
23.75	620.0625	too big

Answer: $x = 23.7$ to 1 d.p.

2 a

b

(number line from 2 to 8, open circle at 3, filled circle at 6)

c

(number line from 0 to 6, line to open circle at 4)

d

(number line from −2 to 4, filled circle at −1, open circle at 2)

3 For $7 \leqslant x < 11$, x can be 7, 8, 9, 10.

4 For $x < 7$, the highest whole number value of x is 6.

5 For $x \geqslant 8$, the lowest whole number value of x is 8.

6 a $x + 3 < 7$

$x + 3 - 3 < 7 - 3$

$x < 4$

b $x - 4 \geqslant 1$

$x - 4 + 4 \geqslant 1 + 4$

$x \geqslant 5$

(number line from 0 to 8, filled circle at 5, line to 8)

7 a $3x \geqslant 18$

$\frac{3x}{3} \geqslant \frac{18}{3}$

$x \geqslant 6$

b $\frac{x}{4} \leqslant 2$

$\frac{x}{4} \times 4 \leqslant 2 \times 4$

$x \leqslant 8$

8 a $2 \leqslant x < 4$

b $-10 < x \leqslant 5$

CHAPTER 16

1

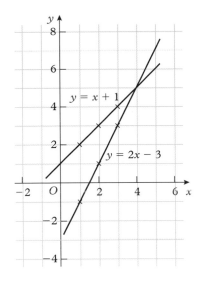

a (1)

x	1	2	3
y	2	3	4

b (1)

x	1	2	3
y	-1	1	3

c The coordinates of the point of intersection are (4, 5)

2 a $x + y = 7$
When $x = 0$
$0 + y = 7$
$y = 7$
This gives $(0, 7)$

When $y = 0$
$x + 0 = 7$
$x = 7$
This gives $(7, 0)$

b $2x + y = 4$
When $x = 0$
$2 \times 0 + y = 4$
$y = 4$
This gives $(0, 4)$

When $y = 0$
$2x + 0 = 4$
$2x = 4$
$x = 2$
This gives $(2, 0)$

c $x + 3y = 6$
When $x = 0$
$0 + 3y = 6$
$y = 2$
This gives $(0, 2)$

When $y = 0$
$x + 0 = 6$
$x = 6$
This gives $(6, 0)$

d $3x + 2y = 12$
When $x = 0$
$3 \times 0 + 2y = 12$
$0 + 2y = 12$
$2y = 12$
$y = 6$
This gives $(0, 6)$

When $y = 0$
$3x + 2 \times 0 = 12$
$3x + 0 = 12$
$3x = 12$
$x = 4$
This gives $(4, 0)$

383

3

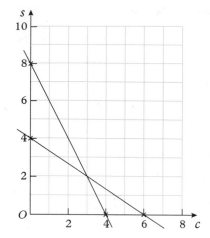

b $2c + 3s = 12$
   $4c + 2s = 16$

c $2c + 3s = 12$
   When $c = 0$
   $2 \times 0 + 3s = 12$
         $3s = 12$
          $s = 4$
   This gives $(0, 4)$

   When $s = 0$
   $2c + 3 \times 0 = 12$
         $2c = 12$
          $c = 6$
   This gives $(6, 0)$

       $4c + 2s = 16$
   When $c = 0$
   $4 \times 0 + 2s = 16$
         $2s = 16$
          $s = 8$
   This gives $(0, 8)$

   When $s = 0$
   $4c + 0 = 16$
        $4c = 16$
         $c = 4$
   This gives $(4, 0)$

The point of intersection is $(3, 2)$. This means that $c = 3$ and $s = 2$.
So chicken and chips cost £3, sausage and chips £2.

d If $c = 3$ and $s = 2$, Steven will buy two chicken and chips at
   $2 \times 3 = £6$ and three sausage and chips at $3 \times 2 = £6$ making a total
   of £12, Keeley will buy four chicken and chips at $4 \times 3 = £12$ and
   two sausage and chips at $2 \times 2 = £4$ making a total of £16.

Exercise 1

1	34	**6**	661	**11**	211
2	44	**7**	433	**12**	310
3	62	**8**	945	**13**	523
4	175	**9**	95	**14**	1621
5	299	**10**	141		

Exercise 2

1	19	**5**	104	**9**	139
2	37	**6**	468	**10**	183
3	27	**7**	135	**11**	108
4	218	**8**	108	**12**	88

Exercise 3

1 227 **2** 569 **3** 7636 **4** 2672

Exercise 4

1 46 **2** 639 **3** 208 **4** 993

Exercise 5

1	74	**6**	3185
2	90	**7**	1314
3	184	**8**	1602
4	372	**9**	1785
5	518	**10**	3212

Exercise 6

1	390	**5**	6840
2	450	**6**	15 620
3	1280	**7**	50 000
4	7560	**8**	80 070

Exercise 7

1	7500	**5**	319 000	**9**	5 004 000
2	8200	**6**	420 000	**10**	8 150 000
3	36 000	**7**	524 300	**11**	3 020 000
4	17 800	**8**	800 000	**12**	83 500 000

Exercise 8

1	560	**5**	1740	**9**	3100
2	720	**6**	1040	**10**	4260
3	810	**7**	3320	**11**	11 130
4	1020	**8**	2250	**12**	29 750

Exercise 9

1	95	**3**	178.3	**5**	107
2	282	**4**	863.1	**6**	9

Exercise 10

1	4291	**3**	7160	**5**	6059
2	5704	**4**	13 740	**6**	708

Exercise 11

1	850	**5**	9485	**9**	17 985
2	2142	**6**	13 621	**10**	39 780
3	5166	**7**	16 813	**11**	45 994
4	8164	**8**	14 448	**12**	96 922

Exercise 12

1	4	**5**	8	**9**	7
2	9	**6**	3	**10**	7
3	5	**7**	5	**11**	5
4	5	**8**	8	**12**	6

Exercise 13

1	42	**3**	11	**5**	32
2	31	**4**	32	**6**	221

Exercise 14

1	29	**5**	12	**9**	106
2	18	**6**	19	**10**	138
3	18	**7**	16	**11**	207
4	16	**8**	16	**12**	52

Exercise 15

1	74	**4**	83	**7**	500
2	8	**5**	904	**8**	70 000
3	596	**6**	720		

Exercise 16

1	78	**4**	42	**7**	200
2	53	**5**	780	**8**	20
3	64	**6**	78		

Exercise 17

1	32	**4**	47	**7**	21
2	8	**5**	377	**8**	303
3	142	**6**	94		

Exercise 18

1	5.17	**3**	0.43	**5**	0.402
2	8.62	**4**	0.569	**6**	1.05

Exercise 19

1	1.934	**3**	0.385	**5**	0.106
2	3.628	**4**	0.169	**6**	0.2704

Exercise 20

1	2.5	**5**	0.37	**9**	0.072
2	5.7	**6**	0.93	**10**	0.349
3	7.22	**7**	0.234	**11**	0.0167
4	2.44	**8**	0.036	**12**	0.0039

Exercise 21

1	250	**5**	19	**9**	2000
2	310	**6**	78	**10**	3900
3	67300	**7**	1840	**11**	917
4	24500	**8**	7460	**12**	6300

Exercise 22

1	$\frac{4}{5}$	**5**	$\frac{12}{13}$	**9**	$\frac{13}{12} = 1\frac{1}{12}$
2	$\frac{5}{7}$	**6**	$\frac{5}{8}$	**10**	$\frac{7}{5} = 1\frac{2}{5}$
3	$\frac{8}{9}$	**7**	$\frac{7}{9}$	**11**	$\frac{11}{8} = 1\frac{3}{8}$
4	$\frac{7}{11}$	**8**	$\frac{9}{12} = \frac{3}{4}$	**12**	$\frac{14}{11} = 1\frac{3}{11}$

Exercise 23

1	$\frac{3}{4}$	**5**	$\frac{7}{12}$	**9**	$\frac{11}{15}$
2	$\frac{3}{10}$	**6**	$\frac{8}{9}$	**10**	$\frac{33}{35}$
3	$\frac{7}{10}$	**7**	$\frac{8}{15}$	**11**	$\frac{31}{56}$
4	$\frac{7}{8}$	**8**	$\frac{11}{14}$	**12**	$\frac{13}{12} = 1\frac{1}{12}$

Exercise 24

1	$\frac{5}{8}$	**5**	$\frac{3}{8}$	**9**	$\frac{4}{21}$
2	$\frac{1}{5}$	**6**	$\frac{3}{12} = \frac{1}{4}$	**10**	$\frac{1}{12}$
3	$\frac{4}{11}$	**7**	$\frac{1}{20}$	**11**	$\frac{9}{40}$
4	$\frac{5}{10} = \frac{1}{2}$	**8**	$\frac{1}{6}$	**12**	$\frac{25}{88}$

Exercise 25

1	$\frac{1}{2}$	**5**	$\frac{2}{3}$	**9**	$\frac{2}{3}$
2	$\frac{2}{3}$	**6**	$\frac{2}{5}$	**10**	$\frac{3}{5}$
3	$\frac{2}{3}$	**7**	$\frac{2}{3}$	**11**	$\frac{1}{3}$
4	$\frac{2}{3}$	**8**	$\frac{2}{3}$	**12**	$\frac{2}{5}$